Globalizing India

D1715526

Anthem South Asian Studies
Series Editor: Crispin Bates

Other titles in the series:

Brosius, Christiane *Empowering Visions* (2005)

Mills, Jim (ed) *Subaltern Sports* (2005)

Joshi, Chitra *Lost Worlds: Indian Labour and its Forgotten Histories* (2005)

Dasgupta, Biplab, *European Trade and Colonial Conquest* (2005)

Kaur, Raminder *Performative Politics and the Cultures of Hinduism* (2005)

Rosenstein, Lucy *New Poetry in Hindi* (2004)

Shah, Ghanshyam, *Caste and Democratic Politics in India* (2004)

Van Schendel, Willem *The Bengal Borderland: Beyond State and Nation in South Asia* (2004)

Globalizing India

Perspectives from Below

Edited by

JACKIE ASSAYAG AND C. J. FULLER

Anthem Press

Anthem Press
An imprint of Wimbledon Publishing Company
75-76 Blackfriars Road, London SE1 8HA
or
PO Box 9779, London SW19 7ZG
www.anthempress.com

This edition first published by Anthem Press 2005.
This selection © Wimbledon Publishing Company 2005;
individual chapters © individual contributors.

British Library Cataloguing in Publication Data
A catalogue record for this book is available from the British Library.

Library of Congress Cataloging in Publication Data
A catalog record for this book has been requested.

1 3 5 7 9 10 8 6 4 2

ISBN 1 84331 194 1 (Hbk)
ISBN 1 84331 195 X (Pbk)

Cover illustration: Computer classes at the School of Aruna Raghavan,
courtesy of Mira International.

Typeset by Footprint Labs Ltd, London
www.footprintlabs.com

Printed in India

CONTENTS

List of Contributors   vii

Acknowledgements   ix

1 Introduction   1
   Jackie Assayag and C. J. Fuller

Part One: Economy and Agriculture

2 On the History of Globalization and India: Concepts, Measures
   and Debates   17
   G. Balachandran and Sanjay Subrahmanyam

3 In Search of 'Basmatisthan': Agro-nationalism and Globalization   47
   Denis Vidal

4 Seeds of Wrath: Agriculture, Biotechnology and Globalization   65
   Jackie Assayag

5 Weaving for IKEA in South India: Subcontracting, Labour Markets
   and Gender Relations in a Global Value Chain   89
   Geert De Neve

Part Two: Education and Language

6 'Children are Capital, Grandchildren are Interest': Changing
   Educational Strategies and Parenting in Calcutta's Middle-class
   Families   119
   Henrike Donner

7 Of Languages, Passions and Interests: Education, Regionalism and
   Globalization in Maharashtra, 1800–2000   141
   Véronique Bénéï

Part Three: Culture and Religion

8 Maps of Audiences: Bombay Films, the French Territory
   and the Making of an 'Oblique' Market   165
   Emmanuel Grimaud

9 Malabar Gods, Nation-Building and World Culture: On Perceptions
   of the Local and the Global   185
   Gilles Tarabout

10 Globalizing Hinduism: A 'Traditional' Guru and Modern
   Businessmen in Chennai   211
   C. J. Fuller and John Harriss

LIST OF CONTRIBUTORS

Jackie Assayag is Director of Research at the Centre National de la Recherche Scientifique (CNRS) and a member of the Maison Française, Oxford.

Gopalan Balachandran is Professor of International History and Politics at the Graduate Institute of International Studies, Geneva.

Véronique Bénéï is a Research Fellow at the Centre National de la Recherche Scientifique (CNRS), a member of the Laboratoire d'Anthropologie des Institutions et des Organisations Sociales, Paris, and a Research Fellow in Anthropology at the London School of Economics.

Geert De Neve is a Lecturer in Anthropology at the University of Sussex.

Henrike Donner is a Research Fellow in Anthropology at the London School of Economics.

Chris Fuller is Professor of Anthropology at the London School of Economics.

Emmanuel Grimaud is a Research Fellow at the Centre National de la Recherche Scientifique (CNRS) and a member of the Laboratoire d'ethnologie et de sociologie comparative at Nanterre.

John Harriss is Professor of Development Studies at the London School of Economics.

Sanjay Subrahmanyam is Professor and Doshi Chair of Indian History at the University of California at Los Angeles.

Gilles Tarabout is Director of Research at the Centre National de la Recherche Scientifique (CNRS), a member of the Centre d'Études de l'Inde et de l'Asie du Sud (CEIAS), and Director of the India and South Asia Programme of Collaboration in Social Sciences at the Fondation Maison des Sciences de l'Homme, Paris.

Denis Vidal is a Research Fellow at the French Institute of Research for Development (IRD), Paris, and a member of the Centre d'Études de l'Inde et de l'Asie du Sud (CEIAS).

ACKNOWLEDGEMENTS

This book is the product of two research projects, one supported by the British Economic and Social Research Council (ESRC) and the other by the French Centre National de la Recherche Scientifique (CNRS). The ESRC, with a grant for a project entitled 'An anthropological study of globalization and its local impacts in India', supported the research of the contributors in the Department of Anthropology at the London School of Economics (who then included Geert De Neve), although Véronique Bénéï and John Harriss were also supported by their own independent grants. The Direction des Relations Internationales of the CNRS, through its Programme International de Coopération Scientifique, provided a grant for a project entitled 'Perspectives critiques sur la "globalisation": localité, nation et mondialisation à partir de l'Asie du Sud', which was based at the Centre d'Études de l'Inde et de l'Asie du Sud (CEIAS), École des Hautes Études en Sciences Sociales, in Paris (with the LSE as the collaborating partner). The CNRS grant supported the research of the contributors affiliated to the CEIAS (who then included Sanjay Subrahmanyam and the other French scholars). Two project workshops, in Paris in 2000 and London in 2001, were supported by the CNRS and ESRC respectively.

On behalf of all the contributors, the editors thank the ESRC and CNRS for their invaluable financial support. They also thank Jenny Hammond for her excellent editing work on earlier versions of many of the chapters.

1

INTRODUCTION

Jackie Assayag and C. J. Fuller

To say that globalization has become the global cliché of our time has itself turned into a cliché in academic writing on the subject. By the end of the twentieth century, however, most social scientists, including anthropologists, acknowledged that globalization is a genuinely important topic of enquiry and that – despite its often ill-defined, catch-all connotations – it does label a distinctive transformative process that appears to have taken hold in many parts of the contemporary world, including India.

Definitions of globalization abound, but paraphrasing Held and his co-authors (1999: 14–15), we may initially define it as the widening, deepening and speeding up of global interconnectedness, a spatio-temporal process of change that links local or national social relations and networks with worldwide, global ones and thereby transforms 'the organization of human affairs'. A particularly important aspect is the 'deepening enmeshment of the local and global', so that distant events may have more and more local significance, and vice versa (ibid.: 15). This aspect is one to which anthropologists can particularly contribute, and introducing their volume on the anthropology of globalization, Inda and Rosaldo point out that anthropology 'is most concerned with the artic-ulation of the global and the local' (2002: 4), with how globalization interacts with particular societies and cultures, and how ordinary people themselves experience and understand the process.

In discussing the local and global, however, several pitfalls should be avoided. Obviously, no human being can be in more than one place at a time, and even if some people today really are 'hybrid' transnationalists, the vast majority of the world's population are not, because they continue to live and work in one locality only – and commonly do so for all or most of their lives. Secondly, and related to the last point, global interconnectedness is extremely uneven. At one extreme, some groups of people in some places engaged in some kinds of activity – international bankers, for instance – are globally linked with each other, whereas at the other extreme, many other groups – notably those formed by the marginalized poor – tend to be very isolated. Indeed, their marginalization, and hence their disconnection from even locally existing networks of people and resources, may be increasing as a direct consequence of 'structural adjustment' policies or other developments that are part of economic globalization.

Thirdly, and of more general relevance to the studies in this book, reified distinctions between 'local places' and 'global forces' need to be avoided, so that, as Tsing observes, we are not misled by 'globalist fantasies'. Instead, we must recognize that 'the cultural processes of all "place" making and all "force" making are *both* local and global – that is, both socially and culturally particular and productive of widely spreading interactions' (Tsing 2002: 477). Thus the local and global – and, *a fortiori*, the national, regional or other spatial levels – are always enmeshed or entangled, not separate and preformed, because they are always mutually constituted vis-à-vis each other through social relationships and cultural patterns.

As Inda and Rosaldo observe (2002: 4), most academic work on globalization is about large-scale economic, political and cultural processes, and the anthropological literature, though growing, is still fairly limited. Certainly this is true for India, where pronouncements about globalization in general are far more plentiful than detailed documentation about 'the different meanings and consequences that [it] may have for social groups located differently along the axes of caste, class, gender, ethnicity, nationality and so on' (Deshpande 2003: 155). On the whole, too, as Deshpande observes, even when the globalization literature mentions the need for such details, it still 'continues with business as usual' (ibid.: 156), so that the 'grass-roots' view from below – the 'folk understandings of the global, and the practices with which they are intertwined' (Tsing 2002: 469) – remain mostly neglected. Interrupting the usual business is the first objective of this book, which is designed to present a selection of ethnography that explores different aspects of globalization from below, and in so doing sheds light on the relationship between the different spatial levels on which globalizing processes unfold. The book opens with an essay on the history of globalization in India that supplies a context for the mostly contemporary material discussed in the subsequent chapters.

Held *et al.* distinguish three broad schools of thought about globalization, which they label 'hyperglobalists', 'sceptics' and 'transformationalists' (1999: 2). For hyperglobalists, contemporary globalization is an entirely new epoch mainly defined by global market capitalism and the consequent weakening of the nation-state. Sceptics, by contrast, contend that globalization is an exaggerated myth, because economic integration across the world today is not unprecedented and is probably less than it was in the late nineteenth century; nor are nation-states actually in decline. For transformationalists – among whom Held *et al.* effectively include themselves – contemporary globalization is genuinely new, but it is a 'long-term historical process which is inscribed with contradictions and which is significantly shaped by conjunctural factors' (ibid: 7); as they recognize, world history has seen a series of earlier phases of globalization (ibid.: 414–24), and the long-term history of globalization, punctuated by reduced integration during phases of deglobalization, has been carefully and critically examined in recent historical scholarship (Hopkins 2002). Moreover, contemporary globalization must be seen as 'a highly differentiated phenomenon' (Held *et al.* 1999: 27), partly because (as already noted above) 'global interconnectedness is not experienced by all peoples or communities to the same extent or even in the same way' (ibid.: 28). There are, in other words, multiple forms of globalization, just as, with comparable but not identical empirical and conceptual problems, there are multiple forms of modernity.

Among commentators, activists and public intellectuals in India, hyperglobalists are prominent, although they vehemently disagree about whether globalization is good or bad. For well-disposed optimists, like the business commentator Gurcharan Das, whose views typify those now expressed throughout the Indian business press, information technology and globalization can transform India in the twenty-first century, and he concludes: 'Never before in recorded history have so many people been in a position to rise so quickly' (2002: 357). For hostile pessimists, like the journalist P. Sainath (2000), whose perspective represents much radical and left-wing opinion, globalization is the manifestation of 'market fundamentalism', an assault on democracy and the harbinger of worsening inequality. Both Das and Sainath grossly overstate their case, but they are not at all unusual. Anthropologists, on the other hand, tend to be professionally resistant to the sweeping generalizations of hyperglobalism, as all the writers in this book certainly are. Assayag in particular explores the flaws in one version of radical hyperglobalist thought pertaining to agriculture and biotechnology, a particular *bête noire* for anti-globalization protestors.

On the whole, anthropologists, in common with historians, tend to be sceptics or transformationalists, although not all the contributors to this book are of one mind and some are more sceptical than others. To some extent, our divergence reflects different theoretical perspectives, but it is also related to the different kinds of evidence that we discuss. From the outset, the main objective of the research project was empirical investigation of a variety of cases that are, at least on the face of it, examples of contemporary globalization – of new entanglements between the global and the local in the economic, agricultural, educational, linguistic, cultural and religious domains. Our principal task, therefore, was and is ethnographic: to collect and present evidence about how very diverse groups of Indians imagine globalization, real or apparent, and how they think and act in relation to its different aspects in different parts of the country. At the same time, though, we wanted to explore critically the extent to which developments that are ostensibly manifestations of globalization are actually driven endogenously by local, regional or national forces, which have often been in place since the colonial period or even earlier.

Also important are 'the resilient but unspectacular continuities present in every specific context' (Deshpande 2003: 153), which ought to be studied precisely to counteract the bias towards evidence of rapid change characteristic of the globalization literature (ibid.: 155). All the anthropologists contributing to this book had considerable previous experience of the people and places they discuss, which greatly helped them in detecting stability and slow continuity, as well as quicker change. The tendency to ascribe to globalization all manner of changes, real or imaginary, that have little to do with it is undoubtedly most prevalent in hyperglobalism. Nevertheless, misleading generalization is a constant danger in 'macro' studies that pay insufficient attention either to ethnographic particularities or to changes and continuities that exist below the global level on a local, regional or national scale. In the field of globalization, anthropologists have no monopoly on truth, but they do have a valuable role to play in counterbalancing large-scale generalizations – often too reliant on evidence about the modern west – with the documented experiences of ordinary men and women in all parts of the world.

Globalization in India

In India, it is generally agreed, globalization becomes a significant process in the late 1980s or early 1990s. In 1985 Rajiv Gandhi's government started to liberalize the economy by removing some controls, restrictions and high taxes that had long been part of the Nehruvian planned economy. In 1991 Manmohan Singh, the finance minister in Narasimha Rao's government, initiated a more determined policy of liberalization and dismantlement of state control, so that during the 1990s, for better or for worse (and opinion varies sharply), India was increasingly integrated into the global economy – at the lumbering pace of an elephant rather than with the spring of an Asian tiger. Thus, for example, foreign direct investment increased, barriers to foreign trade were reduced, growing numbers of Indians began to work for global enterprises – from outsourced textile production to software engineering – and a huge range of 'foreign' consumer goods, from Coca-Cola to Mercedes-Benz cars, went on sale throughout the country, though mainly for consumption by the well-off middle class.

In spite of the conceptual problems discussed by Assayag (2000), the rise of the mainly urban 'great Indian middle class', as Varma (1999) calls it, certainly is one of the most important developments associated with economic liberalization. Middle-class consumer demand is not only a significant stimulus for economic growth, it has also gone hand in hand with the rapid spread of consumerist ideology. Economic liberalization and the globalization of the Indian economy will almost certainly continue to speed up for the foreseeable future, although there are widely divergent views about the prospects for prosperity or poverty for different sections of the population in different parts of the country.

The political concomitants of these economic developments are complicated and sometimes paradoxical. In brief, economic liberalization has been accompanied by the rise of Hindu nationalism and the Bharatiya Janata Party, which looked set to expand its support steadily until its surprising defeat in the 2004 general election. As several scholars have shown (e.g. Corbridge and Harriss 2000; Hansen 1999; Rajagopal 2001), economic liberalization is significantly linked to the rise of Hindu nationalism. Rajagopal, for example, observes that: 'The Hindu nationalists' appeals echoed and reinforced those of an expanding market economy, both expressing the cultural and political assertion of newly rich classes' (2001: 42), especially the urban middle class. Hindu nationalism is plainly chauvinistic and anti-globalist in many ways, but it is also driven by the desire to make India into a modern nation – with its own nuclear bomb – so that it is 'recognized as [one of the] respected members of that elusive global "comity of nations"', the 'object of desire' for even parochial nationalists (Hansen 1999: 234).

Also important in many regions of India has been an intensification of caste-based politics and regional parties, which the BJP and the Congress have sought to accommodate. These regional political developments have multiple causes too complicated to discuss here, but some of them are directly linked to economic liberalization, such as the increased power of regional state governments over their own economies as intervention from New Delhi is reduced, or the complex ramifications of structural adjustment policies on local caste and class systems. If one thing is clear, though, it is that the modern, postcolonial, Indian nation-state is not about to wither away, as some hyperglobalist speculation suggests, so that any cogent analysis of how the local and global are enmeshed will also have to take into account the national and regional levels.

In tandem with economic liberalization and partly enabling it has been a rapid development of electronic communications technology, which is a crucial dimension of contemporary globalization in India. For anyone who knew the country more than 20 years ago, one of the most startling changes was the sudden appearance of public telephone booths in the late 1980s – and the discovery that the telephones often worked. As never before, it then became possible to dial a number for anywhere in India or overseas and expect to get through on an audible line. A working telephone system has now expanded enormously – even though many rural areas are still connected only minimally, if at all – and in most towns and cities connection to the Internet is now fairly easy. In some cities these developments have allowed a new information technology sector to grow very rapidly since the late 1990s, although we still have little hard data (as opposed to copious rhetoric) about the real economic and social effects of this growth.

Television is another modern technology that has grown quickly, so that it can now be received almost everywhere in the country. Since the early 1990s, privately-owned satellite channels have attracted large audiences at the expense of the state-owned Doordarshan channels. As studies in various parts of the world have shown, working telephones and numerous television channels – along with videotapes, computers and other electronic equipment – do not give rise to the global homogenization of cultures. So although these media and technologies, at one level, do enhance the interconnectedness of people and communities – locally, regionally and nationally, as well as globally – they simultaneously generate new appropriations, translations or mutations that in turn create new divisions and differences between people and communities. New forms of imagination continually convert global, cosmopolitan cultural forms into vernacular ones, and vice versa. Across India and its regions, and among the Indian diaspora overseas, therefore, the outcome is that cultural diversity is certainly not being eradicated by global uniformity, let alone by the 'Americanization' feared by some alarmed commentators.

An Outline of this Book

The first chapter, by G. Balachandran and Sanjay Subrahmanyam, discusses the Indian history of economic globalization. Its main part consists of a detailed, critical examination of the early modern Indian economy's connections with the rest of the world, primarily through its trading links, between about 1500 and 1800, and then during the colonial period, focusing on both trade and capital movements. Apart from being a valuable contribution in its own right, Balachandran and Subrahmanyam's essay is a powerful antidote to the presentist bias in some studies of contemporary globalization, which tend to exaggerate its novelty and uniqueness by ignoring the historical evidence on long-term developments. Anthropologists are better attuned to history than once they were, but their fieldwork-based methodology can still encourage them to neglect the significance of the past for understanding the present. In the Indian case, misunderstanding may be made worse by hyperglobalist claims about the country's radical transformation during the last two decades, whereas the evidence shows that the period of state control of the economy, from the 1950s to 1980s, was actually exceptional in a long-term history of relatively open markets and global economic integration.

The next two chapters explore aspects of economic globalization that have received a lot of attention in the Indian and international mass media. Denis Vidal investigates the case of basmati rice and an American company's controversial attempt to patent it – an ostensibly flagrant act of biopiracy by global capitalism. Considered in historical and comparative perspective, however, the issue becomes more complicated. Plant varieties have been transported between countries and continents for centuries, even if patenting is novel, and Vidal makes some interesting comparisons between basmati rice and French wine (similarly the object of only partly effective government protection) and also apples in Himachal Pradesh, which were introduced from America in the 1920s and have made many Himachali farmers prosperous.

These comparisons highlight some of the inconsistencies in the basmati controversy as it has developed in India. For example, basmati rice has been portrayed as the authentic 'traditional' creation of generations of small farmers in the Himayalan foothills, the denizens of 'Basmatisthan', although basmati has actually been developed primarily for export since the 1980s. Thus the market for basmati rice is in fact mainly the product of economic globalization. As demand has risen to exceed supply, disputes among exporters, different groups of farmers, agronomists and the Indian government have repeatedly emerged about whether, for example, hybrid varieties of rice grown in different regions of India can also be labelled as basmati. It is a tangled tale, vividly recounted by Vidal, that is full of ironies and contradictions, whose latest twist is that since 2003 small farmers have been given the 'freedom' to sell their rice to multinational agricultural companies, a development all too likely to mean that production of 'traditional' basmati will indeed come to be controlled by foreign firms like the one that tried to patent it.

Jackie Assayag's contribution is also about globalization and farming, in particular the often rhetorical claims about globalization advanced in connection with the widespread distress among Indian farmers made evident by thousands of suicides. Assayag particularly discusses the situation in Karnataka, where he did his research. He describes the activities of Monsanto, the giant biotechnology firm notorious for pioneering genetically modified crops and sterile 'terminator' seeds. Monsanto, inevitably, is a major enemy of the Karnataka State Farmers' Association, a leading organization in the state's anti-globalization movement, which helped to run a 'seed council' in Bangalore in 2000 to denounce the global conspiracy to take over the seed market and destroy small farmers' rights.

Among these farmers, the new seeds have increasingly come to symbolize their dependence on and exploitation by external forces beyond their control. One patent sign of the farmers' distress is worsening debt levels, to which a considerable number have responded by selling their kidneys in the expanding bodily organ market. Yet despite all these dramatic and often tragic developments, scrutiny of the evidence in a wider perspective clearly shows that contemporary economic globalization is only a small part of the story. Thus, for example, severe distress among farmers has several clear precedents, such as the great depression of the 1930s. Moreover, the Indian government's price stabilization and stockpiling policies have helped to keep the poor hungry for decades, and the serious inequalities in rural society that have existed since at least the nineteenth century are a major factor in the current crisis. These, together with other local factors, produce an 'entangled complexity' that only ideological myopia could reduce to a 'seamless garment' made by globalization.

A similarly entangled complexity is analysed in Geert De Neve's ethnographic study of the relationship between globalized production and a local labour force in and around the weaving town of Bhavani in Tamil Nadu. The Sri Murugan Rug Export company, which supplies rag rugs to the Swedish chain store IKEA, subcontracts their production to rural weavers. Whereas much of the literature assumes that there is always a largely passive pool of readily exploitable labour for global commodity production, De Neve shows that in the Bhavani area the workforce is a mixed group of people – male and female, old and young, high- and low-caste – whose decisions about whether to weave rugs are shaped by diverse factors in a fragmented, differentiated local labour market. The rug company's success also depends on its network of agents who can supervise the workforce and ensure a steady, high-quality output to satisfy IKEA. By comparing several villages, De Neve shows, too, that the new opportunities opened up by rug production can modify the preexisting sexual division of labour and conventional beliefs about gender, skill and work.

How rugs are woven for IKEA therefore depends on local social structures, which actually vary considerably between neighbouring villages, but these are now being altered by incorporation into the global market. Whether the alterations will be consolidated may depend, however, on how many western customers carry on buying rag rugs – if and when flooring fashions change in Europe, all sorts of unpredictable consequences may ensue near Bhavani.

The next two chapters, by Henrike Donner and Véronique Bénéï, are about globalization's impact on local ideas and practices relating to children's education. In Calcutta, in common with many places in India, middle-class people are more and more convinced that their children must be well educated in privately-run English-medium schools, because otherwise they cannot hope to secure good jobs in the multinational companies and other new businesses that economic liberalization and globalization have recently brought to the city. To ensure such an education for their children, young middle-class mothers devote a great deal of time and energy to the task, partly by establishing good connections with a wide range of institutions and people, including their own natal families. (Marriage is virilocal, so that a married woman normally lives with her husband and his parents.) As a result, these mothers assume less domestic responsibility, which must now be taken over by their mothers-in-law, so that a new division of labour has emerged: young mothers mainly look after school-going children and older mothers-in-law run the household.

This in turn has increased young women's independence vis-à-vis their mothers-in-law, who often understand very little about modern schooling, but it also means that the older women's workload remains high because they cannot delegate household tasks to their daughters-in-law, as the previous generation had done. In the household, therefore, an important outcome of economic globalization as mediated through education is a change in the old balance of power between senior and junior women, for young mothers are no longer dominated by their mothers-in-law as they were in the past, and grandmothers are having to work as never before.

In contrast to the Bengalis, the Maharashtrians discussed by Véronique Bénéï are unenthusiastic about English-medium schooling and strongly favour Marathi. The vast majority of primary-school children are taught in Marathi and most private schools, as well as government schools, are Marathi-medium. In Maharashtra, unlike many other parts of India, private education does not imply that English must be the language of instruction, and in the growing private sector new schools are as likely to be Marathi- as English-medium.

As Bénéï explains, various factors account for parents' reluctance to have their children educated in English, even though they recognize that it is an asset in the modern job market. But this was true, especially in an economically developed state like Maharashtra, long before economic liberalization began, and in India, of course, English has a history dating back to colonial times. Moreover, in Maharashtra, English is still widely seen as a colonial, foreigners' language and, still more significantly, people also have strong, emotional feelings about the Marathi tongue, which plays a key role in the exceptionally powerful sense of regional patriotism and identity found in the state. Maharashtrian regional 'nationalism' is symbolized by Shivaji, the heroic warrior-king, who is indeed portrayed as the guardian protector of Marathi as *swabhasha* ('one's own language'). Among minority language groups, as well as the upper middle-class elite fluent in English, attitudes are rather different, but for the majority of Maharashtrians, their commitment to Marathi and ambivalence towards English display a relationship to the region and nation under conditions of globalization that is a complex mixture of emotion and interest.

The last section of the book is devoted to examples of cultural and religious globalization. With a range of funny stories from his own personal experience in the studios, Emmanuel Grimaud discusses the case of a Hindi film dubbed into French in Bombay, a fascinating variation from the usual commentary on Hollywood films and the extent to which they are vehicles of globalization or westernization. For Bombay film producers, 'Overseas' is one sector of their distributional map, which lumps together traditional audiences in Africa, the Middle East and among the Indian diaspora. In the 1990s, though, producers started to talk about their films 'going global', as new markets and audiences were found across the world.

Yashraj Films decided to dub one of their popular Hindi films into French, initially to market it in Mauritius and among French-speaking Indians, and then gradually to the wider French public. The dubbing process was a 'curious experiment' that generated an often weird Hindi-French hybrid language, but in Paris, as Grimaud saw, the dubbed film was quite favourably received, though for different reasons, by Mauritian Indians living there and by some French film enthusiasts. As Grimaud shows, between Bombay and Paris, 'a new form of relation between a film and an audience had emerged', which illustrates just how heterogeneous the 'overseas' market can be. It also shows how the market can be transformed, fragmented and reassembled in myriad ways as producers play with real and imagined audiences that have different languages, cultures and film-going experiences in different localities across the world.

Gilles Tarabout's chapter, on the transformation of a local religious cult into a regional, national and global cultural performance, explores the ways in which different groups of people have been imagining the relationship between the local and global during the twentieth century. *Teyyam* is a popular local deities' cult in Malabar, north Kerala, which is patronised by all castes, but its characteristic feature is that ritual specialists, who mainly belong to low castes, become possessed and engage in spectacular dances during festivals. In the twentieth century, *teyyam* was criticised as irrational and superstitious by colonial officials, foreign and local Christians, Hindu reformers and other members of Kerala's elite, but instead of disappearing, the cult changed and prospered. Kerala Marxists started to praise *teyyam* as a true expression of 'people's culture', while some Indian ethnologists described it as a richly authentic folk tradition. *Teyyam* then joined other folk dances as a strand in India's composite national culture, so that it was incorporated into India's

Republic Day parade in New Delhi and other national celebrations, as well as into Kerala state festivals and tourist promotion events. By these means, *teyyam* became 'art', to be packaged as short shows staged for foreign tourists and audiences in international concert halls, or at folk festivals in Kerala itself, which may be supported by the Ford Foundation.

Teyyam is still part of popular religion in Malabar villages, but now it is also a dance performance all over the world – the villages included – in which almost every variety of discourse about the relationships between the authentically local and the regional, national and global can be articulated. Notwithstanding this diversity, though, there are clear continuities through time in how these relationships have been imagined, more or less consistently, among both Kerala villagers and the outsiders celebrating or condemning *teyyam*.

The final chapter, by C. J. Fuller and John Harriss, is also about transforming religion, but their focus is on a Hindu guru, Swami Dayananda Saraswati, popular among leading businessmen in Chennai who belong to the managerial-professional upper-middle class. Dayananda, in his own and his followers' eyes, is a 'traditional teacher' of the monistic Hinduism conventionally labelled today as Vedanta and he consistently stresses the value of Sanskrit, but he is actually a quintessentially modern guru, who mainly preaches in English and is popular both in India and the United States, where he spends much of his time. In many respects, Dayananda's version of Vedanta is similar to that of his predecessors since the nineteenth century, including the earlier and more famous Dayananda Saraswati, founder of the Arya Samaj. Yet the guru's message also resonates with modern, mainly American, notions of individualism and self-help, so that, Dayananda explains, Krishna in the *Bhagavad Gita* teaches us as individuals that there are 'no failures in life', but 'only varieties of experience'. At the same time, Dayananda insists that Hinduism (unlike other religions) is not stuck in the past, so that Hindus actually become truly modern by more fully embracing their own cultural and religious traditions.

The guru's message about individualism and modernity is very attractive to contemporary businessmen who, in the new epoch of economic liberalization and globalization, have become increasingly confident about their own and their companies' success, not only in India but also overseas. On the other hand, these men are also preoccupied with their own meagre knowledge of Hinduism, and even more with the ignorance of their children, educated in elite English schools and heavily influenced by the USA and the west. In these respects, the Chennai businessmen share the same worries as Hindu Non-Resident Indians, who fear the 'cultural vacuum' in America. Fuller and Harriss argue, however, that both groups now belong to a new, globalized upper-middle class, and it is to this new class – simultaneously self-confident about success and anxious about religious ignorance – that Dayananda's globalized version of Hinduism so powerfully appeals.

Conclusion

As we have said, this volume's main purpose is to provide a series of ethnographic studies of globalization in India, as conceptualized and experienced by a diverse range of ordinary Indian people, which also entails examination of the dialectical relationships between developments occurring at different spatial levels from the global to the local. The men, women and children discussed in this book are surely not typical or representative of the population as a whole, and firm generalizations about beliefs and practices relating to globalization in India would be premature. Nonetheless, each chapter presents material, reaches conclusions and raises questions that challenge many of the sweeping claims made by both the 'hyperglobalists' and the extreme sceptics who pretend that there is nothing new under the Indian sun. Because we have just summarised the book's contents, we shall not restate every chapter's argument, but a few of the most prominent overall findings can be usefully recapitulated.

Balachandran and Subrahmanyam's economic history of globalization in India contains a lesson that is reiterated in the ethnographic contributions. This is that every real or imagined instance of globalization – despite the tendency to exaggerate novelty and rapid change in the globalization literature – has a history that must be uncovered if the process is to be described intelligibly and analysed cogently. Even for anthropologists investigating the ethnographic present in a particular locality, the past matters, if only because it is impossible to assess how new current developments actually are unless we know what went before. Although this point may seem banally obvious, it has been blithely ignored by those who claim, for example, that biopiracy over basmati rice or chronic distress among farmers using 'terminator' seeds is without precedent, as well as by those who suppose, for example, that Kerala *teyyam* rituals or Swami Dayananda's teachings display a traditional continuity untainted by contemporary transformations. Evaluating what is or is not genuinely new often also requires close attention to ethnographic detail, which may reveal that what looks the same is actually different, and vice versa. Such detail, however, is indispensable for understanding the variable beliefs and practices, and meanings and consequences, of globalization that exist among people who belong to different genders, castes, classes, linguistic communities, regional groups, and so on. Anthropologists, of course, always draw attention to diversity at the local level, and sometimes deny that valid large-scale generalizations about societies and cultures can ever be made. We do not take this position, but we do insist that no such generalizations can hold good if they are contradicted by ethnographic evidence, and that many proclaimed truths about globalization – in India or the world as a whole – fail on these grounds.

Just a few examples from this book, which undermine some fairly typical general claims, are our findings that the labour force for outsourced production in rural Tamil Nadu is not a passive, readily exploitable mass of people; that economic liberalization and globalization is increasing the demand for English-medium education in middle-class Calcutta, which requires mothers and mothers-in-law to assume new domestic responsibilities, but globalization is certainly not promoting nuclear families or encouraging women to go out to work; that in Maharashtra many middle-class people do not want their children educated in English anyway, despite the pressures of the job market, and they continue to prefer Marathi-medium; and that an apparently idiosyncratic project to dub Bollywood films into French turns out to be a qualified success, though not entirely as planned, in spite of widespread claims that cinema audiences everywhere have now fallen victim to Hollywood's monoglot Americanization.

Earlier, citing Tsing, we indicated that global 'forces' and local 'places' must be understood as mutually constituted at both global and local – and national and regional – levels. Consistently with this formulation, how local or regional social and cultural systems are entangled with national and global ones is a central theme throughout this book, as our chapter outlines show. Reiterating our insistence on the indispensability of ethnography, let us also emphasize here that the fieldwork-based ethnographic investigation of globalization is in no way a contradiction in terms. Nor is it intrinsically harder to carry out than a lot of earlier ethnography was, because even a 'traditional' village was always part of a ramifying regional system that could not be directly investigated by the resident anthropologist. As Tsing also rightly notes (2002: 470–2), seductive talk about globalization's 'circulations' and 'flows' exaggerates the novelty of today's world, but it can serve, too, as a spurious theoretical justification for avoiding any intensive long-term fieldwork at all. Whether this counts as *trahison des clercs* is debatable, but it is certainly a failure to undertake the kind of work that anthropologists should be best qualified to do – and must do, if ordinary people's experiences of globalization are to be recorded at all.

Finally, let us raise a couple of more provocative issues that are discussed, with more or less directness, in the following chapters. First, we suggest that it is still an open question how much empirical reality – and in particular how much of ordinary people's lived experience – is adequately described or captured by the concept of globalization. Certainly, there are some telling parallels with 'modernization', a comparable concept that was once widely favoured and is now almost entirely discarded. Will globalization go the same way soon?

A second question, which is perhaps the other side of the same coin, is about how far globalization is mostly an ideology, a myth, a millennial fantasy, or even an occult cosmology productive of conspiracy theories, so that hyper-globalist exaggerations are actually influencing people's beliefs and practices far more than, say, policies of economic liberalization or the development of electronic communications technology. Hard though it is to answer this question, the chapters in this book all clearly demonstrate that in constituting social action in India today, people's disparate ideas about globalization – and more specifically about its relationship with their own locally situated lives – are playing a central role. In the end, maybe, globalization is a latter-day equivalent of the Polynesian *mana*, a type of thought whose characteristic is precisely its indeterminate value as a signifier, because 'in itself it is devoid of meaning and therefore liable to receive any meaning at all' (Lévi-Strauss 1950: xliv). And concepts like *mana*, as Lévi-Strauss observes, are not restricted to 'archaic' societies at all; they are 'universal and permanent' (ibid.: xliii).

Bibliography

Assayag, J. (2000) 'En quête de classe moyenne en Inde: grandeur, recomposition, forfaiture'. *Annales HSS*, 6: 1229–53.

Corbridge, S. and J. Harriss (2000) *Reinventing India: Liberalization, Hindu Nationalism and Popular Democracy*. Cambridge: Polity.

Das, G. (2002) *India Unbound: From Independence to the Global Information Age*. New Delhi: Penguin.

Deshpande, S. (2003) *Contemporary India: A Sociological View*. New Delhi: Viking Penguin.

Hansen, T. B. (1999) *The Saffron Wave: Democracy and Hindu Nationalism in Modern India*. Princeton: Princeton University Press.

Held, D., A. McGrew, D. Goldblatt and J. Perraton (1999) *Global Transformations: Politics, Economics and Culture*. Cambridge: Polity.

Hopkins, A. G., ed. (2002) *Globalization in World History*. London: Pimlico.

Inda, J. X. and R. Rosaldo (2002) 'Introduction: a world in motion', in J. X. Inda and R. Rosaldo, eds, *The Anthropology of Globalization: A Reader*. Oxford: Blackwell.

Lévi-Strauss, C. (1950) 'Introduction à l'oeuvre de Marcel Mauss', in Marcel Mauss, *Sociologie et Anthropologie*. Paris: Presses Universitaires de France.

Rajagopal, Arvind (2001) *Politics After Television: Religious Nationalism and the Reshaping of the Indian Public*. Cambridge: Cambridge University Press.

Sainath, P. (2000) 'The age of inequality', in R. Thapar, ed., *India: Another Millennium?* New Delhi: Penguin.

Varma, P. K. (1999) *The Great Indian Middle Class*. New Delhi: Penguin.

PART ONE:
ECONOMY AND
AGRICULTURE

2

ON THE HISTORY OF GLOBALIZATION AND INDIA: CONCEPTS, MEASURES AND DEBATES

G. Balachandran and Sanjay Subrahmanyam

Introduction: A Problematic Category

Over the last decade, globalization has become the great shorthand description for a vast variety of social and economic processes in almost every part of the world. It is deployed to explain phenomena as diverse, often contradictory, and in a few instances also long-lived, as poverty, unemployment, environmental degradation, decline in public health and education, reduction in social spending and welfare measures, caste-based, religious or other forms of social violence, terrorism, the recrudescence of nationalism, and the loss of national sovereignty to market forces and international institutions. It is a 'hegemonic category' in that, although used in a staggering variety of ways and for diverse ends, both protagonists and critics alike usually take the term for granted and its meaning as self-evident. Three quite recent scholarly volumes on globalization open identically by describing the term either as a 'catchword' or a 'cliché' or both.[1]

Yet scholars in the humanities and the social sciences feel irresistibly drawn to it: according to A. G. Hopkins, justifying his own venture into the area, and deprecating the reluctance of historians to even 'recognize the subject', 'the analysis of the origins, nature, and consequences of globalization [is] (...) currently the most important single debate in the social sciences'.[2]

According to a widely cited definition, globalization refers to the 'widening, deepening, and speeding up of worldwide interconnectedness in all aspects of contemporary social life, the cultural to the criminal, the financial to the spiritual'.[3] As discussed in greater detail below, conceptions of globalization

reflect not merely an academic desire to pin down an elusive 'thing', they also
reflect expectations and fears arising from many diverse, and no doubt inter-
connected, processes under way across the world. However it is defined or
viewed, it is clear that most if not all conceptions of globalization share an
underlying premise that expanding economic flows and integration represent
one of its main elements.

A few years ago, the prestigious Brazilian publisher Companhia das Letras
launched a series to mark the millennium made up of a set of extended essays –
each devoted to the turning of a particular century (the series is entitled
Virando Séculos), and to a theme that seemed to mark or encapsulate that particular moment. Invited to set out over a hundred-odd pages what had defined
the period around 1500, the French historian Serge Gruzinski chose to enti-
tle his own volume *At the Origins of Globalization*.[4] Gruzinski argued that globalization was by no means a recent phenomenon, and that in fact it had its
roots at the moment when an economy on a world scale came to be defined
with the Great Discoveries to the east and west, crowned by the voyage
around the world in 1519–21 under the command of the Portuguese Fernão
de Magalhães, better known as Ferdinand Magellan. From this moment on,
the 'four quarters of the world' – Asia, Africa, Europe and America – were
linked together as never before. The world had been 'encompassed' for the
first time, and even the imaginary globe had been filled out in a definitive
sense that was simply not the case with the medieval *mappae mundi*.[5] It just
seemed to him perfectly justified to think of the years from 1480 to 1520 as
the first, and foundational, moment of globalization as we know it today.

At much the same time as Gruzinski's small work, his colleague and fellow
Latin Americanist Nathan Wachtel produced a far more extensive work, this
one on the fate of the so-called 'Marranos' or New Christians who had
emerged after the forced conversion of Jews in Iberia in the late fifteenth century.[6] Having painted an evocative portrait-gallery of a series of individuals,
largely based on the archives of the Inquisition, Wachtel mused in his work
on the modernity of what he termed *la condition marrane*. His conclusion was
once more that the peculiarly modern subjectivity of the cast of characters he
traced was linked to the fact that they inhabited a new sort of world, one that
allowed them to navigate ceaselessly, and with a certain world-weary scepti-
cism between Medina del Campo, Mexico, Lima, Goa and Manila. Once
more, this work evoked the idea that the origins of both globalization and
modernity lay in the sixteenth century, and not in the very recent past.

The retort to works such as these by those who believe that 'we have never
been modern' might well be that 'we have never been global' either. But the
problem does remain for the historian, as well as for the economist and the
social anthropologist, of asking how old the processes are that are so often

described of late under the sweeping head of 'globalization'. This question can in turn be addressed in a variety of different ways, and at a number of distinct scales. Our endeavour in this essay will be to address the problem primarily from a South Asian vantage point, rather than from Brazil or Mexico. But rather than simply adducing a set of empirical materials from South Asia in order to challenge the canonical positions in the debate that have emerged, say, around the NBER (National Bureau of Economic Research) orthodoxy of writers such as Jeffrey Williamson, Kevin O'Rourke and Peter Lindert, we also wish to address problems regarding the very conceptualisation of the idea of 'globalization'.[7] Our purpose here is not necessarily to join Marxist analysts such as Frederick Cooper, who have bluntly asked 'What is the Concept of Globalization Good for?', but rather to point to a serious myopia in the manner in which recent events and processes have been privileged as compared to longer-term ones.[8]

The Perspective from World Economic History

Before proceeding further, it may be useful to summarise what we have termed the NBER orthodoxy, as set out by Williamson himself. Williamson argues that 'globalization in world commodity and factor markets has proceeded in fits and starts since Columbus and de Gama [sic] sailed from Europe more than 500 years ago'.[9] He then proposes that the centuries since 1492 can be divided into 'four distinct globalization epochs', two of which are 'pro-global', and two 'anti-global'. But he goes on to claim (in our view, rather illogically) that globalization itself began with a long 'anti-global' phase, running from 1492 to 1820, largely on account of what he terms 'mercantilist restriction'. Presenting a somewhat gross caricature of world trade trends in the sixteenth and seventeenth centuries, which derives entirely from a slanted reading of European trade in the epoch (Asian trade is thus wholly neglected), Williamson tells us that since commodity prices did not converge internationally in these centuries, there is no 'irrefutable evidence that global commodity market integration is taking place'. To all intents and purposes, then, the centuries before 1800 are a non-starter according to this version.

Things begin to become interesting only after 1820 (Phase II), and this is the familiar story of the 'first global century', lasting up to 1913, and corresponding largely to the hagiography of the emergence of the gold standard under the benevolent effect of the imperialism of free trade in the heyday of the British Empire. Transport costs decline, and 'the liberal dismantling of mercantilism and the worldwide transport revolution worked together to produce truly global commodity markets across the nineteenth century'.[10] Hence, even if there were minor pockets of 'anti-global reaction', the broad trend to be read was one of increased capital and commodity flows, and even of increased labour migration.

We then move to Phase III, that of the second 'anti-global retreat' between 1913 and 1950, punctuated by a particularly low point in the form of the Great Depression of the 1930s. Tariffs rose and 'gains from trade' were apparently largely choked off. The end of World War II and the creation of the Bretton-Woods institutions then reverse this trend.

And so, finally, we have Phase IV, or the 'second global century', beginning in 1950, corresponding to European reconstruction, the emergence of the worldwide dollar, and enhanced commodity and capital flows, though Williamson does admit that 'the second global century has been much more enthusiastic about commodity trade than about migration'. It would appear in this view that the period after about 1985, associated in the Indian case notably with the opening of certain markets and the decline of centralized economic controls, should merely be seen as a part of a far longer trend, if only one were to take the totalising global perspective.

We can thus immediately observe that Williamson's view is quite distinct from that of Gruzinski and others, who are not primarily concerned with economic questions, and also remain convinced of the significance of processes in the sixteenth, seventeenth and eighteenth centuries. Williamson does grudgingly concede that 'there was a world trade boom after 1492', but believes that all forms of improvement were in the final analysis 'offset by trading monopoly mark-ups, tariffs, non-tariff restrictions, wars and pirates'.[11] Globalization for Williamson and his collaborators is above all a form of economic integration, and must be verified using the data thereon. The justification for focusing on economic integration is that the intensification of economic exchanges across the world is to be regarded as the driving force of all the wider processes to which the term 'globalization' is often applied. Yet it may also conversely be argued that if *economic* globalization as a process is shown to be theoretically unoriginal and empirically dubious, the category of globalization itself becomes more difficult to sustain. The challenge, instead, becomes one of explaining its ubiquity and purchase, especially in the media and public discourse.

To the extent that they are possible and useful, economic indices of globalization are obviously more amenable to measurement than others. Economists have traditionally regarded commodity price convergence and the share of trade to national gross domestic product (GDP) as shorthand measures of market integration and an economy's openness to trade respectively. Tariff rates also provide some idea of the latter. The share of trade to global GDP and other such more detailed measures as the share of inter-industry trade in total world trade yield some estimates of the global importance of trade to various forms of economic activity.

It is useful to bear in mind here that many of these measures by their very nature privilege national borders and the nation-state. Yet these national units and frontiers are often regarded by globalization theorists as no longer providing a relevant framework for understanding the constitution of global society today. Where they exist, though, historical data for trade, prices, monetary and capital flows, labour and entrepreneurial movements, etc., for modern nation-states are also structured and determined by the territorial imagination of the nation-state. The latter promotes the neglect of connections and processes that are not assimilable to the nation-state, and of the diverse processes of articulation between regions and the wider zones surrounding them. Thus ironically, while suggesting the emergence or creation of structures and 'scapes' that supersede the nation-state, theorists of globalization discursively also promote the latter's centrality to the project of globalization itself.

Measures of inter-industry trade which reflect the dispersal and re-integration of industrial production processes across national borders may appear to argue the borders' irrelevance more strongly and convey the globalization of economic space more decisively than other measures of trade openness. But in the absence of other supporting evidence, which even when advanced tends largely to be anecdotal, it requires a leap of faith to conclude from high or rising levels of inter-industry trade that industrial firms routinely disperse their production processes across several countries. Besides, while more and more goods on supermarket shelves may be described by their packers as the 'product of many countries' and the nationality of individual brands may have little to do now with location or ownership, such uncertainties of provenance and the locational and other business strategies that give rise to them are as likely to be the outcome of various forms of *regional* integration as that of a *global* reduction or elimination of barriers to trading and industrial re-location with which they are commonly associated.[12]

The proportion of capital flows to GDP is also used to measure economic openness. This measure is open to the same qualifications as measures of trade openness. Furthermore, both in theory and internationally sanctioned practice, no country can indefinitely sustain capital inflows (or for that matter outflows) amounting to a high proportion of GDP. There have no doubt historically been partial exceptions to this condition, most notably Britain, a large exporter of capital throughout the four decades before World War I. But in general and for most parts of the world, 'globalization' by this measure might describe at best a phase of a cycle during which a large gap opens up between domestic savings and domestic investment in the borrowing and lending countries and many profitable avenues of overseas investment develop. This expansionary phase may last as long as the gap and profitable investment opportunities persist, 'long cycles' offering the closest approximation to a condition of worldwide expansion of capital markets that is reflexively associated with financial globalization.[13]

This is not a problem with the so-called Feldstein-Horioka measure of financial integration which is based on the premise that in a perfectly integrated financial system there will be no systematic correlation between national savings rates and investment rates because capital will flow towards countries that offer the highest returns, without regard to the state of domestic investment.[14] But this is not to be confused with the globalizer's nirvana – a world of perfect capital mobility in which there would be no differences between national rates of return (other than differential risk premia and transaction costs), because arbitrage will instantly extinguish whatever other differences might arise in these rates. In this world, as in the world of zero capital mobility, national savings and investment rates will be perfectly correlated. The Feldstein-Horioka measure, however, can only compare states of global financial integration without telling us anything about the direction of movement, which it leaves to be deduced independently from other indicators, and thus from pre-existing histories of globalization or 'de-globalization'. This, as we see below, can lead to some odd results, including facile chronologies of financial globalization and misleading comparisons of states of financial integration across different periods.

The empirical evidence usually advanced to argue that a process of globalization has been historically under way, whether since the early or mid-nineteenth century or since the 1980s, is also far from unambiguous. While urging the need for better research into commodity market integration (CMI) in the recent period and suggesting that commodity markets may be better integrated today than in 1913, Kevin O'Rourke has observed that the evidence for CMI is 'ambiguous' at best for the twentieth century compared to the 'pervasive late-nineteenth century evidence of commodity price convergence'. He also notes that when regarded as a process, rather than merely a condition, 'globalization' was much more decisive during the nineteenth century, which saw a nearly eight-fold increase in the share of trade to global GDP.[15]

The evidence on capital market integration, according to O'Rourke, is also similarly ambiguous. On the one hand, reduction in the dispersion of real interest rates in the nineteenth century was followed by a period of disintegration and then one of recovery lasting until the present. In the range of financial assets traded, as well as the ratio of gross to net capital flows, financial markets in the present may be more integrated than in the past. On the other hand, both these variables reflect the dramatic increase in the volumes of short-term capital flows since the late 1980s. While the stock of total foreign direct investment (FDI) to world GDP is higher now (16 per cent in 1999) than in 1913 (9 per cent), FDI is a smaller proportion of developing countries' GDP now (18 per cent) than in 1913 (40 per cent) because they play host to a smaller proportion (about a third) of FDI now compared to 1913 (two-thirds). Consequently, the high FDI to global GDP ratio may also point much more strongly towards closer regional integration or integration among the major industrial countries than towards the integration of the world economy as a whole.[16]

As we have seen, most historical accounts of globalization argue for a U-shaped trajectory and a chronology according to which the intensification of global exchanges in the nineteenth century and the early twentieth century was followed by a period of dis-integration inaugurated by World War I. This period of dis-integration gave way in due course to a period of accelerated integration that is presumed to continue till the present. But there is no general agreement on the starting and terminal points of these three phases, while the choices made in this regard have interesting implications for wider arguments about the historical, political, and institutional correlates of processes associated with globalization and the latter's discursive constitution.

Conventionally, nineteenth-century globalization was thought to run from about the 1870s to the eve of World War I. This is the period associated with the expansion of trade between Europe and the rest of the world (especially the United States and other so-called regions of recent settlement), larger flows of labour and capital, improvement and cheapening of transport and communications, and the spread of an international monetary system in the form of the gold standard. Thus, for Richard Baldwin and Philippe Martin (unlike for Williamson cited above) the period from 1870 represents the 'first wave' of globalization.[17] But O'Rourke appears to prefer a longer nineteenth century that began in about 1820 because of the tripling thereafter of the annual rate of growth of world trade from the (largely hypothetical) 1 per cent rate of the previous three centuries to about 3.5 per cent.[18]

The share of merchandise exports to GDP rose from 1 per cent to 4.6 per cent between 1820 and 1870, and to 7.9 per cent in 1913. It would therefore appear that trading integration in the five decades after 1820 was more intense than in the following four decades. On the other hand, trading expansion perhaps became more global after 1870 in that many more countries were brought under its sway, and flows of both capital and labour (the latter however largely from Europe to regions outside Asia and Africa) expanded.

How we date the expansive phase of nineteenth century integration of the world affects the way we read the relationship between this process and political structures, institutions and ideas. For if the expansion of trade between 1820 and 1870 took place within the context of a largely liberal world economy, characterized (outside the colonies, China and Japan) by a widening sphere of free trade and the emergence of independent nation states in

Europe, rising trade between 1870 and World War I took place amidst rising tariff barriers and other restrictions to trade, imperialist rivalries, growing militarism, and the colonial partition of the world.[19] From about 1870 a relatively pluralistic silver or bimetallic standard also gave way to a more singular, asymmetrical, rigid gold standard that is often viewed nostalgically, if also misleadingly, as the first truly spontaneous and self-regulating global monetary regime.

Chronologies of integration and dis-integration become more complicated once we move into the interwar and post-World War II periods. It is almost universally held that the interwar years were a period of global dis-integration, when trade and incomes slumped, tariff barriers increased, capital flows turned volatile or ebbed away, barriers to migration went up, and countries in general turned their backs on the rest of the world. As is argued below, this story of interwar dissolution of external links fits some countries' experiences better than others, and in the case of India, for instance, the interwar period was one of persisting openness rather than closure until the onset of World War II. But it is clear that even for the world as a whole, the extent of dis-integration through the 1920s is largely exaggerated in conventional literature.

For example, it is clear with respect to trade from O'Rourke's own data that the share of merchandise exports to GDP rose quite significantly from 7.9 per cent to 9 per cent between 1913 and 1929. Even by the standards of 1870–1913 this is not unimpressive, especially if one considers the decline in this share during the war and the immediate postwar years. Furthermore, this level of world trade to income was not exceeded, reading between the lines of O'Rourke's data, until four decades later, at the height of the postwar boom.

With respect to financial integration it is widely accepted that international financial markets were a great deal more integrated in the late nineteenth century than they have been since, and that global capital flows (expressed as current account surplus or deficit as percentage of GDP) were considerably higher between 1870 and 1913 than later. Though Baldwin and Martin acknowledge this, the estimates of the Feldstein-Horioka measure of financial integration that they reproduce tell an interesting and somewhat counter-conventional story.[20] According to these estimates, international financial markets were actually *better* integrated in the 1920s than during any decade between 1870 and 1990 with the exception of the 1880s.[21] The difference between the 1880s and the 1920s was also quite small, and much smaller than the difference between the 1880s and the following decades that are conventionally regarded as the heyday of nineteenth-century globalization. The degree of financial integration according to this index was also higher or about the same in the depressed 1930s as between 1950 and 1979.

The onset of the so-called 'second phase' of globalization (Williamson's Phase IV) is usually not all that clearly dated either. The expression itself arose as management jargon in the 1970s and was popularized, according to David Harvey, by an American Express advertising campaign.[22] The relaxation of capital controls, first by the United States and then by Britain, is also believed to have something to do with expanding trading and capital flows from the 1980s. Similarly, the intellectual framework for opening up economies and transforming the postwar regulatory framework is supposed to have been laid by a combination of global monetarism and a micro-theoretical approach to macro-economics that stressed the impact of incentives and incentive structures on economic individual and aggregate economic behaviour. The West's victory in the Cold War, the further liberalization of financial markets beyond Europe, and the loss of national sovereignty in important areas of policy to markets and international institutions both old and new reinforced these trends. Consequently, the onset of globalization is often associated conventionally with the Reaganite and Thatcherite 'revolutions' of the 1980s.

There is, however, another view, according to which much of the ground-work for the present phase of globalization was laid at the end of the war, thanks to the Bretton-Woods agreement and the gradual reduction of tariffs under GATT.[23] This institutional infrastructure, together with liberal US economic policies, would have encouraged western Europe to abandon current account controls and move to make their countries' industries competitive and export-oriented. Implicit in this history is a stylized account of the post-war re-emergence of industrial capitalism, according to which expanding trade and foreign direct investment since the 1950s led, from the 1970s onwards, to the development of other types of financial flows, the integration of global financial markets, and complementary changes in financial and banking institutions, as well as in economic policies and attitudes. These developments helped initiate and shape the globalizing transformations that materialized in the 1980s and the 1990s.

In this materialistic view of recent and contemporary history, the postwar expansion of trade brought in its wake globalizing processes in the spheres of finance, values, culture and communication, politics, and institutions (including the development of international juridical and regulatory mechanisms and institutions) at the expense of old-fashioned national sovereignty. In this stylized history, once lower barriers, expanding trade, increased capital flows and income growth become entrenched in a virtuous cycle, production and financial operations become internationalized. This process is accelerated by new communication technologies and underpinned, besides its own success, by international institutions and regimes needed to regulate and oversee the system.

This or similar stylized models inform most popular accounts of globalization. Beyond their reductionist determinism, these models paradoxically assimilate to the history and processes of globalization regimes and institutions (such as the postwar trading and financial system) that were explicitly designed in the immediate aftermath of World War II to avoid the perils of unrestricted trade and capital flows.[24] Thus while the outcome of the Cold War may have provided the ideological justification for globalization, globalization's history as it is now constructed presents the West's victory in the Cold War itself as a product and realization of the project of globalization. In this narrative, then, globalization represents a natural flow of modern human history not only because it has prevailed over most of the last 150 years and represents the intensification of processes that began five centuries or more ago, but also because it confronted and defeated a resolute ideological, political, and institutional challenge to it.[25]

There is something of a paradox here. The globalizer's history of globalization is a history not only of modern capitalism but of a capitalism with the energy, sway and expansiveness imagined by Marx and nineteenth-century Marxists.[26] Furthermore, while Marxists today may hesitate to acknowledge this history, let alone appear to endorse it as a social or political agenda, they share its imaginings of the past. And the images evoked by nineteenth-century Marxists of the present and future also evoke the vision of the modern globalizers.

If the logic of globalization in its economic, political, and cultural dimensions (on which more is said below) might be a realization of the logic of capital as imagined by Marx, the intellectual and imaginary grounds for thinking of globalization as an inevitable historical process have also been reproduced by ideas about a globally rampant and transformative capitalism as a 'modern world-system' and in other similar forms.[27] A vast array of political parties, activists and scholars, even self-proclaimed opponents of globalization, have also helped, each in their own way, to reify the phenomenon. Against such tides the chronological disjunctures underlined above appear only as wrinkles in the broad sweep of history that globalization is thought to represent.

It is tempting to argue that as a category, globalization merely re-presents international capitalism by another name. Students of economic thought would recognize, for instance, how economic 'common sense' today accords with conventional economic wisdom in the nineteenth century. Whether it is the role of trade, of capital flows, the role of incentives and penalties, especially in labour markets and with regard to labour contracts – or indeed the terms in which the dominant premises, attitudes, and policies in these spheres are often popularly represented (for example, the notion of 'tough love' with its evocation of the filial principles of nineteenth-century utilitarianism) – striking parallels may be found between the present and a hundred years ago.[28] In this vein one may speculate that the category of globalization is a re-invention of international capitalism in search of a new image after 'capitalism' and 'modernity' had become politically compromised or passé, while democracy – which once preceded capitalism in the West's order of battle during the Cold War – has become too subversive.

On the other hand, because it has not acquired any canonical meaning at least yet, and means different things to different people and in different places, globalization has also become hostage to interventions of diverse kinds to shape its meaning and course. Thus it is not only a 'neo-liberal' economic programme reminiscent of nineteenth-century capitalism that is sought to be promoted in its name. Globalization is also the mascot for new global legal, criminal, business, trade and competition regimes. It underlines the strategy not only of international business but also of individuals and agencies that represent the 'non-governmental sector' (which is itself is often institutionalized in the image of the state), with not dissimilar implications for such features of the international system as national sovereignty.[29] Thus although the constitution of the international order may be affected whatever the outcome, globalization is clearly becoming a hegemonic category, and conflicts over its meaning and content actually help to reify the category itself at every step.

This makes it all the more necessary, therefore, to recognize the contextual and contingent use of the term and idea of globalization as a description of the present and as a challenge or programme for the future. A few examples of such contexts should suffice.

Globalization is the danger and opportunity CEOs routinely invoke to announce mergers, rationalization, retrenchments and layoffs, while in doing so they also encourage workers to network their resistance. Globalization is the danger and opportunity that aid agencies evoke to nation-states resisting their reform packages and that national elites evoke to frighten their domestic opponents to accept such reform packages. Globalization is equally the political-institutional condition many in Europe, most notably in the EU, would like to see promoted to rein in the United States and discipline its global weight through a welter of international rules and institutions.[30] Conversely, globalization creates unease not only in developing countries that fear the loss of sovereignty, national cohesion and hard-won economic or political freedom, it is also challenged in many respects by the country that has the most sovereignty to lose in a rule-based international regime – viz. the United States.[31] But globalization is also the hopeful slogan of those within the United States who do not wish this tendency to lead to America's turning its back on the rest of the world and returning to isolation, or moving towards unilateralism.[32] For all these political, social and economic actors, globalization is a category that represents a condition that they seek to promote by the very act of affirming its validity, relevance, and indeed presence in everyday life and beyond.

Thus whether or not it is yet an 'objective condition', globalization can also be usefully regarded as a category that is used to represent a whole range of perceptions about the contemporary world and its trajectories into the present and the future. Whatever their level of coherence, these perceptions have also helped produce and reproduce globalization as a category with no clear or fixed meaning in a whole range of discursive, economic, political, social, and cultural contexts.

The World and Early Modern India

The range of meanings of 'globalization' necessitates delimiting this section with particular clarity, as we narrow our focus from broad concepts to a concrete case-study. The long-term historical trajectory of India, and whether it should be seen as having been largely 'closed' or 'open' to external influence, is of course a matter not only academic debate but of pressing political significance.[33] The following paragraphs discuss India's historical experience in the wider networks of trade since the beginning of the sixteenth century. While remaining sceptical about the usefulness of globalization as a category, we believe that such a discussion could offer interesting insights into current chronologies of globalization and detail in useful ways the processes that are often argued to underlie the phenomenon. Besides, while we may debate whether the world as a whole can become more or less 'globalized', it is possible to achieve a more carefully balanced view of wider regional or global processes by understanding one country's historical experience in the international economy.

In about 1500, the Indian subcontinent already enjoyed extensive links with its neighbouring regions to both west and east, by way of both overland and maritime trade. It is generally agreed that after a period of slump in the early and middle decades of the fifteenth century, these trading links were on the upswing at the moment that the first European maritime expeditions rounded the Cape of Good Hope and entered the Indian Ocean.[34] Yet it is currently impossible to estimate in a plausible way the quantitative relationship between long-distance trade and 'domestic product'.[35] What can be asserted confidently is that this relationship varied considerably from one region to another. Four maritime regions – Gujarat, south-western India, the Coromandel coast to the east, and Bengal – dominated the overseas trading profile, while the upper Gangetic valley and the Punjab played a crucial role in supplying the trade routes extending into Central and West Asia.

There is equally little doubt that this trade expanded between 1500 and 1750. The best documented aspect of this expansion concerns European trade, but it is clear that even in those commodities in which the Europeans were keenly interested, they accounted for only a small proportion of overseas demand. Thus, of the expanding pepper production on the Kerala and Kanara coasts, less than 10 per cent seems to have found its way in 1600 to European markets, the rest being consumed in upper India or in other regional Asian markets.[36] In a similar vein, European demand for Indian cottons, which began to pick up in the late sixteenth century and then witnessed a phase of rapid expansion after about 1680, still remained smaller in 1750 than the demand from Southeast and West Asian markets. A similar argument could be made for such products as Indian silks, or indigo, or opium. In short, what drove Indian external trade to a very large extent in the three centuries after the voyages of Columbus and da Gama was the relationship not to Europe but to other Asian markets, a point that we shall develop below.

There were obviously some spheres in which trade between India and Europe was already crucial by 1700. Yet even here the story is more complex than it appears at first sight. For instance, it was usually assumed that after the great bullion famine of the fifteenth century, the silver- and gold-based monetary expansion in India of the sixteenth and seventeenth centuries was premised above all on the import via the Cape Route of precious metals from the mines of the New World, then under Spanish control. The Mughal tri-metallic monetary system, of which the lynchpin was undoubtedly the silver rupee coin of unusual purity and stability, was thus often taken to be a by-product of the opening up of trade relations with the European chartered trading companies.[37] However, doubts arose some two decades ago, when it was argued that trade between India and West Asia (Safavid Iran and the Ottoman Empire) was far more crucial than direct trade with Europe.[38] In other words, even when silver from the great Bolivian mine of Potosí reached Mughal India in 1680, it was likely to have passed via the Red Sea or the Gulf rather than have arrived directly from Europe.

A further step was taken in the debate when broad quantitative comparisons were made between the Japanese production of precious metals in the seventeenth century and that of the mines of the New World, when the latter was found to be less significant in relative terms. Thus, historiography has gradually shifted to conclude that even in the matter of the trade in precious metals, the history of trading integration cannot simply be one of intercontinental commercial flows, with Europe at the epicentre. India's links with Japan, Southeast Asia, Iran, the Ottoman Empire and East Africa must be factored in for the nature and rhythms of external trade to become clearer.

We have noted above that the canonical narrative of globalization by writers such as Williamson assumes that the centuries between 1500 and 1800 were marked by 'trading monopoly markups, tariffs, non-tariff restrictions, wars and pirates'. Does this correspond to the regime that obtained in India at the time, either in the Mughal Empire or elsewhere?

The evidence in fact clearly suggests that until 1750 tariffs were remarkably low, and that the only significant trading monopoly markups, other than those imposed by the European companies, were to be found on those rare occasions when Mughal officials decided to corner the market in particular goods (the so-called *sauda-yi khass* regime).[39] Nor indeed were 'wars and pirates' of greater significance in the centuries preceding 1750 than in those that followed. Rather, we can broadly characterize this period as one of 'free trade', save when conflicts broke out between the European Companies and one or other Asian power. Certainly, tariff barriers were never imposed to limit the import into South Asia of Chinese, Japanese or Southeast Asian products. The situation on the overland trading routes leading from northern India to Central and West Asia was one where raiding and banditry were undoubtedly periodic features, but once again we cannot see this as a 'mercantilist trading regime' in the sense of Eli Heckscher. It is therefore incorrect to generalize from a limited view of a few European states to all early modern trade.

The trading regime of the centuries from 1450 to 1750 in the Indian Ocean was one where 'free trade' was the rule, with the accompanying buoyancy and overall expansive tendency that characterizes such a regime. Yet we can also identify clear cycles, linked to a number of different factors. Some phases of trade depression, such as in the 1540s and 1630s, can be identified with massive crop failures and famines that have repercussions for the production even of manufactured trading goods. Other cyclical movements, notably in the 1570s, are more difficult to attribute to a single cause. Furthermore, the regional emphasis of trade too tended to shift. If the late sixteenth century was a period of unusual trade dynamism in the Bay of Bengal area, the seventeenth century saw a shift to the western Indian Ocean. The great growth in trade between India and Japan in the seventeenth century, mediated in some measure by the Dutch East India Company, could not be sustained into the next century, when it was opium export from Bihar and Malwa into Southeast Asia and China that provided a major impetus to expanding trade.

A significant debate of the 1970s and 1980s attempted to resolve the question of the importance of such external trading links for the South Asian economy in the early modern period. It is clear that inflows neither of capital nor of labour were of much significance in the centuries before 1800. Rather, Indian capital markets were drawn upon even by Europeans to finance their external trading activities, save in certain areas such as the diamond trade, where capital was sent out from Europe to finance purchases. The significance of the external sector in this period must hence hinge above all on commodity trade. Here, one set of historians – notably K. N. Chaudhuri and Om Prakash – favoured the view that external demand for crucial commodities such as Indian cotton textiles in fact permitted the expansion of both incomes and employment in key regions like Bengal.[40] In their view, the 'bullion for goods' pattern of trade that was favoured by the East India Companies created a steadily expanding economy based on a form of 'export-led growth'. Naturally, such processes of growth were seen as more significant for maritime manufacturing regions like Bengal than for others, but a similar pattern was posited for the Coromandel coast of southeastern India and for Gujarat.

Critics of this view have taken several distinct positions. Some have argued that external trade was too insignificant in quantitative terms to play such a role, suggesting that India at this time was a massive, primarily agrarian economy, with a tiny external sector. Others have argued that this view overstates the role of overseas trade to the detriment of overland trade into Central and West Asia, and thus also allows too central a role to the European trading companies. And finally, it has been pointed out that the model of 'export-led growth' is somewhat inappropriate to deal with the situation in this period, since it assumes that significant 'slack' resources existed (notably labour) that could be drawn upon, as in the poor economies of the twentieth century. Thus, the Keynesian assumptions of the theoretical model have been called into question.[41]

Be that as it may, the central question remains an empirical one, and almost impossible to address at the present moment. For it is simply not feasible to produce a set of plausible figures that might represent the evolving relationship between the external trade sector and gross domestic product in South Asia over the years between 1500 and 1800. We simply cannot say whether the share of the external sector in total productive activity was larger or smaller in 1750 than in 1850 (when the figure was probably of the order of 12 to 15 per cent). This presents a major impediment for a smooth Williamsonian narrative of a phase of 'anti-globalization' prior to 1820 that is followed by the economic integration of South Asia with the outside world thereafter.

A further set of remarks may be in order on the human dimensions. Large-scale labour flows into and out of South Asia are not a marked feature of the early modern period, although labour circulation into Sri Lanka from India can certainly not be underestimated. Indian slaves did enter the Indian Ocean traffic periodically, and can be found both in island economies such as Mauritius and in great port-cities like Jakarta in the seventeenth and eighteenth centuries.[42] These slaves were recruited from Bengal, southeastern India and the Malabar coast, and some of them could even be found as far afield as Lisbon. Still, it is with the nineteenth century, and the colonial indenture system, that such labour flows assume more major dimensions. On the other hand, the movement of elites was a marked feature of the period, and we are aware that the Mughals, as well as other regional polities, welcomed migrants from Central Asia, Iran and the Ottoman domains. Again, the African presence in India is largely to be linked with the elite slave traffic of the medieval and early modern periods, when such Afro-Indian elites as the Maliks of Ahmadnagar and the Sidis of Janjira played a pivotal role.[43]

In respect of these forms of circulation and integration, it can even be argued that the years from 1780 to 1830 represent a reversal, and the establishment of the British Empire in India in fact reduces the human contacts that had linked South Asia to other parts of the Indian Ocean littoral.

Colonial Trade and Globalization

It is widely acknowledged that India's engagement with the international economy underwent major changes during the course of the nineteenth century. Between 1800 and about 1850 the subcontinent was transformed from an exporter of manufactures, especially cotton cloth, to an exporter of predominantly agricultural products. It made little difference to this picture that India began to export modest quantities of low-grade machine-made yarn by the end of the nineteenth century, nor that its basket of primary product exports was quite diverse by the standards of other colonies or even of similarly-sized or placed economies such as, say, China. In the monetary and financial spheres, too, this century saw several notable changes, including the entry in a big way of European agency houses and later of exchange banks, which increasingly took over the financing and moving of Indian trade, and by doing so exerted a key influence on relative prices, patterns of production and specialization, and the eventual standardization of the monetary system.

Apart from the well-surveyed issue of de-industrialization in the Gangetic basin and the growth of commercial agriculture in some parts of nineteenth-century India, much more remains to be learnt in economic history about the effects of these transformations and the accompanying rearticulations of occupational structure, and labour, entrepreneurial, trading and financial networks on the Indian economy and society. A major explanation for this inadequacy lies in the hegemonic assumption that a Euro-centric world economy was created and that traditional trading and financial networks were fundamentally transformed by western colonialism and modern capitalism in the late nineteenth century. This assumption may not be fundamentally wrong.

Yet it is worth asking how far this assumption itself may have encouraged the neglect of large swathes of economic activity in India that bore a relatively more open-ended relationship with their external networks. Whether as a discursive strategy or because they were convinced liberal anti-imperialists, India's late nineteenth-century nationalists took a British-centric view of the world that ceded agency to Britain and its traders, bankers and entrepreneurs, protected or supported by the imperial state.

Most modern scholarly writings on India's engagement with the world faithfully reproduce this view, but several issues of significance for the making of the late nineteenth century world are thereby obscured. These include the contested processes that characterized the formation of the international economy in the nineteenth century; the many layers that existed in what is simplistically understood to be a single, integrated, and in some respects even centralized global economy; conflicts and other connections between these layers; the roles of peasants, workers and entrepreneurial agents in diverse parts of the world who experienced these conflicts and forged these connections; and not least, the politics of the discursive production, both contemporary and historical, of a single, 'modern' and 'rational' world economy that superseded earlier forms of economic organization and was so manifestly superior that the rest of the world had to adjust or adapt to it.

Quantitatively-based research in economic history is even more deeply implicated in the modalities of colonial rule. Writing about trade in the Indian Ocean in the seventeenth and eighteenth centuries, Ashin Das Gupta remarked on the 'absence of statistics' being a 'fact of life with which the student of India's medieval economy has learned to live ...', and which made a history of foreign trade of this period into a 'discussion of the structure of commerce and the role of the merchant in it'.[44] However, thanks in particular to the colonial state's interest in meeting its external obligations and managing the currency, we are somewhat better served in the matter of colonial India's foreign trade and capital movements (the latter notably after the formation of the League of Nations) than about earlier periods or about most other aspects of its economy. There have also been several estimates of India's national income since about the middle of the nineteenth century.

Working with the trade data compiled by the colonial state and estimates of India's national income at various times, several attempts have been made to work out the extent of the Indian economy's engagement with the world economy and the trends therein. According to K. N. Chaudhuri, using V. K. R. V. Rao's estimate of India's national income in 1931–2, exports (9.54 per cent) and imports (7.73 per cent) together accounted that year for about 17.3 per cent of the national income. In the middle of the Great Depression this probably represented a lower-bound estimate for the interwar period, with trade as a proportion of national income in the 1920s not far off the estimated prewar ratio of about 20 per cent.

The trend in this ratio during the preceding half-century appears to have been remorselessly upwards. According to Nabendu Sen's estimates, the average proportion of foreign trade to national income rose from less than 12 per cent between 1858–9 and 1871–2 to about 14 per cent over the next two decades. The average ratio of foreign trade to the *gross* national product rose during the two decades before World War I to about 18 per cent (peaking at over 22 per cent in 1912–13).[45] If we conservatively assume a rate of growth of national income of 1 per cent through out this period, Sen's estimate is consistent with a rate of growth of foreign trade of about 2 per cent per annum. Tirthankar Roy estimates a faster increase in the share of foreign trade to national income than Nabendu Sen, with this share rising from 4 per cent in 1857 to over 20 per cent in 1913.[46] At the same growth rate of aggregate incomes of 1 per cent per annum, this presumes a rate of growth of foreign trade of about 4 per cent per annum.

On the other hand, K. N. Chaudhuri estimates that Indian foreign trade 'more than quadrupled in value and volume' between 1814 and 1858.[47] If this is right, and if income growth in India during this period was not greatly out of line with the 1 per cent rate assumed for the second half of the nineteenth century, the share of trade to income that year would have been in the region of about 1.5 per cent.[48] Since this appears implausible on the face of it, it is likely that while Nabendu Sen may well have underestimated the extent to which the Indian economy became oriented towards foreign trade between 1858 and 1913, Roy probably rather overestimates the phenomenon.

Because the coverage of foreign trade statistics is uneven, and national income data for the nineteenth and early twentieth centuries are largely informed guesswork, it is difficult to arrive at any definitive conclusion about the role of foreign trade overall in the Indian economy. Yet it seems reasonable to assume that the share of foreign trade to national income in 1858 lay somewhere between Sen's and Roy's estimates. It also seems reasonable to conclude that the Indian economy grew more exposed to world trade in the second half of the nineteenth century and in the years leading up to World War I. This trend was interrupted during World War I, but the mid-1920s appear to have seen a spurt in this share at least to prewar levels if not higher, before experiencing a rather longer-lasting decline, due in turn to the Great Depression, World War II and the strategy of import-substituting industrialization necessitated by the foreign exchange crisis that independent India faced with the implementation of the Second Five-Year Plan.

Not surprisingly, India's trade accounts in the century prior to 1950 displayed a distinctly 'colonial' character. As is well-known, India ran a surplus on the trade account (excluding treasure) during most of this period. The trade surplus is estimated to have fluctuated between 2 per cent and 4 per cent of the gross national product between the 1860s and 1913 and between 0.5 per cent and about 2 per cent during 1921–46. The 'home charges' and imports of gold and silver between them left little room for other service payments that were largely met through capital imports.[49]

Estimates of the ratio of capital imports (or exports) to national income have to be regarded with particular caution because of the quality of the underlying data. According to Goldsmith, foreign investment in India was 'small' before 1857 and consisted primarily of British investors' holdings of East India Company stock. Thereafter, annual investment inflow is estimated to have amounted to about 1 per cent of the national income between 1860 and 1913, with this proportion doubling from about 0.7 per cent between 1860 and 1898 to 1.5 per cent in the next 15 years. The increase in foreign investment was 'moderate and irregular' after 1913 and is estimated by Goldsmith to have averaged about 1 per cent of the national income between 1921 and 1929. He also estimates net capital *exports* of 0.5 per cent of GNP in the depressed 1930s and nearly 5 per cent during World War II, so that for the 1921–46 period as a whole, India appears to have faced a net foreign investment *outflow* amounting to 1.6 per cent of the GNP.[50]

Capital imports averaged about a fifth of gross domestic capital formation during 1860–1913. This proportion rose from about one-seventh during 1860–*c*.1900 to one-fifth during the next few years. In relation to net capital formation, capital imports rose from about one-fourth in the earlier period to one-third in the later one, with the proportion averaging about one-fourth for the period as a whole. As against estimates for gross capital formation of 6 to 8 per cent of GNP and net capital formation of 4 per cent of GNP for 1901–13 'with only small year-to-year variations', we have estimates for the 1914–46 period averaging some 7 per cent in the case of the ratio of gross capital formation to GNP (with a range for annual rates of 5 per cent to about 9 per cent) and a more or less stable 2.25 per cent in the case of the ratio of net capital formation. While the low ratio of net capital formation is definitely curious and India's record in respect of gross capital formation in the post-World War I period anything but spectacular, it is interesting, nevertheless, to observe the rather limited impact of the withdrawal of foreign capital in the later period on India's overall rates of gross capital formation.[51]

The readily available price data do not allow us to estimate the extent of price convergence as a measure of India's integration with the world economy. Likewise, savings and investment data have been estimated for long periods of several decades rather than for individual years, so that it is not possible to estimate, for example, the Feldstein-Horioka measure of financial integration for India during our period. In their absence we may briefly summarize India's economic engagement with the rest of the world during the six decades or so between the middle of the nineteenth century and the beginning of World War I to point out that while trade and capital inflows expanded more or less steadily throughout this period, they did so at a considerably faster clip during the second half of this period than during the first. The post-World War I period saw a slower expansion of trade and capital inflows in the 1920s followed by a period of decline during the 1930s.

India's engagement with the world economy was strongly conditioned by its colonial status. Indeed, many aspects of this engagement, including the transformation of India's trading basket during the course of the nineteenth century, would be impossible to understand outside this colonial context. India's colonial status also determined the nature of its macro-institutional articulation with the global economy until the eve of World War II, and it is to two aspects of this articulation that we turn in the remainder of this section.

As noted above, even at the height of the trading boom on the eve of World War I, and despite India's determinedly staying the course as a small, open economy with no barriers to trade (other than perhaps extreme poverty), the external sector was not particularly overwhelming or preponderant in relation to domestic economic activity. Nevertheless it exerted a disproportionately large influence on the Indian economy and the livelihood of its people because of the colony's macro-institutional structure.

Even if they did not necessarily represent it in these terms, until the late 1910s India was perceived as a 'small, open economy' by successive generations of colonial economic officials.[52] Doing so predisposed them to adopt a passive macro-economic stance and pro-cyclical behaviour that intensified the impact of external influences on the Indian economy. Although peace-time experiments in macro-economic management are of later origin, few non-industrial countries in the nineteenth and twentieth centuries pursued their commitment to preserving an open economy (including allowing destabilizing short-term capital movements to take place without let or hindrance) and discharging external obligations with the same tenacity and consistency as colonial India. Thus India's vulnerability as a passive victim of trade and economic shocks originating overseas, more than the intrinsic exposure of its economy to foreign trade or capital flows, describes the colonial Indian economy's experience of 'globalization'.

It is useful at this stage in our discussion to look separately at two aspects of this tenacious openness – that is, short-term capital movements and the discharge of *current* account obligations. The latter has attracted a certain amount of attention in the context of discussions of the so-called 'drain' and will not be further discussed here, but the importance of the former has been less well recognized even when it has not been conflated or confounded with the latter.[53]

The principal component of short-term capital movements to (and from) India was banking or trading capital. This was primarily the funds that flowed to India to finance trade during each busy season (running roughly from October to April) when interest rates tended to rise, and returned to London at the end of the season. In addition, asset and liquidity management decisions by European-owned and managed banks that mobilized deposits in India and kept a large portion of them as reserves in London might also lead to substantial movements of short-term funds. Although short-term seasonal inflows helped finance trade, they also accentuated India's economic and institutional weaknesses and vulnerability to external pressures in several directions. These included the persistent under-development of the Indian banking system and promoting the centralization of Indian banking resources in London. Both factors reinforced India's dependence on overseas short-term capital and exchange banks to finance trade. These flows, needless to stress, were extremely sensitive to global trading conditions and helped transmit them directly to the Indian producer.[54] India's dependence on London-based banks for financing trade also disabled it from imposing controls on destabilizing short-term capital *outflows* because of the risk of endangering *future inflows*.

Finally, the effects of variations in these flows were not confined to the Indian producer of exportables. In the virtual absence of commercial banking, India's monetary system almost wholly comprised currency and coin until the 1920s. Even this under-developed monetary system was all but inelastic, because currency expansion was determined by the inflow of funds to finance trade.[55] Consequently, trading shocks that affected the quantum (or direction) of short-term capital inflows immediately exerted a severe monetary and macro-economic impact on the colony.

The colonial imprint on India's macro-institutional articulation with the world economy is also evident in the context of its historical counter-cyclical role in this economy. It is well-known, thanks principally to S. B. Saul, that India played a balancing role in the late nineteenth-century international economic system by helping to finance Britain's deficits with the rest of the world.[56] It is also well-known that India was (as in the early modern period) a large importer of precious metals, and after the price of silver relative to gold began to decline from the 1870s, increasingly of gold. India's gold imports were feared to have a destabilizing impact on the world economy in the short run by driving up interest rates in the advanced money markets, but it was believed to be a stabilizing force globally in the longer run, because it helped to depress the world rate of inflation and to regulate or check a world boom. The mechanism for this, as Keynes underlined in his *Indian Currency and Finance*, was that as the world economy expanded and output and prices rose, Indian exports and export revenues also increased. This translated into higher incomes in India, especially for households involved in the export sector, some proportion of which they preferred to hold in the form of gold; their preference for the metal usually grew, other things remaining the same, as the global (and Indian) rate of inflation rose. Consequently, gold outflows to India from the rest of the world increased during a global boom. But such outflows also helped to promote tighter monetary conditions in the gold exporting countries (mainly the industrial countries) and to arrest an inflationary spiral there.[57]

Conversely, in theory, Indian gold holdings could also ease the effects of a slump as Indian households liquidated their savings in the form of the metal to finance consumption and meet fixed debt obligations. But in the 1920s and the 1930s, as Britain's external financial problems deepened and it became dependent on a global inflationary spiral to bring its own economy back into equilibrium with the rest of the world and particularly with the United States, India's counter-cyclical propensity became a basis for official policy. Consequently, official policy focused on restricting Indian gold imports during the boom years of the interwar economy (mainly the mid-1920s), and on promoting Indian gold dissaving and exports during the depression of the 1930s. Although the former policy was far from successful in achieving its intended object, it nevertheless worked well enough, despite the expansion of its exports especially in the mid-1920s, to insulate India from the global booms of the decade.[58] And conversely, although Indian became a large net exporter of gold in the depression, and by contemporary estimation, a major reflationary influence on the world economy, these gold exports did very little to ease India's plight in the Great Depression.

Conclusion

We have had two principal objectives in this chapter. First, we attempted to provide a sceptical survey of the recent uses of the concept of 'globalization', as well as of certain grand narratives produced by economic historians. These narratives are in turn clearly linked to the prevailing ideologies of the day, which seek to portray the emergence of the global market in the form of a *telos*, perhaps linked in turn to ideas such as the 'end of history' that have been propagated since the end of the Cold War. The eschatological tone of some of these writings, in which the market invariably appears as the central axis, can be compared to the tenets of many a millenarian movement. Thus we being told of 'a final world in which there would be "cosmos without chaos", a world of "making wonderful" without imperfections, an eternal peace beyond history, [and] a changeless realm ruled by an unchallenged god', with the resolution of the Cold War being presented as 'a final apocalyptic battle between two forces, a battle in which, after much agony, the good would triumph and the evil be driven from the earth'.[59] From our viewpoint, then, it is rather disingenuous to believe that 'the discourse of globalization differs from that of modernization by relinquishing a Eurocentric teleology to accommodate the possibility of different historical trajectories in the unfolding of modernities'.[60] On the contrary, the discourse of globalization in the hands of its market-obsessed proponents renders the processes even more mechanical.

Secondly, we took a long view of the economic relationship between India and the rest of the world, in order to question the received wisdom that sees recent 'globalization' and its attendant 'liberalization' as processes without precedent before the planning system and the so-called licence-permit raj were dismantled in fits and starts from the mid-1980s onwards. A persistent cliché, especially prevalent amongst liberal economists, has been that India had for centuries had a closed, highly regimented economy, which Deepak Lal described in a polemical work as 'the Hindu equilibrium'.[61] Instead, we have suggested that through much of the early modern period, as well as in colonial times, India experienced a relatively high degree of openness, in its commodity markets and for other factor flows. To this extent the control system put in place in the 1950s, whether with respect to labour export, capital import or the free flow of commodities, must be seen as an aberration, and the roots of the political economy that produced it cannot be sought in the depths of Indian culture. Rather, we must look to a specific political conjuncture that emerged under successive Congress governments, involving a form of implicit collaboration between powerful rural interests, indigenous capitalists with a protectionist bent of mind, and a bureaucracy that eventually came to be constituted itself as an interest group.[62]

The changes of the past decade and a half in India must not be seen therefore as the first time the 'market' has played a significant role in Indian history. What is new is the conjuncture, and the institutions – both internal and external – that underpin the market today. This should undoubtedly encourage us to 'look for state processes and effects in sites less obvious than those of institutionalized politics and established bureaucracies'[63] – but it should not lead us to the illusion that the market has somehow replaced politics.

Notes

1 'At the end of the twentieth century, globalization became an all-purpose catchword in public and scholarly debate': Frank J. Lechner and John Boli, eds, *The Globalization Reader* (Oxford, 2000), p. 1; 'Globalization is the catchword of the day': A. G. Hopkins, ed., *Globalization in World History* (London, 2002), p. 1. Lechner and Boli (p. 1) also describe it as a 'cliché', as do David Held, Anthony McGrew, David Goldblatt and Jonathan Perraton, *Global Transformations: Politics, Economics, and Culture* (Stanford, 1999), p. 1.

2 Hopkins, ed., *Globalization in History* (see note 1), p. 1.

3 Held *et al.*, *Global Transformations* (see note 1), p. 2.

4 Serge Gruzinski, *Virando Séculos 1480–1520. A passagem do século: Às origens da globalização* (São Paulo, 1999).

5 Cf Andrew Gow, 'Gog and Magog on *Mappaemundi* and early printed world maps: orientalizing ethnography in the apocalyptic tradition', *Journal of Early Modern History*, Vol. 2, no. 1, 1998, pp.61–88.

6 Nathan Wachtel, *La foi du souvenir: Labyrinthes marranes* (Paris, 2001).

7 Kevin H. O'Rourke and Jeffrey G. Williamson, *Globalization and History* (Cambridge, Mass., 1999); O'Rourke and Williamson, 'When did globalization begin?', *European Review of Economic History*, Vol. 6, Part 1, 2002, pp. 23–50; Peter H. Lindert and Jeffrey G. Williamson, 'Does globalization make the world more unequal?', in Michael Bordo, A. M. Taylor and J. G. Williamson, eds, *Globalization in Historical Perspective* (Chicago, 2002).

8 Frederick Cooper, 'What is the concept of globalization good for?: an African historian's perspective', *African Affairs*, No. 100, 2001, pp. 189–213.

9 Jeffrey G. Williamson, 'Winners and losers over two centuries of globalization', NBER Working Paper No. 9161, 2002, p. 1.

10 Williamson, 'Winners and losers' (see note 9), p. 5.

11 Williamson, 'Winners and losers' (see note 9), p. 2; also see Kevin O'Rourke and Jeffrey G. Williamson, 'After Columbus: Explaining Europe's overseas trade boom, 1500–1800', *Journal of Economic History*, Vol. 62, 2002, pp. 417–56.

12 Thus Kevin H. O'Rourke's otherwise careful comparison of merchandise trade shares relative to GDP and value added ignores the regional aspect of trading integration: O'Rourke, 'Europe and the causes of globalization: 1790–2000', in Henryk Kierzkowski, ed., *Europe and Globalization* (London, 2002), p. 70; note in this connection that regional integration is often regarded as a substitute or defensive response to economic 'globalization' rather than as part of the latter process.

13 Recent advances in macro-economic coordination and management and institutional design may prolong this cycle while retaining within its regime countries that in earlier or other circumstances may have fallen out, such as Argentina during its latest financial crisis. But such features of the contemporary regime highlight the political constitution of institutions and practices glibly associated with globalization, simplistically understood as a spontaneous and historically unstoppable process.

14 According to the Feldstein-Horioka measure, the higher the correlation between domestic investment and saving, the lower the degree of financial market integration; conversely, 'with perfect world capital mobility, there should be no relation between domestic saving and domestic investment'. See Martin Feldstein and Charles Horioka, 'Domestic saving and international capital flows', *The Economic Journal*, Vol. 90, No. 358 (June 1980), pp. 314–29.

15 O'Rourke, 'Europe and the causes of globalization' (see note 12), pp. 68–70; the ambiguity arises because the share of merchandise to GDP has gone down during the last century, so that a lower share of merchandise trade to GDP is consistent with a higher share of merchandise trade to value added. But as argued above, a higher ratio of the latter might arise from regional integration rather than globalization.

16 O'Rourke, 'Europe and the causes of globalization' (see note 12), p. 71.

17 Baldwin and Martin, 'Two waves of globalization: superficial similarities, fundamental differences', National Bureau of Economic Research Working Paper No. 6904 (Cambridge, Mass., 1999).

18 O'Rourke, 'Europe and the causes of globalization' (see note 12), p. 68.

19 In a paradox that has not received the attention it deserves, countries that followed protectionist policies during 1870–1914 grew faster than those that did not: Paul Bairoch, 'European trade policy, 1815–1914', in P. Mathias and S. S. Pollard, eds, *The Cambridge Economic History of Europe*, vol. 8: *The Industrial Economies: The Development of Economic and Social Policies* (Cambridge, 1989), pp. 69–70.

20 Baldwin and Martin, 'Two waves' (see note 17), pp. 9–10, for the relevant Feldstein-Horioka measures. According to the estimates they reproduce, the decennial correlation coefficients between 1870 and 1990, are roughly as follows:

1870–79	0.6	1900–09	0.78	1930–39	0.9	1960–69	0.95
1880–89	0.4	1910–19	0.78	1940–49	1.05	1970–79	0.95
1890–99	0.59	1920–29	0.5	1950–59	1.0	1980–89	0.7

Note: these numbers are read off from histograms charted against a Y-axis marked at intervals of 0.2.

21 The argument that the interwar period is one of 'de-globalization' is implicit in Baldwin and Martin (see note 17). For a more explicit statement, see James Foreman-Peck, ed., *Historical Foundations of Globalization* (Cheltenham, 1998) pp. xxiii-iv and Part VI.

22 David Harvey, *Spaces of Hope* (Berkeley, 2000), pp. 12–14.

23 This view is argued in different degrees by Baldwin and Martin (see note 17), and by O'Rourke (see note 12).

24 Thus the IMF articles of agreement allowed member countries to impose capital controls (VI.3) and disallowed the use of fund resources to finance 'large or sustained outflow of capital' (VI.1).

25 To this defeated challenge is also assimilated, in turn, all historical and contemporary opposition to modernity and capitalism.

26 It is often forgotten that until after World War I Marxian economists viewed capitalism as an expansive system capable of self-renewal. How they came to view it thereafter as a system enmeshed in a terminal crisis remains insufficiently researched. Note in this connection that the original Russian subtitle of V. I. Lenin's *Imperialism* was *The Latest Stage of Capitalism*.

27 Note here that André Gunder Frank's 'alternative history' of globalization does not challenge the process but only displaces its location while curiously affirming its modern logic: *ReOrient: Global Economy in the Asian Age* (Berkeley, 1997).

28 But there are important differences: the international monetary and financial regimes are more closely regulated through formally independent international institutions while national monetary and fiscal policies now have greater degree flexibility than under the pre-1913 gold standard (though less flexibility compared to the first three decades after World War II). There is also greater recognition now of market imperfections in world trade.

29 On the implication of non-governmental organizations with a global regulatory regime that attempts in certain contexts to sidestep governments in developing countries, see Julia Elyachar, 'Mappings of power: the state, NGOs and international organizations in the informal economy of Cairo', *Comparative Studies in Society and History*, Vol. 45, No. 3, 2003.

30 Thus not only the rule-based WTO that disciplines US unilateral impulses with respect to international trade, but also such European concerns as an international competition law.

31 Thus the US efforts to explore the scope for unilateral action within the WTO regime, and its repudiation of international agreements like the Kyoto protocol on climate

change and the Rome convention on the international criminal court, both of which are justified as cooperative international efforts to deal with global challenges.

32 For example, Thomas L. Friedman, *The Lexus and the Olive Tree* (New York, 1999), and his *New York Times* columns on a suitable US foreign policy in a globalized world; and Joseph S. Nye, Jr, *The Paradox of American Power: Why the world's only Superpower can't go it alone* (New York, 2002).

33 See Sanjay Subrahmanyam, 'Inde ouverte ou Inde fermée', in Yves Michaud, ed., *Qu'est-ce que la culture?* Université de tous les savoirs, Vol. 6 (Paris, 2001), pp. 69–79.

34 Ashin Das Gupta and M. N. Pearson, eds, *India and the Indian Ocean, 1500–1800* (Calcutta, 1987).

35 For a wholly unconvincing attempt, see Shireen Moosvi, 'The Gross National Product of the Mughal Empire, *c.*1600', *The Indian Historical Review*, Vol. 13, Nos 1–2, 1988, pp. 75–87.

36 Jan Kieniewicz, 'Pepper gardens and market in pre-colonial Malabar', *Moyen Orient et Océan Indien*, Vol. III, 1986, pp. 75–87; also A. R. Disney, *Twilight of the Pepper Empire: Portuguese Trade in Southwest India in the Seventeenth Century* (Cambridge, Mass., 1978).

37 J. F. Richards, 'Mughal state finance and the pre-modern world economy', *Comparative Studies in Society and History*, Vol. 23, No. 2, 1981, pp. 285–308.

38 See Sanjay Subrahmanyam, 'Precious metal flows and prices in western and southern Asia, 1500–1750: Some comparative and conjunctural aspects', *Studies in History*, (N.S.), Vol. 7, No. 1, 1991, pp. 79–105.

39 For a discussion, see Sanjay Subrahmanyam, 'Persianisation and mercantilism: Two themes in Bay of Bengal history, 1400–1700', in Denys Lombard and Om Prakash, eds, *Commerce and Culture in the Bay of Bengal, 1500–1800* (New Delhi, 1999), pp. 47–85.

40 K. N. Chaudhuri, *The Trading World of Asia and the English East India Company, 1660–1760* (Cambridge, 1978); Om Prakash, *The Dutch East India Company and the Economy of Bengal, 1630–1720* (Princeton, 1985).

41 Sanjay Subrahmanyam, *The Political Economy of Commerce: Southern India, 1500–1650* (Cambridge, 1990).

42 For a rapid survey, see S. Arasaratnam, 'The slave trade in the Indian Ocean in the seventeenth century', in K. S. Matthew, ed., *Mariners, Merchants and Oceans: Studies in Maritime History* (New Delhi, 1995), pp. 195–208.

43 Shanti Sadiq Ali, *The African Dispersal in the Deccan, from Medieval to Modern Times* (New Delhi, 1996); also Sonia Miegakanda Bouketo, 'Des Africains à leurs descendants en Inde: les Siddhis du Nord Kanara du XVIème siècle à nos jours', *DEA Memoir*, EHESS, 2002.

44 Das Gupta, 'Indian merchants and trade in the Indian Ocean', in Tapan Raychaudhuri and Irfan Habib, eds, *The Cambridge Economic History of India*, vol. 1: *c.*1200–1750 (hereafter *CEHI I*) (Cambridge, 1982), p. 407.

45 K. N. Chaudhuri, 'Foreign trade and balance of payments 1757–1947', in Dharma Kumar, ed. *The Cambridge Economic History of India*, vol. 2: *c.*1757–1970 (hereafter *CEHI II*) (Cambridge, 1983), pp. 804–5; Nabendu Sen, *India in the International Economy, 1858–1913: Some aspects of trade and finance* (Calcutta, 1992), pp. 34–7. The proportion of foreign trade to national income for Sen's last period would have been higher.

46 Tirthankar Roy, *The Economic History of India, 1857–1947* (Delhi, 2000), pp. 34–5. A 1 per cent growth rate of national income is assumed not because it is more realistic but because a higher rate of growth of national income would have required an even higher rate of growth of foreign trade for the postulated proportions for the two dates to hold.

47 K. N. Chaudhuri, *Economic Development of India under the East India Company, 1814–1858: A selection of contemporary writings* (Cambridge, 1971), p. 1.
48 According to Prinsep's estimates of trade from the port of Calcutta, for instance, 1814 was the first year of a post-Napoleonic war boom that saw the value of Calcutta's trade rising by nearly 60 per cent in next five years: George Alexander Prinsep, 'Remarks on the external commerce and exchanges of Bengal, with Appendix of accounts and estimates (1823)', in Chaudhuri, ed., *Economic Development of India* (see note 47), pp. 110–11. Although Prinsep's figures include Calcutta's trade with ports on the Coromandel and Malabar coasts, such trade does not appear to have been very significant, amounting perhaps to about 7 per cent of the port's total trade (pp. 82–3).
49 Raymond Goldsmith, *The Financial Development of India, 1860–1977* (Delhi, 1983), pp. 16–17 and 76–7.
50 Goldsmith, *Financial Development* (see note 49), pp. 17–18 and 76–8.
51 Goldsmith, *Financial Development* (see note 49), pp. 19, 79.
52 This reflected the influence upon officials of a kind of liberal economic theorizing that was still relatively recent (and not yet well established) even in Britain, let alone elsewhere. See J. Maloney, *Marshall, Orthodoxy and the Professionalization of Economics* (Cambridge, 1985). This recalls to mind the greater grip of economic orthodoxy today on policy-makers in developing countries, generally, than in the industrially developed countries, especially the United States.
53 For a discussion of the 'drain' and an elaboration of this argument, see 'Introduction', in G. Balachandran, ed., *India and the World Economy* (Delhi, 2003).
54 D. E. Moggridge and E. Johnson, eds, *The Collected Writings of John Maynard Keynes*, Vol. 1, *Indian Currency and Finance* (London, 1971) (hereafter *JMK I*) pp. 151–6; on the vulnerability of these funds and of the Indian financial system generally to a crisis in London, see pp. 149–51.
55 Chaudhuri, 'Foreign trade', *CEHI II*, p. 805; Goldsmith, *Financial Development* (see note 49), p. 9; A. G. Chandavarkar, 'Money and credit, 1858–1947' in *CEHI II*, p. 774; *JMK I*, p. 40.
56 S. B. Saul, *Studies in British Overseas Trade, 1870–1914* (Liverpool, 1960).
57 *JMK I*, pp. 70–1.
58 Derek. H. Aldcroft, *From Versailles to Wall Street, 1919–1929* (London, 1977), p. 216. This argument about India's counter-cyclical role in the world economy is explored in G. Balachandran, *John Bullion's Empire: Britain's gold problems and India between the wars* (London, 1996).
59 These quotations are taken from Jonathan D. Spence, *God's Chinese Son: The Taiping Heavenly Kingdom of Hong Xiuquan* (London, 1996), p. xx, and refer to the standard vocabulary of millenarian movements.
60 Arif Dirlik, 'Modernity as history: post-revolutionary China, globalization and the question of modernity', *Social History*, Vol. 27, No. 1, 2002, p. 25. Dirlik's essay is remarkable for its continual complicity with the very views it claims to critique.
61 Deepak Lal, *The Hindu Equilibrium*, Vol. I: *Cultural Stability and Economic Stagnation, c.1500 BC–AD 1980* (Oxford, 1988).
62 For a useful schematic argument, see Pranab Bardhan, *The Political Economy of Development in India* (Oxford, 1984).
63 Michel-Rolph Trouillot, 'The Anthropology of the state in the age of globalization: close encounters of the deceptive kind', *Current Anthropology*, Vol. 42, No. 1, 2001, p. 133.

Bibliography

Aldcroft, Derek H. (1977) *From Versailles to Wall Street, 1919–1929*. London: Allen Lane.

Ali, Shanti Sadiq (1996) *The African Dispersal in the Deccan, from Medieval to Modern Times*. New Delhi: Orient Longman.

Arasaratnam, S. (1995) 'The slave trade in the Indian Ocean in the seventeenth century', in K. S. Matthew, ed., *Mariners, Merchants and Oceans: Studies in Maritime History*. New Delhi: Manohar; pp.195–208.

Bairoch, Paul (1988) 'European trade policy, 1815–1914', in Paul Mathias and Sidney Pollard, eds, *The Industrial Economies: The development of economic and social policies* (The Cambridge Economic History of Europe, vol. 8*)*. Cambridge: Cambridge University Press.

Balachandran, G. (2003) *India and the World Economy*. Delhi: Oxford University Press.

—— (1996) *John Bullion's Empire: Britain's gold problems and India between the wars*. Richmond, Surrey: Curzon.

Baldwin, Richard and P. Martin (1999) 'Two waves of globalization: Superficial similarities, fundamental differences'. National Bureau of Economic Research Working Paper No. 6904.

Bardhan, Pranab (1984) *The Political Economy of Development in India*. Oxford: Blackwell.

Chandarvarkar, A. G. (1988) 'Money and credit', in Dharma Kumar, ed., The Cambridge Economic History of India, vol. 2: 1757–1970. Cambridge: Cambridge University Press.

Chaudhuri, K. N. (1983) 'Foreign trade and balance of payments', in Dharma Kumar, ed., *The Cambridge Economic History of India*, vol. 2: 1757–1970. Cambridge: Cambridge University Press.

—— (1978) *The Trading World of Asia and the English East India Company, 1660–1760*. Cambridge: Cambridge University Press.

—— (1971) *The Economic Development of India Under the East India Company, 1814–1858: A selection of contemporary writings*. London: Cambridge University Press.

Cooper, Frederick (2001) 'What is the concept of globalization good for?: An African historian's perspective'. *African Affairs*, 100: 189–213.

Dirlik, Arif (2002) 'Modernity as history: Post-revolutionary China and the question on modernity'. *Social History*, 27 (1): 16–39.

Disney, A. R. (1978) *Twilight of the Pepper Empire: Portuguese trade in southwest India in the seventeenth century*. Cambridge, Mass.: Harvard University Press.

Das Gupta, Achin (1982) 'Indian merchants and trade in the Indian Ocean', in Tapan Raychaudhuri and Irfan Habib eds, The Cambridge Economic History of India, vol. 1: *c.*1200–1750. Cambridge: Cambridge University Press.

Das Gupta, Achin and M. N. Pearson, eds (1987) *India and the Indian Ocean, 1500–1800*. Calcutta: Oxford University Press.

Elyachar, Julia (2003) 'Mappings of power: The state, NGOs and international organizations in the informal economy of Cairo'. *Comparative Studies in Society and History*, 45 (3): 571–605.

Feldstein, Martin and Charles Horioka (1980) 'Domestic saving and international capital flows'. *The Economic Journal*, 90 (358): 314–29.

Foreman-Peck, James, ed. (1998) *Historical Foundations of Globalization*. Cheltenham: Edward Elgar.

Frank, André Gunder (1998) *ReOrient: Global Economy in the Asian Age*. Berkeley: University of California Press.

Friedman, Thomas L. (1999) *Lexus and the Olive Tree*. New York: Farrar, Straus, Giroux.

Goldsmith, Raymond (1983) *The Financial Development of India, 1860–1977*. London: Yale University Press.

Gow, Andrew (1998) 'Gog and Magog on *Mappaemundi* and early printed world maps: Orientalizing ethnography in the apocalyptic tradition'. *Journal of Early Modern History*, 2: 61–88.

Gruzinski, Serge (1999) *Virando Séculos 1480–1520. A passagem do século: Às origens da globalização*. São Paulo: Companhia das Letas.

Harvey, David (2000) *Spaces of Hope*. Berkeley: University of California Press.

Held, David, Anthony McGrew, David Goldblatt and Jonathan Perraton, eds (1999) *Global Transformations: Politics, economics, and culture*. Stanford, CA: Stanford University Press.

Hopkins, A. G., ed. (2002) *Globalization in World History*. London: Pimlico.

Kieniewicz, Jan (1986) 'Pepper gardens and market in pre-colonial Malabar'. *Moyen Orient and Océan Indien*, 3: 75–87.

Lal, Deepak (1988) *The Hindu Equilibrium*, vol. 1: *Cultural Stability and Economic Stagnation, c.1500 BC–AD 1980*. Oxford: Clarendon.

Lechner, Frank J. and John Boli, eds (2000). *The Globalization Reader*. Oxford: Blackwell.

Lindhert, Peter H. and Jeffrey G. Williamson (2002) 'Does globalization make the world more unequal?', in Michael Bordo, A. M. Taylor and J. G. Williamson eds, *Globalization in Historical Perspective*. Chicago: Chicago University Press.

Maloney, John (1985) *Marshall, Orthodoxy and the Professionalisation of Economics*. Cambridge: Cambridge University Press.

Miegakanda Bouketo, Sonia (2002) 'Des Africains à leurs descendants en Inde: les Siddhis du Nord Kanara du XVIème siècle à nos jours'. *DEA Memoir*, EHESS, Paris.

Moggridge, D. E. and E. Johnson, eds (1971) *The collected writings of John Maynard Keynes*, vol. 1: *Indian Currency and Finance*. London: Macmillan for the Royal Economic Society.

Moosvi, Shireen (1988) 'The Gross National Product of the Mughal Empire, c.1600'. *The Indian Historical Review*, 13 (1–2): 75–87.

Nye, Joseph S., Jr (2002) *The Paradox of American Power: Why the world's only Superpower can't go it alone*. New York: Oxford University Press.

O'Rourke, Kevin H. (2002) 'Europe and the causes of globalization, 1790 to 2000', in Henryk Kierzkowski, ed., *Europe and Globalization*. Basingstoke: Palgrave.

O'Rourke, Kevin H. and Jeffrey G. Williamson (1999) *Globalization and History: The evolution of a nineteenth century Atlantic economy*. Cambridge, Mass.: MIT Press.

—— (2002a) 'After Columbus: Explaining Europe's overseas trade boom, 1500–1800'. *Journal of Economic History*, 62: 417–56.

—— (2002b) 'When did the globalization begin?' *European Review of Economic History*, 6: 23–50.

Prakash, Om (1985) *The Dutch East India Company and the Economy of Bengal, 1630–1720*. Princeton: Princeton University Press.

Prinsep, George Alexander (1971) 'Remarks on the external commerce and exchanges on Bengal, with Appendix of accounts and estimates', in K. N. Chaudhuri, ed., *The Economic Development of India Under the East India Company, 1814–1858: A selection of contemporary writings*. London: Cambridge University Press.

Richards, J. F. (1981) 'Mughal state finance and the pre-modern world economy'. *Comparative Studies in Society and History*, 23 (2): 285–308.

Roy, Tirthankar (2000) *The Economic History of India, 1857–1947*. Delhi: Oxford University Press.

Sen, Nabendu (1992) *India in the International Economy, 1858–1913: Some aspects of trade and finance*. Calcutta: Orient Longman.

Spence, Jonathan D. (1996) *God's Chinese Son: The Taiping heavenly kingdom of Hong Xiuquan*. London: HarperCollins.

Subrahmanyam, Sanjay (1990) *The Political Economy of Commerce: Southern India, 1500–1650*. Cambridge: Cambridge University Press.

—— (1991) 'Precious metal flows and prices in western and southern Asia, 1500–1750: Some comparative and conjectural aspects'. *Studies in History* (N.S.), 7 (1): 79–105.

—— (1999) 'Persianisation and mercantilism: Two themes in Bay of Bengal history, 1400–1700', in Denys Lombard and Om Prakash, eds, *Commerce and Culture in the Bay of Bengal, 1500–1800*. New Delhi: Manohar; pp. 47–85.

—— (2001) 'Inde ouverte ou Inde fermée', in Yves Michaud, ed., *Qu'est-ce que la culture?* Université de tous les savoirs, vol. 6. Paris: O. Jacob; pp. 69–79.

Trouillot, Michel-Rolph (2001) 'The anthropology of the state in the age of globalization: Close encounters of the deceptive kind'. *Current Anthropology*, 42 (1): 125–38.

Wachtel, Nathan (2001) *La foi du souvenir: Labyrinthes marranes*. Paris: Seuil.

Williamson, Jeffrey G. (2002) 'Winners and losers over two centuries of globalization'. National Bureau of Economic Research Working Paper No. 9161.

3

IN SEARCH OF 'BASMATISTHAN': AGRO-NATIONALISM AND GLOBALIZATION

Denis Vidal

Every society has to decide on the degree of reforms it may accept by opening itself to others. It is a choice that is greeted with more or less optimism and anxiety depending on cultural and historical circumstances. When the balance is tilted in favour of anxiety, what might at other times have been considered an opportunity worth seizing begins to take on the character of threat or inescapable fate. And when it comes to discussions of globalization, however sophisticated they might appear, much of what is written is simply a reflection of the deepening sense of unease felt with this sort of dilemma.

There can be few other domains in which such anxiety is so palpable as the domain of agriculture; where what is presented as defence of tradition may be easily confused with the invention of new identities, new natural species and new definitions of place. This may be partly due to the curious fact that even the greatest enthusiasts of hybridity in other domains of culture seem considerably less willing to embrace this doctrine when it comes to the issue of what they eat. But it no doubt has even more to do with the actual inability to decide, in all sincerity, what is the most desirable path for developing countries: to stick to the policy of localism, the defence of traditional agricultural practices, and self-subsistence, or to recognize the limitations of such a strategy, concurring with Amartya Sen's view that 'food self-sufficiency is a peculiarly obtuse way of thinking about food security' (2002).

It is not my intention here, however, to enter into the intricacies of this debate but rather to try to broaden our perspective on it by exploring different elements of the globalization process in this area from a historical and comparative perspective. This I shall do by focusing in particular on a controversy which arose at the end of the 1990s when an American company owned by Hans-Adam II of

Liechtenstein – one of the last reigning merchant princes of Europe and one of its most important farmers – tried to patent basmati rice in the United States.

In recent years some American companies have tried to make use of some of the intrinsic ambiguities of American patent laws in order to appropriate commercial rights over various agricultural products and natural species that originate from developing countries. In particular, attempts have been made to patent turmeric, *neem* and basmati as 'novel' inventions in the United States, despite the fact that all of these products have long been known and consumed for all sorts of purposes in India. Needless to say such dubious practices have not gone unnoticed. According to Vandana Shiva, a well-known social and environmental activist in India, such activities are not just opportunistic – they signify a new form of colonialism (Shiva 1998; cf Shiva 2000; 2001):

> This epidemic of piracy is very much like the epidemic of piracy which was named colonialism 500 years ago. I think we will soon need to name this round of piracy through patents as new colonization; as a colonization which differs from the old only in this – the old colonization only took over land; the new colonization is taking over life itself.

Many other people, even if they do not go quite so far as Shiva, insist on the necessity of doing something against this type of appropriation. For example, one of the main objectives of Indian representatives at the World Trade Organization is to obtain an extension of the application of 'geographic indication' to specific Indian products like basmati rice, Darjeeling tea and others. All of this helps to explain why it was considered such a dramatic 'victory' against the perils of globalization when the American company that seemed to threaten the traditional South Asian monopoly over basmati finally withdrew most of its patent claims because of the vocal public campaign and legal battle that had been conducted against it.

In this chapter I argue that the whole episode is better understood if one extends the analysis beyond the time-frame of the controversy itself, considering also what happened before and immediately after it. By adopting a more inclusive and also more comparative approach, one may acquire, I believe, not only different insights into the specificities of this case but also a more comprehensive understanding of what is actually going on under the overused label of 'globalization'.

Globalization and Delocalization

Plenty of myths, all over the world, assume the existence of some sort of exclusive relationship between a particular place and the people who are supposed to have originated from it. But this does not prevent us from realizing, whether we like it or not, that migration and displacements of all sorts are the stuff of history. It would seem, however, that whenever it comes to the products of the soil, we seem to lose our sense of historicity. Instead we celebrate and rejoice in the exclusivity of the relationship between the appearance, consistency, colour, flavour, smell and taste of myriads of foods or beverages and the places from which they come – places for which they supposedly become the expression and emblem.

The Basmati Controversy (1997–2001)

The adaptation of rice varieties from India to the United States is not exactly a recent trend. If one believes the historians specialising in this question, we may argue that such a process began about 3,600 years ago, when Malaysian traders introduced rice from eastern India to Indonesia. A next step followed when, some time in the first millennium BC, Austronesian traders apparently took rice from Indonesia to Madagascar. A more decisive move took place around 1645 when Dutch or English traders (depending on different versions of the account) took rice with them from Madagascar to South Carolina (Dethloff 1988).

All of this would suggest that contrary to what Vandana Shiva implies in her discussion of biopiracy, there is nothing very new in appropriating 'forms of life' rather than 'land' in the history of international trade and colonialism. Moreover, one could even argue that one of the most spectacular examples of this sort of behaviour has been precisely the way in which Americans appropriated not only rice of Asiatic origin during the second half of the seventeenth century, but also African slaves, who represented not only a free source of labour but also an equally precious source of expertise in the practice and know-how of rice cultivation (Littlefield 1981).

Viewed from this long-term perspective, when Hans Adam II of Liechtenstein decided, through his American company, to adapt and patent basmati varieties of rice in the United States, it seemed little more than an extension of a long-established historical trend – something Norbert Elias might describe as a slow continuation of the same civilization process. Similarly, retaining the native name of a plant in this sort of case may not be seen as necessarily worse or more amoral than giving it an alternative name. Retaining names has moreover always been a common habit, as we see from the Inca (Nahuatl) origin of the term *tomato* and the Afghan origin of the term *carrot*.

However, as one might imagine, the basmati controversy has not been perceived and interpreted so leniently in India. One has only to consult a

fragment of the extensive literature on the topic to get a sense of the outrage
that prevailed when it was announced in Indian newspapers in 1997 that an
American-based company had been granted a patent for 'Basmati' in the
United States. Most commentators in India seemed to interpret this as
the selling-off of exclusive rights to basmati rice in the United States, even
if the claims included in this patent seemed to be, in reality, slightly less
outrageous.

I do not intend here to enter into the raging polemic which has taken place
in recent years to try to determine more exactly the extent of the exclusivity
and commercial privileges that the applicant could gain by a patent.[1] Rather,
I would simply like to recall two essential elements of the case. First, it
appeared that RiceTec, the American company that had asked for the patent,
had tried effectively to appropriate and commercialise in the United States
varieties of rice that originated from South Asia and were close replicas of the
ones previously developed by farmers as well as by agronomists in South Asia.
Second, it appeared that the company had also tried to legalize the right to
retain the term 'basmati' to define in a general manner these varieties as
grown on American soil, whereas the term had until then been informally but
exclusively associated with the superior varieties of basmati rice grown in
South Asia itself.

Such attempts have rightly been considered scandalous, both in India and
abroad. And in 2001, three years after the patent had been granted, a legal challenge and a particularly vigorous public campaign by various personalities and
non-governmental organizations in India and abroad, as well as by institutions
directly associated with the Indian government, left RiceTec little choice other
than to withdraw nearly all its claims in order to avoid losing the case.

A New Form of Colonialism?

Viewed retrospectively, perhaps the most striking thing about this campaign,
and to a large extent the key to its success, was the unexpected alliances it succeeded in creating between the most unlikely partners. Thus, for example,
although the relationship between India and Pakistan had probably never
been so tense in recent times as during the period of the basmati controversy,
this was one of the few instances when the two countries showed a certain
amount of solidarity and cooperated against the common threat. This is still
more surprising when one realizes that until this time, India and Pakistan had
in fact been the two main competitors in the basmati rice market.
Furthermore, agronomists who had promoted the green revolution now allied
themselves with those who had most vehemently opposed it. And in the same
vein, personalities and organizations which had formerly systematically

denounced the globalization and liberalization of the economy now allied themselves with governmental organizations and the lobby of Indian exporters, whose main function was precisely to promote globalization.

What was particularly interesting about this case was the way in which it was formulated not so much in terms of a neo-liberal policy versus a socially and ecologically conscious one, but rather as some sort of national affront to India, or even a wider regional affront to the whole of South Asia. In India, people were asked to rally behind the defence of basmati as they might be asked to rally behind the defence of the flag. Comments like 'India is basmati, and basmati is India' were heard in the Indian parliament. People who might under normal circumstances be at loggerheads seemed suddenly to unite against this common threat, and, as I mentioned before, this seemed to promote not just a surge of nationalism but also the development of something akin to a form of pan-South-Asian patriotism.

Until recently basmati was, in fact, traditionally associated with very specific regions of India and Pakistan. Because of such associations, it would have been difficult to imagine that basmati – even if one takes into account the Sanskrit origins of a term said to be associated with ideas of 'earth' and 'fragrance of the earth' – could suddenly acquire the status of a national and quasi-religious icon in India. And it is still more surprising to notice that it was not only Indian or Hindu nationalists who were involved, but also well-known personalities who would not normally be associated with such nationalistic rhetoric. As already mentioned, there is a certain irony in the fact that the very people who celebrate all forms of hybridity in culture seem largely unwilling to contemplate it with the same enthusiasm in agriculture.

The unusual alliances that the basmati controversy evoked were made possible because the whole episode was seen not only as an act of commercial piracy but, more fundamentally, as the expression of a new form of colonialism. There is little doubt that such rhetoric had a powerful impact. However, it is important to remember that such historical parallels can be misleading. I will argue that one cannot effectively understand the issues at stake in controversies like the one concerning basmati by analysing it solely through the prism of the asymmetrical relationship between developed and developing countries, or even that between the interests of the small farmers of the South and the multinationals of the North.

One Trend May Hide Another One

The rapid delocalization of production undoubtedly constitutes one of the most important and explicit dimensions of globalization. This is as true for agriculture as for any other domain. When the delocalized products are ones that were previously associated with a particular part of the world and a specific culture, the visibility of the process becomes especially apparent. The basmati case was so spectacular because until recently this rice had been so obviously identified with South Asia. It was also significant that the basmati controversy appeared to present a perfect demonstration of the point that globalization is the latest device for exploiting post-colonial countries. But while the exploitation of the South by the North should be taken into consideration in analysing globalization, one should not forget that the delocalization of production is a much larger, multi-directional process in which all sorts of strategies are simultaneously implemented. This is best demonstrated by moving away from basmati altogether for a moment to consider the delocalization and relocalization of products elsewhere in the world. How, then, might an understanding of French wines and Himalayan apples aid our comprehension of the basmati case?

The Case of French Wines

At least four elements are supposed to determine the quality of French wine: *le terroir* (the terrain with all its specificities where grapes grow), the year of production, *le cepage* (the variety of grape used for making the wine) and the process of wine-making itself. It is certainly admitted by connoisseurs that each of these elements should be considered equally important for defining the quality of a wine. In the French tradition, however, with the exception of a few regions like Alsace or Champagne, it is usually only the place of origin of a wine, and to a lesser degree its age, that are taken into consideration explicitly by consumers when selecting wine to buy or drink. For example, until recently, most French people ignored the fact that Burgundy wines are made with only one variety of grape (Pinot Noir) while Bordeaux wines combine a variety of them in diverse proportions (Merlot and Cabernet Sauvignon, in particular).

The exclusive importance given to place of origin and age helps to explain why a strict correlation can be made in France between the reputation and price of a particular wine, and the ability to pinpoint as precisely as possible the exact location of the grapes used to make it. Such an emphasis is not necessarily ancient or particularly representative of French culture. It is true that the place of production has never been ignored, especially in the case of the most prestigious vintages, but the systematic importance given to geographic indication throughout the twentieth century has been a relatively recent development, linked on the one hand to the history of the French vineyard, and on the other to the evolution of legislation in this domain from the end of nineteenth century. More recently, however, another paradoxical consequence of this 'tradition' has emerged.

Many of the relatively new wine-producing countries all over the world are now adopting – as a deliberate strategy – different criteria from the French ones for defining and classifying wines. They put commercial emphasis not so much on the place of origin or age but on the grape, the company brand or the wine-making process. The advantage of this strategy is that it undermines the hierarchy that benefits the countries with a long-established reputation for wine-making. If such a strategy can be successfully imposed globally – in the way that it has been imposed in the British market, for example – then France may lose much of its comparative advantage in the wine-making industry and will have to try to reconstruct its primacy (Berthomeau 2001). Traditionally less renowned wine-producing regions like the Languedoc have already begun to follow these trends, thus shaking up the wine hierarchy and suggesting that the new fashion may take off even in France. We are witnessing here the delocalization of wine from its former territorial strongholds.

The case of French wines is relevant here not simply because I am French, but also because the example of French wines and Champagne have constantly been advanced in India during the basmati controversy. The French case was cited regularly to demonstrate the different levels of legal protection granted to exclusive agricultural products in developed and developing countries. The idea behind this comparison was to demonstrate that if the Indian government had given more effective legal protection to Indian agricultural products, like the French government did, no American company would have dared to appropriate such products as basmati and turmeric.

The comparison seems fair enough. It is indisputable that because of the insistence of successive French governments, alcoholic drinks now benefit from a unique level of legal protection in the international trade. It is only in more recent times that legal and institutional processes have begun at the international level for extending to other specific agricultural and food products the sort of legal protection which had formerly been exclusively granted to wines and spirits.

However, the conclusions that may be drawn from the basmati-wine comparison are not as clear as they may at first appear.

The first point is that in order for such a comparison to be effective, varieties of rice should be compared, at least until recently, with the varieties of grape used for making wine rather than with wines as such. It then becomes clear that the new focus on varieties of grape rather than place of origin is in fact a strategy for overcoming the advantages that countries like France have had in the wine market. One may also notice, then, that the French names of the best-known varieties of grapes (Sauvignon, Pinot, Cabernet, Chardonnay, Merlot, Gamay, etc.) have been imported and retained by the new wine-producing countries which compete with the French on the international market, and this may parallel the Americans' desire to retain the term 'basmati' for the rice grown in the United States. Furthermore, not only are most of these names of varieties of grape actually French words, but in some cases they are also geographical place references in France. Moreover, just as in the basmati case, wine producers in other countries do not hesitate to claim, quite openly, that their Merlot, Sauvignon and Chardonnay wines are better and often less expensive that the French equivalents.

This comparison therefore demonstrates not only that there is a difference in how products of the North and the South are protected, but also that such legal protection is less effective than many would like to believe. In today's global economy we therefore find systematic attempts, in both the North and the South, to dissociate the previously exclusive links between certain products and places, and to adapt the production process elsewhere for commercial purposes. While in the basmati case it is a product of the South that is being transplanted and produced in the North, in the wine case it is a product of the North (France, Italy, etc.) being transplanted and developed by countries of the South (Argentine, Chile, etc.), as well as other areas of the North (United States, Australia, etc.).

Now that we have 'delocalized' the debate surrounding basmati, let us move on to examine another case of relocalization of an agricultural product, into a region very close to the place where basmati is traditionally grown. I shall consider the transplantation of apple production to Himachal Pradesh in India – a case which seems to exemplify the reverse trajectory of basmati.

The Case of Himachali Apples

Before introducing the Himachali apple, I return briefly to the comparison made earlier between biopiracy and colonialism. One point on which the multiple critiques of colonialism during recent decades agree is that the phenomenon of colonialism cannot be explained by a simplistic dichotomy between colonisers and colonised people (Bayly 1983). Rather, we must understand not only how colonialism has been imposed upon diverse societies but also how these societies, or certain sections of their populations, identified at least in part with it. It is in this context that I introduce the case of apples in Himachal Pradesh.

Himachal Pradesh has long been known for the richness of its flora and fauna (or what would be more commonly described today as the extent of its biodiversity). Nowadays, however, Himachal Pradesh is most renowned for its apples, the production of which has considerably increased the prosperity of the state and of its inhabitants. It is significant that these apples bear rather 'exotic' names – such as 'Delicious', 'Golden Delicious' or 'Royal Delicious' – and that nearly all the production is intended for export (mainly to the Middle East), just as in the case of basmati. Hence it is worth briefly explaining here how Himachal Pradesh developed as an apple-growing state.

It began in 1904 when Samuel Evan Stokes, a missionary from a wealthy American Quaker family, came to Himachal in order to preach the Gospel. After a few years in the region, however, it was he who became the convert. Not only did he convert to Hinduism, he also married locally, had several children, took an Indian name and became an Indian citizen. Nevertheless, he retained the enterprising spirit that every American is supposed to possess. With the aim of encouraging local development in the region, in the 1920s he decided to import a few apple trees from the United States to see if they would grow in the part of Himachal where he lived (Sharma 1999). After a few years, his economic success was so marked that many people followed his example, and gained incomes beyond their dreams.

In the early 1980s, I was doing fieldwork in Himachal, where I was impressed by the high levels of self-subsistence people managed to secure with small plots of land. I can also attest to the contrast between the pride and appreciation felt for the best qualities of rice growing on their land and their contempt for apples, which they refused to consider as real fruit. Their only personal use of the apple was to plaster it in salt as a snack to accompany drinks, or to offer generous box-loads to officials and civil servants in the hope of buying their favours cheaply. Yet none of that deterred the people from considering that there was no greater fortune in life than to dispose of a plot of land for profitable conversion into an apple orchard. The farmers I met in Himachal who contemplated the possibility of transforming their small plots into orchards did not appear to ignore the risks and initial costs it would involve. But if the opportunity to convert to an orchard carried the potential of future profit, they complied for the sake of their families and their future.

In Himachal Pradesh, then, following older trends that began in the later phases of colonisation, we find apple varieties originating in the West imported to India and marketed under their western names without anyone appearing to complain about it. The irony, however, is that the structural consequences have not been so different from those in the basmati case when one reconsiders that controversy in its proper context.

Globalization and Relocalization

The basmati controversy has been presented as a dramatic confrontation not only between two opposing ways of practising agriculture but also between two different modes of reasoning in relation to the product. In India, for example, it is often argued that it is reductionist to consider basmati as a mere commodity. Rather, it should be seen as a depository of religious and social values. At another level, the characteristics of basmati have been repeatedly attributed to the particular qualities of the sub-Himalayan soil where it has traditionally been grown. Finally, during the controversy, basmati rice was often described as the collective creation of generations of small farmers who cultivated it. According to opponents of the patent, it was only because of the anonymous labour of poor farmers that the rice had slowly evolved, not only as a rice variety ideally suited for its own part of the world but also into one of the best varieties of aromatic rice existing anywhere. No other rice variety grown in another environment could share the same characteristics as authentic basmati, and to describe pale foreign imitations as 'basmati' not only despoiled Indian cultivators but was also a fraud and a misnomer.

For the American company which tried to patent it, however, the term 'basmati' was simply a generic term, which basically referred to the specific characteristics defining this particular variety of aromatic rice that differenti- ated it from hundreds of other varieties whose samples were equally available in the World Collection of Germplasm in Aberdeen, Idaho, in the United States. The company's argument was that if it could be shown, preferably with the help of 'scientific' tests, that newly-created varieties of rice shared most of the same characteristic as basmati, there was no reason why it could not legitimately define them as basmati, independently of where they were cultivated.

According to this reasoning, the South Asian origin of basmati was merely circumstantial, and if it could be used to prove anything, it was precisely the opposite of what opponents of the patent intended. If one admitted that basmati only corresponded, until now, to a purely South Asian variety of rice the qualities of which were supposed to be linked solely to a specific South Asian environment, then this was surely the best proof that a new rice variety, which shared the same formal characteristics as basmati but was cultivated in the United States, could be legitimately considered as a 'novel' invention in that country. The irony is that in spite of being diametrically opposed, the two definitions of 'basmati' proposed by the defendants and opponents of the patent shared one thing in common, and that was a disdain for serious empirical evidence.

As far as the RiceTec patent was concerned, it soon became clear that their claims had little empirical basis. Most of the claims seemed very notional and the judges who had to consider them in the court case that followed were not impressed by their content. Some of the claims, however, referred more specifically to the hybrid varieties that RiceTec had effectively adapted in the

United States. It was not the company's ability to produce these varieties, nor its right to patent them as 'novel', that was contested, but rather its right to call these varieties 'basmati'. It might be true that some basmati of Asian origin had been used in their development, and that some of their character-istics were close to those of known varieties of Asian basmati, but these had been combined with other varieties of rice of different origins, so that they had many other characteristics that had very little to do with Asian basmati. Even if one ignored the fact that RiceTec's new varieties had been cultivated in the United States and even if one recognized 'basmati' as a generic term, it still therefore seemed a serious misnomer to characterize this American rice as 'basmati'. Once it became evident that it would be legally challenged, RiceTec preferred to withdraw most of its claims, perhaps aware that the evidence on which its claims were based was too shaky to win the case.

Although the dubious nature of this patent had been largely exposed during the controversy, what did not appear so clearly was the equally uncon-vincing representation of basmati advanced by opponents of the patent. In criticising RiceTec's claim that 'basmati' *is* a generic term, opponents of the patent preferred to ignore discreetly the contemporary uses of the term in India itself, because an investigation of the commercial practices associated with basmati in the years immediately preceding the controversy yields a slightly confusing picture.

Before the Controversy

Basmati may have a very ancient and distinguished past in India, but only since the 1980s has its mass production really taken off. Its relatively low production until then was because, in India as in China but in contrast to Pakistan or the United States, most rice cultivation is and was oriented principally towards the domestic market.

Basmati is characterised not only by its taste and quality but also by its relatively low yield compared with other rice varieties; it also matures more slowly than most other sorts of rice. This explains why the production of basmati – always perceived as a luxury food in India – was not considered a priority in the agricultural policies of successive Indian governments. Until the last decade, the main priority of every Indian government has been to ensure the country's self-reliance in terms of agricultural production. This also conversely explains why basmati has long been the only segment of the rice market to escape state control and remain entirely in private hands. Moreover, what really distinguishes the basmati market from the main rice market today is that for many years it has been oriented almost entirely towards export. Far from being threatened by the privatization and liberalization of trade, like many other agricultural sectors in India, the fortune of this particular market has been therefore directly linked from the start to the progressive opening of Indian agriculture to the outside world and, more generally, to trade liberalisation. The basmati market has not only benefited from the development of the world market, it is the export market that has been its key *raison d'être*, at the levels of both production and consumption.

More generally, what characterizes the international demand for basmati, by contrast with the demand for lesser varieties of rice, is the fact that this is a market that is expanding rapidly but is not threatened by overproduction. The growing demand for basmati today is fuelled not only by the increasing number and prosperity of the South Asian diaspora communities in different countries, but also by a more general rise in the appetite for high-quality foods among middle-class populations all over the world (Krissoff *et al.* 2002). Thus, in spite of the harsh competition from Pakistan, the real problem faced by Indian exporters of basmati has little to do with either problems of demand or pricing. According to Indian basmati traders, their real limitation is insufficient production, for Indian basmati is in short supply, in terms of both quantity and quality. This may explain some of the recent problems that traders have had to confront.

While I was doing fieldwork in the wholesale grain market of Delhi in 1997, Indian exporters were concerned that the basmati export trade would suffer because of the dubious quality of some of the shipments sold abroad the previous year.[2] If the numerous reports and comments made public since by Indian exporters are to be believed, the situation does not seem to have improved. One main reason for this is that there have until now been very few controls in India to ensure the consistent quality of the rice labelled 'basmati' when it is sold for export. This has meant that any variety of aromatic rice that more or less fitted the appropriate criteria could be easily labelled 'basmati', and also that less scrupulous exporters were mixing real basmati with cheaper varieties of rice in order to boost their profits.

In the domestic market it is more difficult to get away with such practices in the long term, because the quality of rice is rarely taken for granted and is carefully checked at different stages of the marketing chain by intermediaries and traders as well as by the final buyers. This type of informal control is less effective in the case of exports, however, because huge quantities of rice are sold to distant customers (Vidal 2000). In the absence of more institutionalized quality checks and precise rules of labelling, the general reputation of Indian rice exporters is at stake and the Indian rice trade as a whole may suffer in consequence.

There is, however, another reason which has played an equally important role in changing the definition of basmati in recent decades. It is not only in the wicked world of American companies that one finds the term 'basmati' being used in a more or less generic manner. There is little doubt, for example, that both Indian and Pakistani agronomists had a very similar perspective in mind when they sought to develop new varieties of basmati by cross-hybridising basmati with other rice varieties. As in the American case, their aim was to create new varieties of rice which would retain the qualities of earlier varieties but would also be more resilient, quicker to mature and higher-yielding than the ones which had slowly evolved under the care of small cultivators. Moreover, another potential 'asset' of such hybrid varieties of basmati resided in their adaptability to different soils and climates so that their cultivation could more easily be delocalized, whether in India or, indeed, elsewhere.

As one might imagine, real connoisseurs have been quick to argue that even the best hybrids can only superficially compete with more traditional varieties of basmati. In spite of their similar appearance and more or less similar characteristics, the former are dismissed for their 'blandness' by comparison with the 'real thing'. However, possibly owing to their greater availability and their lower price of production, it has become common practice in India to identify hybrid varieties as 'real' basmati, and they have commonly been sold abroad under this prestigious label. The irony, of course, is that one could argue that the American company RiceTec was simply pushing to an extreme a tendency that began in India itself.

Reinventing Basmati

Largely because of this controversy, there is now a consensus in India that there may be only one way to prevent the term 'basmati' from being used as a generic term abroad in the future, and that is to get basmati officially acknowledged as 'a geographic indication' and recognized as such by the WTO. As the comparison with French wines demonstrated, such a legal status would not prevent all forms of international competition, but at least it would prevent the sort of dubious practices that had been at the heart of the basmati controversy.

Independently of this former point, however, as well as of the many difficulties that such a move might imply in terms of trade negotiations, a prior condition is to make sure that the production of basmati in India fits the official criteria of geographical indication. According to the WTO definition, 'geographical indication' applies to names 'which identify a good as originating in the territory ... or a region or a locality in this territory, where a given quality, reputation, or other characteristic of the good is essentially attributable to its geographic origin'.[3] But paradoxically enough, to prove that basmati corresponds to such a definition is by no means a straightforward process.

During the controversy it became clear that although India is known for all sorts of surveys and gazetteers, there were no reliable inventories of the precise details and distribution of the rice varieties commonly termed 'basmati'. These problems were not caused exclusively by the lack of reliable official information but also because hybrids had always played a significant role, in India itself, in blurring the frontier between what should and should not be labelled as basmati.

It is also interesting, additionally, that it is Indian exporters who in recent times have become the most vocal in their insistence that hybrid varieties should not be labelled as 'basmati' any more, however close their resemblance to the real thing. But the irony is that once this decision seemed to be accepted, traders (in the eternal style of traders) insisted that one should be able still to mix hybrid varieties *with basmati*, on condition that the quantity of hybrids does not exceed 30 per cent of the whole. This is not the sort of concession that helps to restore the reputation of Indian basmati abroad.

Another difficult decision that had to be taken in order to make sense of the notion of a 'geographical indication' was to limit much more precisely the area from which varieties of aromatic rice could legitimately be labelled as basmati. This too was not such an easy task, for it involved a certain degree of controversy and politicking at the border zones, such as parts of Bihar and Rajasthan, where nobody had ever challenged the labelling of the rice pro- duced there as basmati. Finally, another step was taken recently by Indian exporters when they lobbied the government to ban Indian agronomists from interfering with basmati by manipulating it genetically. Genetic modification is of course one of the most important, but also most controversial, trends in contemporary agriculture. As one would expect, a section of the Indian sci- entific community is keen to play a part in its evolution. Nevertheless, Indian traders, as well as Pakistani ones, have argued to the contrary that for the time being it would certainly be a mistake to play this game in the case of basmati, because of the risk of jeopardizing the demand for basmati abroad.[4] It is rightly recognized that alienating the sort of middle-class clientele willing to pay a premium price for the best varieties of rice is not a wise strategy for successful expansion in the food industry.

That Indian agronomists and Indian traders fought shoulder to shoulder in the battle to prevent the American threat to the South Asian monopoly over basmati did not prevent them from rapidly diverging afterwards. In India as elsewhere, many agronomists cannot ultimately resist the temptation to rein- vent nature, and it is this that distinguishes them from the traders who obey a more flexible commercial logic. If there were any economic advantage in completely reinventing what was previously defined as basmati, most traders would accept the logic of doing so. On the other hand, if they identified their commercial interest with maintaining the integrity of the product, then this would be the path to follow. Ideally, of course, they would prefer to benefit from the combination of both commercial logics, as indeed some are already doing when they simultaneously advertise both organic and genetically manipulated rice, but it is not always possible to do this.

In the case of basmati in India we are witnessing a curious shift of alliances among exporters, agronomists and militants. While for decades the interests of agronomists and Indian traders have seemed close, in the recent controversy Indian exporters continued to find common ground for a longer time with ecologists and anti-globalization militants. However, such an alliance might also be only temporary.

Creating a 'Basmatisthan'

For many years now, both Indian traders and the Indian government have been conscious that the main impediment to basmati exportation is not so much the competition but the insufficient supply of quality basmati for sale in the global market (Jasol 1987). Everyone involved in the trade is also painfully conscious that such dubious palliatives as the adulteration of pure basmati or the naming of new hybrid varieties developed by agronomists as basmati are not the best ways of dealing with the problem in the long term.

For several decades both rice exporters and the government have realized that the only real way of increasing basmati production in India is completely to transform the way in which it is cultivated. Furthermore, as I mentioned earlier, when Indian traders objected to the labelling of hybrid varieties and genetically modified rice varieties as basmati, it was not for political or ideological reasons but for economic and commercial ones. Similarly, their willingness to define clearly the geographical area of the basmati label has little to do with a wish to defend biodiversity or the patrimony of local farmers. Yet the specific interests of traders seemed to coincide, for a while, not only with the general policy of the government which is progressively choosing to favour export over self-reliance in agriculture, but also with the objectives of alternative ecological movements. This is obviously no longer the case.

One of the most important state initiatives in this matter has been the administrative effort made in recent years to establish specific areas, known in bureaucratic jargon as *agri-export-zones* (AEZs), where everything should in theory be organized in order to encourage the production and commercialisation of particular agricultural products that may have a real appeal on the international market. The apple-growing valleys of Himachal Pradesh would constitute one of these zones, as would the region of northern Punjab where basmati has traditionally been cultivated but where its production has virtually ceased for simple economic reasons. Now there is little doubt that such a state policy, welcomed by big Indian exporters and agricultural firms in the region, completely contradicts the aims which have been systematically pursued by ecological militants and anti-globalization activists like Vandana Shiva during the basmati patent controversy.

First of all, the idea that any Indian region should be principally dedicated to the monoculture of any agricultural product destined for export is anathema to those whose aim, on the contrary, is to promote ideals of self-subsistence and biodiversity. The situation is made worse because it is also strongly recommended that in such areas farmers should not only dedicate themselves to monoculture but should also cease to take any individual or collective initiative in how they select or cultivate seeds. They are expected to use exclusively the seeds recommended to them by agronomists and to strictly follow their recommendations concerning the cultivation process. It is proposed, for example, in government recommendations about AEZs that 'the government must ensure seed replacement at least once in three years by growers and breeders to identify and remove off-types to sustain seed quality.'[5] In practice this means that the wide variety of seeds considered the common heritage of small cultivators would be wiped out in a few years, and traditional practices, like seed-sharing exchange, which are said to be at the heart of the collective practices of the local farmers, would also disppear.

The general philosophy behind such a government policy is, in reality, the same one that has been promoted for many years now all over the world and has been consistently denounced everywhere, owing to the very unequal relationships it creates between small farmers and agro-commercial firms. It is, quite simply, the logic of contract-farming. Agricultural areas where basmati is cultivated have now become some of the regions of India where contract-farming has developed most quickly, and it is not only Punjab, which has specifically chosen to encourage contract-farming, that is held up as an example for other Indian states to follow.[6]

Conclusion

For many eco-activists, the basmati controversy has become emblematic of successful resistance to globalization. Such an interpretation makes sense as far as biopiracy or the delocalization of indigenous products is concerned. There are, however, other aspects of this controversy which do not fit in so well with the ideology of ecological movements. Even if one rightly condemns the dubious attempt to substitute an American ersatz for real basmati, any attempt – on the part of the American market – to answer a local demand by a local supply would appear to go against the trend of globalization, while on the other hand an agricultural policy like India's that privileges the export of basmati abroad would appear to be promoting global trade. Another consequence of the actual policy followed in India is to redefine the characteristics of basmati according to the expectation of international demand. Such a trend may of course meet with the temporary approval of social activists and ecologists in its intolerance of adulteration and eventual genetic manipulation of basmati, but activists will no doubt be less enthusiastic when they realize that in order to obtain the sort of basmati which satisfies the exacting requirements of Europeans and Americans, cultivation and decision-making are taken out of the hands of small scale local farmers. Traders and exporters are being given the power to ensure the supply of the right stuff on their own terms, even if this means that they control the entire process from the choice of seed to the final stage of marketing.

Finally, the game may now be over, because in 2003 it was agreed by the government that small cultivators can now be allowed to sell their basmati directly to whoever they want, including non-Indian firms.[7] While such a decision may, in the short term, help cultivators to break the monopoly of the intermediary rice millers and Indian traders who exploited them, there remains a long-term danger in establishing, through contract-farming, new forms of unequal relationships between small farmers and Indian or foreign agricultural firms.

If this policy is allowed to prevail, it may not be long before the requirements for Indian basmati are totally defined abroad and its production is largely under the control of foreign firms. Of course Indian people may still find consolation in the fact that basmati will remain a product both of cheap Indian labour and of Indian soil, but can anyone really consider the containment of biopiracy a success if the alternative is to return to something even closer to an earlier form of colonialism? After all, wasn't it one of the main vocations of colonial countries to supply the West with raw delicacies?

Notes

1 For details of the case, see Jamil 1998.
2 On markets in India, see Vidal 2003.
3 Article 22 of TRIPS, July 1995: see Berkey 2000.
4 See 'Ban on genetically modified basmati rice sought', *Dawn*, 20 November 2002; 'Ban on tinkering with basmati', *Economic Times*, 3 June 2003.
5 *Tribune*, 30 September 2002.
6 'Focus Punjab: transforming agriculture', *Frontline*, 12–25 April, 2003.
7 'Basmati farmers allowed to sell abroad', *Economic Times*, 5 April 2003.

Bibliography

Bayly, C. A. (1983) *Rulers, Townsmen and Bazaars: North Indian society in the age of British expansion, 1770–1870*. Cambridge: Cambridge University Press.

Berkey, Judson O. (2000) 'Implications of WTO for food geographic indications'. *Asil Insights*, 43. Washington: American Society of International Law.

Berthomeau, Jacques (2001) *Comment mieux positionner les vins français sur les marchés d'exportation?* Paris: Rapport officiel commandé par le Ministère de l'Agriculture et de la Pêche, 31 Juillet.

Dethloff, Henry C. (1988) *A History of the American Rice Industry, 1685–1985*. College Station: Texas A&M University Press.

Jamil, Uzma (1998) 'Biopiracy: the patenting of Basmati by RiceTec'. Paper for Sustainable Development Policy Institute, submitted to Bio-IPR Docserver.

Jasol, Fateh Singh (1989) 'Augmenting basmati rice exports: no soft options', in Fateh Singh Jasol, ed., (1988) *Papers of the National Conference on Agro-Exports*. New Delhi: Viva Photolithographers; 105–31.

Krissoff, Barry, Mary Bohman and Julie A. Caswell (2002) *Global Food Trade and Consumer Demand for Quality*. New York: Kluwer Academic.

Littlefield, D. (1981) *Rice and Slaves: Ethnicity and the slave trade in colonial South Carolina*. Baton Rouge: Louisiana State University Press.

Sen, Amartya (2002) 'Why half the planet is hungry'. *The Observer*, 16 June.

Sharma, Asha (1999) *An American in Khadi: The definitive biography of Satanyand Stokes*. New Delhi: Penguin.

Shiva, Vandana (1998) 'An interview with Dr Vandana Shiva'. *www.Motionmagazine.com*

—— (2000) *Stolen Harvest: The hijacking of the global food supply*. London: Zed.

—— (2001) *Protect or Plunder? Understanding intellectual property rights*. London: Zed.

Vidal, Denis (2000) 'Markets and intermediaries: an enquiry about the principles of market economy in the grain market of Delhi', in Véronique Dupont, Emma Tarlo and Denis Vidal, eds, *Delhi: Urban space and human destinies*. Delhi: Manohar; 125–42.

—— (2003) 'Markets', in *The Oxford India Companion to Sociology and Social Anthropology*, Delhi: Oxford University Press; 1342–60.

4

SEEDS OF WRATH: AGRICULTURE, BIOTECHNOLOGY AND GLOBALIZATION

Jackie Assayag

'If the *charkha* was the symbol of the Indian Independence, the seed is the symbol for protection of this independence.'

M. D. Nanjundaswamy,
President of the Karnataka Rajya Raitha Sangha, 29 December 1993

South India

Siddeshvara village in Bidar district, Karnataka, contained about 600 house-holds and 4,000 inhabitants in 1997. Its cramped houses, made of a mixture of straw, stones and mortar, are linked by narrow lanes which are filled with water, rubbish, excrement and cow dung during the monsoon. The Siddeshvara temple overlooks the houses. A new statue recently installed by the members of the dominant caste of Virashaiva-Lingayats marks the entrance to the village. The climate is dry, there is little or no irrigation, harvests are disappointing, the local government is inefficient, and the state apparatus appears to be indifferent.

Shivaraj Mainalle lived in Siddeshvara. He was some 40 years old and the father of five children, the youngest of whom was in the primary school in the fifth standard. He owned 1.28 hectares of land and farmed 3.6 hectares as a tenant (*lavani*). In 1995–97, he lost all his harvests because of parasitical worms and the vagaries of the weather. His debt to the local cooperative bank had risen to 24,000 rupees at the end of 1997 and he owed 80,000 rupees to a private moneylender in the village. The purchase of pesticides alone cost him more than 20,000 rupees. Notwithstanding this period of distress, his moneylender demanded his due. Shivaraj Mainalle committed suicide in December 1997. He drank a widely known variety of pesticide prohibited in

Western countries, *endosulphina*, of which the advertising slogan is: 'Friend of friends, enemy of enemies'! Between 1996 and 2000, more than 3,000 suicides of this type were reported in Andhra Pradesh and 2,000 in Karnataka.[1]

Paris, Europe and the World

On the morning of 5 June 1999, 500 members of peasants' organizations gathered below the Eiffel Tower in Paris. Most of them were from the Indian states of Karnataka and Uttar Pradesh and they had come to demonstrate in the Intercontinental Caravan against genetically modified (GM) crops and a type of hybrid seed called 'terminator' because it is sterile. American imperialism, intensive agriculture, the debt of the countries of the South and the international financial system – in short, 'globalization' – were also being denounced. During this weekend in June, peasants, surrounded by activists from the host agricultural countries, led the demonstration – which now also embraced the question of patent rights – to Cologne in Germany to the meeting of the G8. The demonstration then continued to Geneva to protest against the World Trade Organization (WTO) and in front of the offices of the multinational companies Novartis and Nestlé, as well as at the headquarters of the Banque Suisse. In France, in Rennes, Montpellier, Aix-en-Provence, Lyon, Chaumont and Besançon, the rally was mainly organized by the Peasants' Confederation led by the neo-ruralist José Bové. The Intercontinental Caravan had been formed in response to the General Agreement on Tariffs and Trade (GATT), which had drawn to a close with the Uruguay Round in 1994. During this meeting, the WTO was created under the aegis of the G7. At that time, India committed itself to opening its borders to the world food market before 2003.

Often contemptuously referred to as the 'World Tyrannic Organization', the WTO is widely held to be responsible in India for the agricultural crisis. Many see the thousands of suicides committed by farmers as the 'price' of the 'mistakes' of globalization. A majority of the media, national as well as foreign, share this diagnosis. Nevertheless their assertions are contradicted by the structural character of the agrarian inequalities of caste, class, faction, region and gender in the subcontinent. And this is the case even though the opening to the world market (since 1980) and the establishment of the 'structural adjustment programme' (in 1991) have indeed entailed a restructuring designed to end the 'state-centred', 'interventionist' development imposed on the country by Jawaharlal Nehru in the 1950s.

Globalization has become the *Zeitgeist* of the epoch, a cliché, as much in South Asia as elsewhere. This notion, vague and wide-ranging, over-used and largely metaphorical, does not however have the explanatory capacity ascribed to it. Its definition is still more inadequate because globalization is spontaneously understood as a 'total social fact'. In short, globalization gives rise to a speculative bubble, one which the anthropologist is called upon to puncture. With this in mind, research was conducted in Karnataka between 1999 and 2001. My investigation was not a thorough consideration of the agrarian question or of the peasant situation. Rather, it focused on social and biotechnological representations, as well as their diffusion through various practices, by looking at how agrochemistry is perceived, consumed, debated and fought over by a multiplicity of social actors in the subcontinent and beyond. By considering the cultural, social, politico-economic, as well as the dramatic dimensions of globalization, this approach aims to cast light on two questions: first, the nature of the turbulence affecting both the public space and civil society, and, second, the crisis of authority in the democratic nation-state. The aim of this chapter is to clarify the workings of social imagination in India.

This approach covers numerous locations and attempts to be at once descriptive, reticulated and multi-levelled.[2] By 'descriptive', I mean that the tools of the social sciences are applied to recent discordant events and emerging processes in contemporary India, perceived either 'from above' or 'from below'. By 'reticulated' I suggest that the dynamics of the network prevail over the logic of a culture that has for too long been assimilated to ideas of social enclosure or geographical location. Finally, 'multi-levelled', because the use of a variety of contexts of 'globalism', 'globality', and 'glocalized' for the study of 'globalization' reveals a broad spectrum of practices and discourses, as well as a range of political emotions from anxiety to fear and from desire to utopia, which appear as warring fictions, views or cosmologies.[3]

Agriculture in India

Agriculture is an essential component of the Indian economy for at least three reasons. First, it accounts for more than one quarter of the gross domestic product (GDP); second, nearly two-thirds of the active population – approximately 600 million people – are engaged in it; third, the widening gap between agricultural and non-agricultural incomes is a major factor, although not the only one, underlying persistent poverty.[4]

Let us sketch a portrait of the average Indian farmer. He farms between one-and-a-half and two-and-a-half hectares of land, and each half-hectare brings him roughly 5,000 rupees yearly, rising to 10,000 rupees in a good year. Even if one takes the higher figure and then doubles it, the smallest shop assistant in Mumbai, or even a beggar, earns more money (although less in real terms because of the higher cost of living in a big city). When wealthy businessmen and political decision-makers raise the pressing need to tax agricultural revenues, one should remember that few farmers earn enough for inclusion in taxable categories. Although there are subsidies for chemical fertilizers, electricity and water for irrigation, a number of rural zones lack electrical or hydraulic resources, and nearly 40 per cent of villages are not yet linked to roads. This inventory, although brief, nevertheless gives an idea of the seriousness of the situation.

The 'Green Revolution' of the 1970s, with the coordinated use of high-yielding seeds, chemical fertilizers, pesticides and irrigation, transformed India from a large importer of food grains into a country self-sufficient in cereals, and several huge regions became veritable zones of industrial agriculture (producing above all wheat and rice, or 'white gold'). Nevertheless, the paradox remains that in September 2001, for example, while 500 million persons were malnourished and an even greater number susceptible to food insecurity, 63 million tonnes of grains were stocked by the government.

Under the aegis of the International Monetary Fund (IMF) and the World Bank (WB), the Indian government initiated a policy of structural adjustment in 1991. The general objective was opening up the hitherto protectionist economy to the world market. In agriculture, there were several aims: dismantling of the system of state-controlled price-fixing; abolition of subsidies for inputs; liberalization of trade in basic products; abolition of the system of food management and diminution of the corresponding costs; and finally, making the system of public distribution of subsidized food products available only to the poor. All these measures were designed to increase trade with foreign countries, hitherto regulated by the level of customs duties.

Farmers were variably affected by changes in domestic regulations imposed by the WTO – namely the liberalization of the prices of agricultural products and inputs against the background of the increase in prices and risks – in proportion to the reduction of state support to them. Of course, the Food Corporation of India (FCI) has regularly raised the ceiling of agricultural prices. However, in recent years, with the opening of the sector to international trade, the FCI has been little motivated to purchase cereals. In short, uncertainty has increased. Little accustomed to price variations on world markets and unable to accommodate themselves well to new and unforeseen events, few farmers can extricate themselves from debt and many are unable to honour obligations accepted during good years when prices were high. For many local observers, the origin of the farming crisis is to be found in the stagnation in public investment and the emphasis placed on price mechanisms aimed at satisfying the interests of powerful agricultural lobbies. The negligence of the Indian state towards the majority of farmers is, however, a better general explanation for the permanent poverty of rural India.

The Agro-capitalist Cosmology of Seeds

Monsanto or 'My Satan'

The mobilization, both local and international, against globalization was clearly forged in reaction to the restructuring of multinational companies. In fact, a small number of them today dominate the world's agrochemical sector; between five and ten of them control global trade in grains. The leading ten seed-producing companies represent one-third of the 23 billion dollars in this trade, and control nearly 100 per cent of the market in transgenetic seeds. The same companies account for more than 20 per cent of the 30 billion dollars of trade in pesticides, which is equivalent to 44 per cent of total sales. Finally, these ten leading companies retain 61 per cent of the veterinary market, which, according to figures for the year 2000, amounts to 16 billion dollars.

The giant Monsanto bought Cargill International for the sum of 1.4 billion dollars in order to develop its seed activity in Central and Latin America, Europe, Asia and Africa. Monsanto, with its subsidiary, American Home Products Corporation, is one of the largest research enterprises in pharmaceutical and health products in the world. It is one of the best-placed companies and certainly the most dynamic in the production of vaccines, biotechnologies and agricultural products, but also in animal treatments. Even though it got rid of some activities in the agro-industrial sector that were seen as public relations risks, it regrouped the rest of them to become a powerful agrochemical industrial company practising its 'sciences of the living' in competition with the Swiss giant Novartis. Its annual turnover is officially estimated at 12 billion dollars.

Monsanto's publicity claims that it works to satisfy the interests of 'all farmers on all continents' thanks to its technology of genetically modified (GM) crops.[5] Acquisitions, joint ventures and mergers aim at making it 'the world seed company', knowing that its new crops only thrive with the simultaneous use of fertilizers and pesticides bearing its logo. 'We want to consolidate the entire food chain', stated one of the company's media directors at a press conference in 2000. An advertising campaign in Europe, which cost some 1.6 million dollars, made it possible to disseminate this profession of faith:

Worrying about starving future generations won't feed them. Food technology will. The world population is growing rapidly, adding an equivalent of a China to the globe every ten years. To feed these billion more mouths, we can try extending our farming land or squeezing greater harvests out of existing crops. With the planet set to double in number around 2030, this heavy dependency on land can only become heavier. Soil erosion and mineral depletion will exhaust the ground.

Lands such as rainforests will be forced into cultivation. Fertilizers, insecticides, and herbicides use will increase globally. At Monsanto, we now believe food biotechnology is a better way forward.

Monsanto's presence in India goes back to the 1970s. The company began by producing herbicides, such as 'Machete' and 'Roundup', but after its conversion to genetic engineering and the increase in capacity of its seed production under the visionary slogan 'Food, Health, Hope', it became the most powerful actor in Indian agriculture, from growth hormones for livestock to irrigation processes. The company is now present on the Indian market with GM seeds for cotton, wheat, maize, sunflower and rice, as well as with fruits and vegetables. The subcontinent is a field of experimentation for Monsanto. Its ambitions for the region are in proportion to the population of over 1.5 billion. Apart from the purchase of a state-of-the-art centre for research in genetic engineering for 20 million dollars, the company has spent roughly 4 billion dollars to acquire several leading seed enterprises so as to improve access to the Indian market: notably the Indian company Mahyco and the American giant Cargill (already mentioned), which itself owned Rallis, one of the largest Indian providers of food grains.

Seeds of Hope or of Despair?

In 1998, Monsanto took over Delta and Pine Company, the largest cotton seed company in the world, for 1.8 billion dollars. With that company, and in collaboration with the United States Department of Agriculture, Monsanto developed the so-called 'terminator' technology, which makes it possible to create 'sterile seeds'. The patent rights for this type of seed are already applicable in 78 countries! The objective is to introduce this technology to all seeds produced in Indian laboratories, so that farmers will not be able to utilize seeds from the previous harvest, and will be totally dependent on seed companies that will then have a monopoly. This is already the case for all hybrid seeds. However, unlike vegetable hybrids there is no commercialized hybrid wheat in the world, and the rice hybrid is still not prevalent in India, in contrast to China.

To attain its goal, Monsanto orchestrated a vast 'information' campaign. 'Video trucks' crossed the targeted regions to organize the showing of documentary and fictional films in villages as a means of popularizing hybrid seeds among the farmers. The company simultaneously trained hundreds of locally recruited 'field assistants' (*kshetra utsav*) to provide explanations, give demonstrations and advice, and extol the comparative advantages of the new seeds, with the final aim of persuading the small farmers to sign 'loyalty contracts' with

Monsanto for the annual provision of biochemical products. In addition, statistical surveys funded by the company and conducted among a sample of 1,100 small farmers attested to the wish of the latter to use 'hybrid seeds': 92 per cent stated that they unreservedly favoured the employment of biotechnological plants.

When local activists against GM crops conducted a counter-survey, they brought to light the bias of the survey protocol because the survey had been conducted in privileged agro-ecological zones (AEZs) and only among prosperous farmers. Moreover, the expressions 'biotechnology' or 'genetically modified crops' were never translated into vernacular languages. Explanations had recourse to the metaphor of filiation (from grandparents to parents to children) to illustrate that the new basmati rice, for example, transmitted its qualities in a similar manner: flavour, fragrance, colour, reliability, and hardiness from generation to generation.

The company also sponsored sports events and religious festivals. Images of gods and saints were recycled for advertising needs among small farmers who, one should remember, are mostly illiterate. Brochures and leaflets were translated and read aloud in the diverse regional languages. In the South, the figure of the goddess, symbol of fertility and prosperity, was selected to illustrate packets of genetically modified seeds. In Punjab, the seed packages bore images of Guru Nanak, the founder of the Sikh religion. Brahma, the supreme creator, lent his name to a type of hybrid seed. When the peasant leader M. D. Nanjundaswamy launched his 'angry brigades' against Monsanto's experimental fields, he followed the precedent by baptizing his commando operation 'Shiva', after the Hindu god who destroys the world.

Farmers Against Globalization

Peasant Leaders and Unions

My first encounter with M. D. Nanjundaswamy, the charismatic president of the Karnataka State Farmers' Association (KRRS) was on 27 November 1998.[6] It took place at his house, transformed into an office in the Vijayanagar quarter of Bangalore. Nanjundaswamy is a jurist who studied in Holland in the 1960s. In 1989 he assumed the leadership of the powerful farmers' union, which had been formed in October 1980 in the town of Shimoga. At that time, the 'professor' was a member of the regional parliament. Since then he has been involved in the defence of the peasants, the 'mothers of the nation', in his own words. The targets of his campaign are the multinational corporations responsible for the intensive agriculture that he condemns. His ideal is an agriculture which respects the environment and can be realized through 'rural self-management' and the decentralization of agricultural policies.

In the early 1990s Nanjundaswamy led a campaign to preserve biodiversity and to oppose the extension of agricultural patenting in the countries of the South. During the 1990s he organized mass rallies against the GATT (today the WTO) and against the agricultural policy of the Indian government which, according to him, had become its 'instrument'. In 1994, after a number of agricultural decisions had 'subverted democracy', he brought together 6,000 farmers to stand laughing for an entire day in front of the Karnataka parliament. The following week the state government fell. Apart from commando attacks against agro-food seed producers and international food businesses, such as Kentucky Fried Chicken, Pepsico and Pizza Hut, he distinguished himself through his opposition to holding the Miss World beauty contest in Bangalore. 'To fight against the perversion of Indian culture is my mission,' he is fond of repeating.

The International Caravan was his creation. It was formed on the occasion of a meeting of the Food and Agriculture Organization (FAO) in Rome, in 1996. The next year he co-founded, with Sergio Hernandez, the World Peoples' Action (WPA), an 'anti-globalization' network which includes the Zapatista National Liberation Front (Mexico), the Sandinista Organization (Nicaragua), the Brazilian Movement of the Landless, the militant Maori peasants of New Zealand and the ecological associations of the former Soviet Union. The WPA is also connected with the Via Campesina, a federation of more than 200 peasants' organizations established in some 60 countries which was founded in 1993. Defending the food sovereignty of all countries of the South, this network of organizations fights against the 'neo-liberal conspiracy' and the 'harmful effects of globalization in the rural zones'. Today, Nanjundaswamy campaigns against 'Western biopiracy and all forms of (re)colonization of India and the countries of the South'.

In Nanjundaswamy's view, the Western countries are animated by the spirit of capitalism (*chaitanya poorna bandavala*). They therefore preserve their own class societies by means of imperialism: exporting their technologies, invoicing their imports at elevated prices by directing to their advantage the interplay of exchanges between North and South, and, finally, imposing the Euro-American system of production and consumption, which promotes a lifestyle conforming to Western, middle-class market values.[7] India, the victim of colonial powers, is therefore confined to a 'weak capitalism' (*badakalu bandavala*). Nanjundaswamy, a global theorist and visionary, compares the northern hemisphere to the upper castes and India to the *Dalits* (or Untouchables). He describes this relationship as a 'comprador' (*hondanki*) one, because the native political leaders sell 'Mother India' to foreigners – an old nationalist theme that is illustrated by the image of 'the India Cow' milked to exhaustion by the British in the 1880s and conceptualized as the 'economic theory of the draining of riches'.

Alongside his absorption of Marxist doctrine, this denigrator of Western values has readily made use of Hindu nationalist memories. Thus Nanjundaswamy incessantly calls for the revitalization of 'small village republics' and for popular anti-colonial mobilization. In both cases he draws inspiration from Gandhi, the hero of the nationalist movement against the British. Nanjundaswamy thus proclaims loudly and clearly the heritage of the 'insistence on truth' (*satyagraha*) and of 'rural socialism' as formulated by the Mahatma, two aspirations which have today been forgotten by all Indian political parties. Usually dressed in local cotton (*khadi*), following the example of his guru, he asserts 'I am a Gandhian terrorist', both in India and on the BBC. He estimates the adherents of his peasant movement at hundreds of thousands, with millions of sympathizers. According to him, the demonstrations by 'his' militants express 'the anger of the green brigade against globalization'. This invented tradition of ecological protest does not lack efficacy, as is shown by his brigades' destruction of the Cargill offices in 1992 and again in 1998, the burning of Monsanto's experimental fields in 1993, as well as the destruction of a KFC outlet in 1996. The KFC commando operation, a powerful symbolic action against 'Frankenstein junk food', brought him several days in jail and a good opportunity to be elevated to the status of peasant martyr!

Nanjundaswamy's detractors in India underscore the contradictions involved in representing well-off farmers, organized in a lobby for the privileged. Not content to demand subsidies from central or provincial government, the protection of borders against foreign intrusion and the strengthening of the national(ist) framework, he also enters into alliances with militant activist groups in other countries or with otherwise disparate non-governmental organizations. The nationalist rhetoric serves both to attack the neo-liberal project and to defend autochthony (*swadeshi*), despite the fact that he reaches beyond the nation-state to enter transnational coalitions. Thus, KRRS ideology presents itself as a combination of vulgar Marxism and violent Gandhism, a mixture of national populism and identity-based nativism fighting for a return to rural autarchy. The will to protect 'traditional Indian civilization' does not appear to contradict the simultaneous appeal to the internationalism of the 'agricultural *Lumpenproletariat* of the whole world'.

The Tribunal of GM Seeds

The project to introduce the biotechnology of the so-called 'terminator' gene into India thus met with strong opposition. Gandhians, Marxists, Communists, environmentalists, moderate and radical nationalists, as well as various political parties, ecological movements, local and transnational NGOs, farmers' unions and women's associations have periodically mobilized themselves with some success. Thus, on 5 March 1999 a '*satyagraha* of seeds' was organized in Delhi to the cries of 'No ownership rights on life!', and 'No bollart! No terminator!', derived partly from the name of the cotton parasite BT (*Bacillus thuringensis*). Other large towns in the country took up this campaign on the same day to celebrate the anniversary of the march undertaken by Gandhi to break the British salt monopoly in India. 'We shall grow our food ourselves. We reject the agrichemical patents,' declared Vandana Shiva, the director of the Foundation for Research on Scientific Technologies and Ecology. 'We will throw Monsanto out of the country. Free and private trade in food is a recipe for famine and suicide of the peasants,' added this former physicist who became a world inspiration for 'ecofeminism'.

In September 2000, a 'seed council' (*bija panchayat*) was organized in Bangalore. The aim of this widely publicized 'tribunal' was to 'denounce the conspiracy to take over the seed market in India (and other countries of the South) and to destroy the inalienable rights of farmers over seeds'. The next day, a rally brought together some fifty farmers' organizations (notably the Karnataka Rajya Raita Sangha, the Andhra Pradesh Raita Sangha, the Bharata Kisan Union, the All-India Kisan), including some from abroad (such as the Rural Farmers' Confederation of José Bové, who was himself present), as well as NGOs and women's movements. They protested together against the anti-agricultural policy of the central and state governments. Activists from Greenpeace, garbed in 'vegetable' costumes, joined members of the Communist Party of India (Marxist) (CPI[M]) to denounce the arrival in Bangalore of the Asian-Pacific Seed Association, which coincided with the signing of concessions given to agricultural companies by the state government. This international meeting was organized in the capital of Karnataka because this state, which already produces 50 per cent of the seeds in India, would like to become the 'seed superpower of the country'.

At the opening of the 'seed council', Vandana Shiva explained that its convocation finally made it possible to 'hear the testimonies of those who are dramatically affected by the new economy of globalization'. Allowing the victims to speak provided an opportunity to recall the exorbitant cost of 'the Green Revolution and intensive agriculture'. She also denounced in one go the suicides of peasants, weak production and low incomes, agricultural failures, artificial fertilizers, agro-chemical excesses, the debt trap and the trade in kidneys. A forum of experts and concerned groups discussed the issue of control over seeds, the reduced autonomy of research in public agriculture, the growing influence of the industrial sector on rural projects, the cost and risks of genetic engineering and the implications of intellectual property rights and seed monopolies. Their many demands were summarised in the slogan 'End biopiracy organized by foreign countries!'

Among the many poignant testimonies was the story told by Yellappa Gindakal's brother from the village of Kadappati. Having obtained a bank loan, Yellappa saw his crops destroyed by parasites for two consecutive years. In 1997 he borrowed money from a local moneylender. His cotton was once again devastated, and he furthermore harvested only 450 kilograms of peppers from 5.2 hectares (that is, half a [short] ton of peppers from nearly 13 acres). His debt was then nearly 80,000 rupees. Although family members attempted to dissuade him, he took his life by swallowing organophosphate poison.

The recommendations of the tribunal, composed of judges and experts, were voiced by V. R. Krishna Iyer, a retired Supreme Court judge. It proposed a ten-year moratorium on the commercialization of genetically engineered agricultural products. The need to develop the 'indigenous agricultural system of intellectual property' was emphasized as the only way to protect the 'seed sovereignty' of the rural farmers of the South. Krishna Iyer concluded that 'seed racketeering has become a form of genocide [sic] which condemns rural farmers to pay with their lives for the profits made by the companies.'

The Vernacular Cosmology of Seeds

So great have been the transformations in the agricultural world that farmers characterize the period in which they are living as the 'hybrid era' (*hibred kala*). The sense of rupture is so strong that they habitually describe themselves as 'hybrid people' (*hibred people*).[8] Of course, no rural farmer is unaware that the local (*desi*) seeds produce less than half of what is produced by the hybrid seeds, which therefore afford greater profits for landowners unless ill-fortune strikes.[9] However, they tend to view this quantitative performance negatively and refer to it as the sign or cause of a qualitative decline affecting the nature of the crop, as well as Nature in the broader sense. The association of hybrid seeds with the actual human condition is almost always expressed by pejorative epithets such as 'weak' and 'frail' (*sukshme*). People today are said to be more dependent and more often victims of pain and illness than in the past. Rural folk recall with nostalgia the 'robustness' and the 'health' that formerly prevailed. A strictly 'local' culture that once blossomed and bore fruit is described as 'organic' (*javari*), 'strong' (*thakat*) and 'autonomous' (*swantha*), and regarded as belonging to an epoch blessed with a native, hence 'authentic', (agri)culture.

The memory and repeated representations of this cultural past enable one to grasp the magnitude of the cosmological change taking place. This past separates the worldview of poor farmers from the ideology of out-and-out globalization introduced by executives of companies such as Monsanto. The latter support the 'progressive' Indian entrepreneurs, as well as the large landowners who became wealthy during the 'Green Revolution', all of whom are advocates of intensive agriculture.

The rural farmers have for a very long time selected the best seeds for resowing, for the spring (*rabi*) and autumn crops (*kharif*). This system, based on inherited lore, has to a great extent regulated the social reproduction of the daily life of the people. Based on the principles and (supposed) precepts adapted to regional ecological specificities, this is precisely the knowledge on which the harvests depend. It is also a disposition, both cognitive and emotional, that is the expression of accumulated experiences and of the collective incorporation of a cosmology in which humans, the land, fauna, flora and seeds, and indeed certain gods, are intimately linked to each other.

In Karnataka, for example, the new seeds are nearly always objects of ceremonial 'adoration' (*puja*) before being sown or used. The rural farmers also pay homage to the harvest before it is consumed, and they give thanks to the fields and their alliance with the environment (despite causing damage to the latter, for ecological respect is not a *habitus* of the rural folk's world). The rituals addressed to agricultural implements similarly testify to the gratitude felt towards the fertility of the earth. Briefly, during each phase of agricultural operation, from germination to harvest, homage is paid, rituals are performed and ceremonies are shared.

One often hears that 'The field is the mother of the farmer.' This assertion of affiliation and close bonding is exemplarily expressed during the auspicious season for marriage ceremonies, when mothers pass on selected seeds to their daughters who are about to become wives. The reproductive act itself is conceived of in terms of the male seed germinating in the female field.[10] A number of customs and proverbs closely link women, seeds, soil and fertility. Seeds and fields are recurrent symbols in rituals, including those which have no direct relationship to marriage. During the *Dasara* festival at the beginning of the dry season, the women germinate five kinds of seeds in their houses: lentils (*senegalu*), barley (*yavalu*), sorghum (*jonnalu*), sunflower (*kusumalu*) and wheat (*godamalu*). When the seeds have sprouted, they are transplanted into the family field. The farmer's wife then utters a prayer to the seeds: 'May your life-force be undying!'

Conserving, selecting, using and sharing grain plays an essential function corresponding to the importance of exchange within the family or among farmers. These practices are based on the ideas of cooperation, of gift-giving and reciprocity; a giver will receive in return an equal quantity of seeds. The use of numerous seeds and the practice of crop diversification make it possible for women to satisfy food needs by varying menus as much as possible.

Owing to their expert management of the stocks of food grains, they acquire a recognized status and, consequently, an authority within the household and community (even though the asymmetry of sexes, according to which men are in command, is still determinant for property ownership).

Rural ethnography thus illustrates the powerful significance of seeds for several hundred million individuals as material and symbolic supports of continuity and of assured revival: the essence of life itself. According to estimates, nearly 60 per cent of Indian seeds, the best from each crop, are thus collected and resown. This is indeed the fundamental practice in the 'moral economy' of the Indian rural farming world which has been imperilled for more than two decades by the increasing use of hybrid seeds. Paradoxically, the introduction of genetically modified products, as well as the practices of intensive agriculture and commercialization, have increased the importance given to seeds in rural farming cosmology.[11] The comparison of incomparables has, in fact, become commonplace in rural discourse, as is shown by this song from the 1990s:

Pesticides were the milk-rice of the peasantry –
hybrid sorghum is here.
Ills and destruction are more, whereas duties and traditions have been repressed.
Hybrid sorghum is here,
and the pleasant ways of working have gone.
Hybrid sorghum is here.

The quality of local lands and environment is thus measured in terms of seeds, defining both fertility and biodiversity, of human beings as well as the land. For the poor rural farmer, this is because the new seeds mean the coming of a corrupting world and metaphorically represent the transformation of the substantial identity of the group and its environment, that of a rural culture soon to be engulfed by its ethics, its ways of life and all its values. The adulteration of seeds is interpreted as yet another risk to rural farmers' vulnerability – worse, it is seen as a peril overhanging the very existence of farmers. In short, the agrarian community knows the worth of its seeds as much today as in the past.

With the introduction from the outside world of agrochemical products unfamiliar to farmers and over which they have no control, seeds have come generally to characterize either the farmers' autonomy or their dependency. Seeds thus acquire more or less political connotations, above all in relation to what a number of small rural farmers experience as 'giving oneself up to the protective force' of the state, traditionally called 'mother/father' (*maabap*). The farmer's complaint is passed on to their spokespersons, elected or not, who undertake to translate this diffuse nostalgia into political demands. In this way, they give it both voice and credibility in the public space, but also in the media and national and transnational organizations. While unionists see this attachment to the past as the 'silence and shortcomings of those in (central or regional) power' towards farmers, ecological or radical activists prefer to blame 'globalization' as the ultimate cause of the misfortune of the voiceless rural folk.

Moneylenders, Brokers, Sellers

The main cause of rural farming poverty is financial weakness exacerbated by debt. The incomes of a majority of the farmers are low and almost always inadequate. In 1994 a study by the National Council for Applied Economic Research showed that 59 per cent of rural households in India had a net annual income of less than 20,000 rupees. This sum makes it impossible to surmount any crisis. Should the monsoon be weak or a draught animal need to be replaced, should an illness befall the family or a parasitic worm proliferate, recourse to the moneylender becomes necessary.

Apart from these misfortunes, a number of local (or pan-Indian) practices periodically give rise to debt. Money borrowed to provide a girl's dowry or to satisfy customary and indispensable distribution practices on the occasion of religious ceremonies is the most frequent reason for the loan, and the debtor cannot extricate himself from his social obligations without the risk of exclusion. The dowry is, moreover, not only a tradition or obligation; it is a sign of wealth, status and privilege, an opportunity for upward mobility. Further, it is the cause of 'renewed bidding' between families at the cost of those whose daughters are being given. At least in this case, debt affords pride.

The unregulated ad hoc introduction of new technologies has added its share of problems. After the 'Green Revolution', farmers converted to hybrid seeds in their striving for greater profits. But this type of seed is more costly and requires inputs, not only for fertilizers and pesticides but also for irrigation. These crops are also more vulnerable to attacks from pests, whence the bitter reflection of the farmer Yellappa: 'This is a vicious circle because you invest more in the hope that by doing so you will really make more.'

Specialization in certain crops can also lead to debt while increasing at the same time the economic and social exploitation of the rural farmer. The cotton crop is in this respect a textbook example, particularly concerning the purchase of the agrochemical inputs which cotton-growing demands. Devotion to this crop, especially in small areas, necessitates borrowing, mostly in the informal sector. Explains Yadamma:

We prefer the local moneylender because the amounts offered by the bank do not cover the cost of seeds or fertilizers – not even the work invested. The local moneylender lends us all we need. In addition, he tells us what must be done.

One characteristic of the cotton crop is the instability of market prices from one year to the next. For this reason, the government of India has established an 'intervention price' which guarantees a buying price for merchants. However, many marginal farmers prefer to sell to merchants at lower prices.   •

> It costs more to transport the cotton to the Cotton Corporation of India. In addition, you must queue up there for several days at a time. Finally, the interest on loans has to be paid in good time. Cheques from the Corporation take weeks to arrive.

This combination of factors is an obstacle to the improvement of incomes, especially if the farmer depends on informal credit. The rates vary between 36 per cent and 60 per cent per year, but can be as high as 120 per cent! In short, even a small sum may never be paid back. The last resort is to mortgage land or a house, which can be used to pay the increased interest on the loan, despite the fact that in this area (unlike other regions of India) this type of usury is loathed. Custom dictates instead that family members – usually the women and children – work for the creditor without remuneration. With this last form of dependency and exploitation, the cycle of privation is complete. Not only does the capitalist organization of agriculture assimilate the rural farmers into a wider regional market, it also includes them in an even wider system of exploitation.

Who are the moneylenders? In northern Karnataka the majority of them are called *dalal* or *dalali*, which means 'broker'. Generally in Karnataka the moneylenders are not *Kannadigas*, unlike in Mysore, the southern part of the state, where the local merchants called *mandis* are dominant (the term *mandi* meaning 'market'). It sometimes happens, however, that the *dalal* assume control over the *mandi*, including their craft workshops. The loans are most often made far in advance of the harvest, after which the sum must be paid back. The proliferation of private intermediaries reflects the farmers' difficulties in accessing institutional credit because of the burdensome formalities characteristic of banks, particularly for the numerous illiterate rural inhabitants. What is more, the paperwork takes time, which means that by the time the fertilizer can finally be bought the rains have passed. The proliferation is also due to the corruption which afflicts this type of administration at the cost of its clients, as well as to the 'hardening' of loan conditions since the reforms in 1991. The success of the informal moneylending sector can also be explained by the rural farmers' fear of being unable to find a lender who is both 'generous' and accessible, often leading them to underestimate the risks of debt.

The pressure exerted on the debtor varies according to the occupation of the lender, who may be a professional or a farmer. A farmer, unlike a professional moneylender, is generally a native and a powerful agent in the village economy. He can be a landowner who leases (part of) his land to a clientele of farmers, or a local merchant who lets out land in exchange for jewellery from the wife's dowry or for unremunerated work. Distillers and other dealers in alcohol profit from the dependency on drink of the rural folk in the area. Sometimes local landowners convert a financial surplus into capital in the form of a portfolio of loans made in the vicinity. The seed merchant in the village has become a major figure in the theatre of usury. This is because he combines usury with opinions and advice, which the farmers in fact seek, regarding seeds, fertilizers, pesticides and other biotechnologies. The large number of shops selling pesticides in small towns is indicative of the growth of this economic role.

Another factor in this growth is the repeated purchase of fertilizers and pesticides, when the seeds sold on credit are unsuitable or of poor quality, in an attempt to save at least part of the harvest. Persistent rumours suggest that diluted pesticides are in circulation. 'The pesticide merchants drink our blood,' declares Mudavath Jumani from the village of Gairanda. Another rural farmer explains:

> The whole village has debts to a single merchant. We grow cotton on two hectares, and we see what the other farmers do. But he repeatedly tells us that we must use more and more pesticides. Now the harvest is completely destroyed, and we owe him nearly 30,000 rupees.

For his part, the accused merchant attributes this failure to the farmers' inadequate management of agrochemical products. The excessive consumption of pesticides reached its peak in 2002, with the death by poisoning of some 500 rural farmers in South India. Following irresponsible advice, they mixed different corrosive products in order to increase their effectiveness.

Politicians are concerned to avoid paying the financial compensation claimed by the families of victims or union organizations, and they ignore the problem. After the death of her son Sivaiah, Chandramma received 10,000 rupees from the government of Karnataka through the revenue office of the district. She deposited 5,000 rupees in a bank account in her granddaughter's name and took the rest home. The next day, the pawnbroker knocked at her door and claimed 3,500 rupees from Chandramma, whose situation remains desperate. What is worse, the trouble of being in debt and shame of having a relative who committed suicide covers her family with opprobrium, isolating them still more and making things more difficult after the wilful death of the head of the family, which was already a sign of social disintegration – 'anomic suicide' in Durkheim's sociological typology.

Body, Transplantation and Conspiracy

In recent years, no fewer than 100 seriously indebted farmers have sold their kidneys to doctors practising in Delhi, although rumours have spread that their numbers are more like several thousand.[12] The pivotal place for this trafficking is a village in Guntur district in Andhra Pradesh. In Rentachintalsa, Khambhampadu and Machela villages, farmers who admitted to having sold their kidneys made the front pages of the regional, national and occasionally international press. The brokers in this organ trade, the market for which is the Delhi middle classes, preceded them in the promotional race by opening a website with the address *saleof@kidney.com*!

All those who have submitted to this removal are farmers working on leased lands (*ryots*). They are pressured by the landowners to cultivate cotton (not genetically modified) and pepper, the prices of which have not fallen in the market in recent years. More than 75 per cent of them live in subsistence conditions. Venkat Reddy, who cultivates one hectare of land, tells of having accumulated a debt of 50,000 rupees as a consequence of sterile crops from bogus seeds. 'It was an enormous sum for a poor man like me,' he says, 'and I did not know how to pay back my moneylender, who knocked at my door every day.' Finally, 'I met an intermediary who bought kidneys, passing through villages and promising money. Along with two other farmers, we went with him to Delhi. There we authorized the doctor to remove our kidneys illegally.' Venkat Reddy does not even remember the name of the hospital or that of the surgeon who performed the operation. He sold his kidney for 40,000 rupees, which enabled him to pay off his debts. 'I don't regret anything, because it was the best thing I could do as there was no one to help me.' There then came, however, the cruel discovery: 'My health has deteriorated and I can no longer really work. I now depend on the income from my wife, who works in my place as a farm labourer.'

More than a dozen farmers from this village have had similar experiences for the same reasons, explains Venkat Reddy:

We didn't want to commit suicide like the other farmers who were unable to pay back their debts and survive harvest losses. We thought it was better to live and take care of our families, which would have been orphaned [sic] if we had chosen death. I am proud of myself. I didn't commit suicide like the others. I sold a part of my body. I didn't beg, borrow or steal because of my debts. By selling a part of my body, I gave new hope in life to my family.

He also received 40,000 rupees.

This is no isolated case; trafficking in kidneys on a more or less large scale has also been discovered in Karnataka and in Tamil Nadu. The rapid spreading of the news of organ trafficking in the rural communities where a large number of the poor live is often accompanied by wild rumours or mass panic, particularly when obligingly relayed by the media. Names circulate, connections are made, concrete examples are given, the suspicion of conspiracy takes hold. The simple facts as well as their amplified narrations are equivalent to an alarm system. The bodies and lives of the villagers, and those of their children and grandchildren, are endangered. The accounts foster a chronic state of fear and the sense that their earthly survival is threatened.

Of course, the rumour of trafficking is perhaps a fantasy aimed at publicising the real dangers which threaten the bodies of marginalized populations, as if contemporary speech, bringing new life to archaic mythologies, were to follow paths of the social imagination in order to denounce the state of misery and abandonment which is the lot of the poor. But faced with dramatic circumstances, members of vulnerable communities debate and fight with their only available resources: hearsay, eyewitness accounts, gossip, rumours, accusations, beliefs, magic, folklore, cosmologies. All these means of expression, as well as the customs of daily life, give shape to the day-to-day uncertainty and precariousness of their situation, a kind of 'shield of the poor'. These accounts express the aroused subjectivity of subaltern populations forced to live in 'negative zones of existence' where lives and bodies are experienced in a survival or crisis situation, sometimes at their limits or 'facing extremes'. This is so not only because of hunger, disease, misfortune and exploitation, which all exacerbate indebtedness, but also because of the lack of security and hope, too many children or excess mortality, or the threat of disappearing without a trace. The chronic state of fear and urgency in which the poor survive bears witness to the 'structural violence' or 'low-intensity war' characterizing their condition.

Stories are ceaselessly repeated and circulate without any certainty about whether they are fact or fiction, but who would doubt that they are expressions of a tragic situation, both social and existential? In the villages or towns in the underprivileged South, regulated by unequal exchange, the encounter with numerous forms of violence is direct, if not routine. Violence also haunts people's imaginations to the point that social relations are often experienced in a destructive manner; hence the confounding of image and reality, the reality of suffering bodies that are anaemic, broken or bruised, and sometimes mutilated. Such a perspective on life is plainly seen as an emblematic 'massacre of the innocents'.

Trafficking in organs, as well as the international business of child adoption or marriage by e-mail, is experienced by the victims as predation. They recognize in all this a 'new colonization', 'the imperialism of modern times', as their politicised leaders tell them. The rich and powerful drain the villages, 'the nation or Indian civilization', and denounce the radical ideologues, while 'foreigners' appropriate the bodies of others who are poor and powerless. The North, through indigenous representatives, sucks the blood of bodies in the South.

In fact, the flow of transplants follows the routes of capital and mirrors social stratification: from the Third World to the (post-)industrial countries, from blacks to mixed races to whites, from the poor to the rich (and sometimes from women to men). Between 1983 and 1988, the press counted 131 wealthy citizens from the United Arab Emirates or Oman who had come to Bombay to receive transplants of Indian kidneys. Chosen by local intermediaries, the donors were recruited from among poverty-stricken peasants. Each had received the equivalent of 2,000 or 3,000 US dollars. The business caused a sensation and rumours increased. The cases of reported transplants are, however, only ripples on the surface. 'Charter-loads of Muslims from the Gulf countries come to pillage the bodies and organs of Hindus,' proclaim nationalist militants. The well-known British medical journal *The Lancet* has spoken more sombrely of the matter. It published an article analysing the high percentage of mortality among the Arabs who had undergone this transplantation.

Today, the trade in organs (but also in blood, tissues and children) has spread well beyond the South and the Gulf states, to Turkey, Iraq, Israel, Singapore and Korea, to Brazil and Argentina, and after the collapse of the Soviet Union, to Russia, Romania, Bulgaria, Estonia and Croatia. Recently it was even introduced to some hospitals in the United States, and the practice was officially justified in the name of 'donors for dollars'.[13] Such a complex of ideas and transnational behaviour, based on criminal medical practices that authorize unequal sharing between North and South, attests to a greater danger. Worse, it fosters the fear of conspiracy, the possibility that everything could be tied together, connected in the so-called 'new world order' – another take on globalization. This is of course the most immediate way of explaining that the victims are dogged by hard luck. 'Why me? Why now? And why me again?', questioned anthropologist Edward Evans-Pritchard regarding sorcery among the Azande in the 1930s. Every original social situation is known to require new forms of magic.

Globalization, History and Causality

The multiplication of distress scenarios among farmers in India is the symptom of a major crisis. This crisis is at the same time economic, social, institutional and ecological, and all these factors combine to increase the vulnerability of heavily indebted rural farmers with little or no land. It is presently fashionable in the subcontinent to assign responsibility to such diabolical figures as international organizations of world (de)regulation, in particular the WTO, with which the Indian central government has signed an agreement entailing a series of measures authorizing the mass entry of foreign products. Deflationary economic policies combined with (partial) removal of national trade barriers form the core of the policy agenda of finance capital.[14]

India imports today small quantities of rice, wheat and sugar. Horticultural products from Australia, New Zealand and the United States are now sold in large shops in the metropolises, and Chinese silk effectively inundates the market. However, figures support the observation that the terms of exchange have neither suddenly nor completely changed in recent years.[15] The persistence in maintaining a measure of autonomy and the rejection of an abrupt opening to the world market, which were characterized as 'archaic' ten years ago, are today seen more favourably in the subcontinent than in other countries. As far as economic changes are concerned, India likes – not without good reasons – to compare itself to an elephant which is today walking to the rhythm of a new *Zeitgeist*.

History shows that it would be illusory to explain the rural farmers' distress and despair only as the impact of recent globalization, although a crisis of such magnitude has not been seen since the run-up to the Great Depression. There was a cotton crisis in Karnataka and Andhra Pradesh from 1860 to 1870 following the American Civil War, when exports of this raw material to industries in continental Europe and then Japan gave rise to murderous riots against moneylenders by indebted peasants.[16] Later, an agricultural debacle was triggered in the 1960s, when the 'interventionist' state decided to buy up harvests and stock them in order to stabilize prices and so guarantee costs and outlets. Never challenged, this decision made India a country which retains 60 million tonnes of food reserves (in 2001), while the majority is still undernourished – in short, a country able to manage neither poverty nor abundance. Furthermore, the promotion of commercial agriculture – based on the use of hybrid seeds and the intensive use of chemical fertilizers and pesticides in arid and inadequately irrigated regions – only further destabilizes human communities already weakened by great inequalities in land, income, jobs and status, which were exacerbated by nineteenth-century colonial land policy and the later absence of agricultural reforms.

To blame globalization alone for India's tribulations, as is done by a number of militants and populist leaders, makes an economic axiom or historical necessity out of a complex, fragmented and contingent process, the dynamics of which lead in various directions. This alleged explanation for the poverty and misfortune of the peasantry passes over the long history of an extremely segmented social structure (divided by classes, castes, regions, agricultural systems, modes of domination, gender) whose past attests to crises, droughts, famines, and violent conflicts and clashes. To recognize that every phenomenon has a cause does not imply that a determined effect can only be produced in one way. The (Leibnizian) principle of *maxima minimis*, to explain the most by the least, proves here an oversimplification. The establishment of a causal chain leading from globalization to agricultural crisis is as much a cliché as 'butterfly wings' or 'Cleopatra's nose', even though the repetition *ad nauseam* of the word gives it credibility.

Except for confirming reified abstractions, globalization, for better or worse, has only a very indirect impact on the situation of the rural farmers. International flows and world forces are only seen through a set of polychromatic filters, the brightly coloured effects of which are sometimes highly contrasted. Only the mediations, the succession of which can be compared to the outcomes of a game of dominoes, bring about the presence of globalization at different points and with an apparently random tendency, but conforming to the rules of the game. The mediations further accentuate or reduce certain features so that the (supposed) effects of globalization assume new meanings, inasmuch as social agents recode the meanings and behaviours according to contexts, situations and moments. Just as there are several ways to arrange the twenty-eight dominoes, more than one story can be told of this chain of effects, which gives rise to conflicting interpretations of struggles that are more or less violent. In fact, only a close examination of situations in terms of networks, connections and causal chains makes a 'glocal' situation intelligible by showing us the multiple ways social actors have to produce their worlds here and now, knowing that they can change them according to the beliefs that they hold about themselves.

To understand the origins and development of the agricultural crisis in India (and everywhere) thus requires an analysis of the entangled complexity of local factors and the specific milieux in which so-called 'world' phenomena are experienced. A list of these factors summarises a process of disintegration conditioned by globalization: a reduction of the area assigned to food crops; the replacement of local crops by intensive monocultures; the alteration or disappearance of local seed varieties, replaced by non-native seed varieties; a hiatus between the practice of intensive and commercial agriculture and regional ecological specificity; an increase in the use of inputs entailing depletion of the soils, as well as massive recourse to (informal) credit to provide supplies (a tendency favouring richer landowners); the disappearance of an institutional 'safety net' for the provision of credit and a distribution system offering advantageous prices; lack of knowhow in the use of new agricultural products; small peasants' lack of experience in so-called 'entrepreneurial' management systems; ignorance of or aversion to intermediaries and other outside agricultural advisers; and finally, climatic changes, above all variable rainfall patterns, leading to increased uncertainty and risk factors. Only ideologues entertaining a teleological vision (of globalization) could fail to see that this patchwork does not form a seamless garment.

Notes

1 On the issue of suicides, see the articles by Parthasarathy (1990), Assadi (1998), Revathi (1998), Prasad (1999), Vasavi (1999), Menon (2001) and Deshpande (2002).
2 Compare the multi-site approach of Marcus (1995).
3 These contextual distinctions are made by Beck (2000: 9–11). 'Globalism' is the liberal ideology of the world market; 'globality' signifies that we have been living for a long time in a world society; 'globalization' is a process in which the sovereign nation states are undermined in their prerogatives. The notion of 'glocalization' comes from the Japanese term *dochakuka*, which refers to the adaptation of an agricultural technique to local conditions.
4 More than 80 per cent of the farmlands consist of small holdings of less than 2 hectares; India counts approximately 100 million farms.
5 On the strategy of this company, see Tokar (2002) and Shiva *et al.* (1999).
6 For a sociological and historical account of the Karnataka Rajya Raitha Sangha (KRRS) and the Shektkari Sangathana (SS) of Maharashtra and the Bharakta Kisan Union (BKU) of Andhra Pradesh, see Assadi (1997); cf also Brass (1995).
7 On the history of the Indian middle class, cf Varma (1999) and a critique by Assayag (2005: ch.3).
8 On fundamental changes in agriculture, see Vasavi (1994), Appadurai (1989), Gupta (1998) and Panini (1999).
9 For wheat and rice (but not cotton), they confuse the 'hybrids' with the 'high-yield varieties' (HYV), which are not hybrids but were disseminated from the time of the 'Green Revolution'. There are thus three types of 'non-traditional' seeds: the HYV, the hybrids and 'terminators'.
10 On symbolic associations with seed and earth, see Dube (1986), and in relation to gender, Agarwal (1994).
11 A commercialization which developed in the nineteenth century, see Raj et al. (1985), Bharadwaj (1985) and Washbrook (1994).
12 On the question of trafficking in organs in India, see articles by Changappa (1990) and in *Frontline* (1997), but above all the works of Cohen (1999) and Das (2000).
13 On globalization of organ traffic, see Scheper-Hughes (1996, 2000).
14 For details and an explanation of the collapse in prices of globally traded primary products in the last five years, see Patnaik (2002).
15 See, for example, Painak and Chandrashkar (1995), and Bhalla and Singh (2001).
16 For details of the mechanisms of this crisis, see Harnetty (1971); cf Patnaik (2002: 125–8) and the more generally suggestive work by Davis (2001).

Bibliography

Agarwal, Bina (1994) *A Field of One's Own: Gender and Land Rights in South Asia*. Cambridge: Cambridge University Press.

Appadurai, Arjun (1989) 'Transformations in the culture of agriculture', in Carla Borden, ed., *Contemporary Indian Tradition*. Washington DC: Smithsonian Institution Press; 173–86.

Assadi, H. Muzaffar (1997) *Peasant Movement in Karnataka, 1980–94*. Delhi: Shipra.

—— (1998) 'Farmers' suicides. Signs of distress in rural economy', *Economic and Political Weekly*, XXXIII, 14, 4: 747–8.

Assayag, Jackie (1998) 'La culture comme fait social global? Anthropologie et (post)modernité', *L'Homme*, 148: 201–24.

—— (2001) *L'Inde: Désir de nation*. Paris: Odile Jacob.

—— (2005) *La mondialisation vue d'ailleurs: L'Inde dés-Orientée*. Paris: Seuil.

Beck, Ulrich (2000 [1997]) *What is Globalization?* Cambridge: Polity Press.

Bhalla, G. S. and Gurmail Singh (2001) *Agriculture: Four Decades of Development*. New Delhi: Sage Publications.

Bharadwaj, Krishna (1985) 'A view on commercialisation in Indian agriculture and the development of capitalism', *Journal of Peasant Studies*, 12, 4: 7–25.

Brass, Tom, ed. (1995) *New Farmers' Movements in India*. Ilford: Cass.

Changappa, Raj (1990) 'The organ bazaar', *India Today*, July: 30–7.

Cohen, Lawrence (1999) 'Where it hurts: Indian material for an ethics of organ transplantation', *Daedalus*, 128, 4: 135–65.

Das, Veena (2000) 'The practice of organ transplants: networks, documents and transplantation', in Margaret Lock, Allen Young and Alberto Combrioso, eds, *Living and Working with the New Medical Technologies*. Cambridge: Cambridge University Press; 38–55.

Davis, Mike (2001) *Late Victorian Holocausts: El Nino famines and the making of the Third World*. Verso: London.

Deshpande, R. S. (2002) 'Suicide by farmers in Karnataka. Agrarian distress and possible alleviatory steps', *Economic and Political Weekly*, XXXVII, 19: 2601–10.

Dube, Leela (1986) 'Seed and earth: the symbolism of biological reproduction and sexual relation of production', in L. Dube, L. Leacko and S. Ardener, eds, *Visibility and Power. Essays on Women, Society and Development*. Delhi: Oxford University Press; 22–53.

Frontline (1997) Vol. 18, no. 2, 2 February.

Gupta, Akhil (1998) *Postcolonial Developments: Agriculture in the Making of Modern India*. Durham: Duke University Press.

Harnetty, Peter (1971) 'Cotton exports and Indian agriculture, 1861–1870', *Economic History Review*, XXIV, 3: 414–29.

Marcus, George E. (1995) 'Ethnography in/of the world system: the emergence of multi-site ethnography', *Annual Review of Anthropology*, 24: 95–117.

Menon, Parvathi (2001) 'A farm crisis and suicides', *Frontline*, 27 April: 21–4.

Panini, M. Narendar (1999) 'Trends in cultural globalisation: From agriculture to agribusiness in Karnataka', *Economic and Political Weekly*, XXXIV, 39: 2168–73.

Parthasarathy, Shameen (1990) 'Suicides of cotton farmers in AP: an exploratory story', *Economic and Political Weekly*, XXXIII, 13: 720–6.

Patnaik, P. and C. P. Chandrasekhar (1995) 'Indian economy under structural adjustment', *Economic and Political Weekly*, XXX, 47, 2: 3003–13.

Patnaik, Utsa (2002) 'Deflation and *déjà vu*: Indian agriculture and the world economy', in V. K. Ramachandran and Madhura Swaminathan, eds, *Agrarian Studies: Essays on Agrarian Relations in Less Developed Countries*. Delhi: Tulika; 111–43.

Prasad, C. Shambu (1999) 'Suicide deaths and quality of Indian cotton: Perspectives from history of technology and khadi movement', *Economic and Political Weekly*, XXXIX, 5, 30 January: PE-12–PE-29.

Raj, K. N., N. Bhattacharya and S. Guha (1985) *Essays on the Commercialisation in Indian Agriculture*. Delhi: Oxford University Press.

Revathi, E. (1998) 'Farmers' suicides: missing issues', *Economic and Political Weekly*, XXXIII, 20: 1207.

Scheper-Hughes, Nancy (1996) 'The theft of life: the globalization of organ stealing rumour', *Anthropology Today*, 12, 3: 3–11.

—— (2000) 'The global traffic in human organs', *Current Anthropology*, 41: 191–211.

Shiva, Vandana (2000) *Stolen Harvest: The hijacking of the global food supply*. New Delhi: Indian Research Press.

Shiva, Vandana, Ashok Elani and Afsar H. Jafri (1999) 'The seed and the earth: biotechnology and the colonisation of regeneration', in Vandana Shiva, ed., *Minding Our Lives: Women from the South and the North: Reconnected ecology and health*. Delhi: Kali for Women; 38–50.

Tokar, Brian (2001) 'Monsanto: l'arrogance d'une transnationale', in Edward Goldsmith and Jerry Mander, eds, *Le procès de la mondialisation*. Paris: Fayard; 165–87.

Varma, Pavan K. (1999) *The Great Indian Middle Class*. New Delhi: Penguin Books.

Vasavi, A. R. (1994) 'Hybrid times, hybrid people: culture and agriculture in South India', *Man*, 2: 283–300.

Vasavi, R. (1999) 'Agrarian distress in Bidar. Market, state and suicides', *Economic and Political Weekly*, XXXIV, 32: 2226–68.

Washbrook, David (1994) 'The commercialization of agriculture in colonial India: production, subsistence and reproduction in the "dry South", c.1870–1930', *Modern Asian Studies*, 28, 1: 129–64.

5

WEAVING FOR *IKEA* IN SOUTH INDIA: SUBCONTRACTING, LABOUR MARKETS AND GENDER RELATIONS IN A GLOBAL VALUE CHAIN

Geert De Neve

This chapter focuses on the processes by which a rural labour force in Tamil Nadu, South India, is recruited to produce for a global company. The intensification of global sourcing by networked enterprises has led to the mobilization of rural workers across the world to produce for the export market. However, little is known about the manner in which such enterprises subcontract work or about the ways in which rural labourers come to produce for a global commodity chain (Cox 1997: 11). This chapter aims to explore two sides of this issue.

Firstly, it examines the process by which the production of rag rugs for IKEA is subcontracted to weavers in a rural area of Tamil Nadu. It explores the ways in which caste, gender and kinship are central to the generation of a network of rural weavers at the tail end of a commodity chain.

Secondly, it focuses on the rural workers themselves: the opportunities that are available to them, and their decisions to weave or not to weave. It is suggested that the choices made by rural workers have to be understood in the context of local constraints imposed by highly fragmented labour markets and prevailing sexual divisions of labour. It is argued that in the area under consideration the rural labour markets are firmly segmented due to particular caste occupations, perceptions of work, gendered ideologies of skill, and sexual divisions of labour. While these factors shape to a large extent who *can* and who *wants to* join this export labour force, the very introduction of this new job opportunity in the villages also modifies existing sexual divisions of labour and gradually alters ideologies of skill, perceptions of work and values of domesticity.

The study will further point to the ways in which shifting patterns of post-marital residence rather than long-distance migration have resulted from new employment opportunities in the rural villages that were studied.

While very little is known about labour working for export markets and even less about how it is recruited and absorbed into globally sourcing enterprises, a few assumptions reign that are largely left unquestioned in much writing on the subject. Labour is always assumed to be 'there' – that is, to be readily available for deployment by whichever corporation needs it; labour is assumed to be largely passive and without choice; and finally, 'global' labour tends to be stereotyped as predominantly factory-based, young, unskilled, female, migrant, and above all exploited in many ways (see e.g. Ong 1987; Wolf 1992; Rofel 1999). Those who work for the global market as home producers, subcontractors or in small-scale workshops seldom get their share in the study of labour under global economic conditions (for exceptions see Bagchi 1999; Breman 1996, 1999; Cadène and Holmström 1998; Mies 1982; van der Loop 1996; Wilkinson-Weber 1999). This study aims to show that the workers at the supply end of a commodity chain can be old as well as young, male as well as female, and local as well as migrant. The availability of workers, the formation of particular workforces and the activities of labour itself (whether in co-operation, submission or resistance) are often taken as a given, while there is an urgent need for these processes to be described and analysed. Labour, denied both its history and agency, remains unrecognized as a force that can and does make a difference to the evolving processes of globalization.

The process of labour recruitment and labour force formation cannot be understood merely by referring to the needs of global capital (Chandavarkar 1994; de Haan 1999). A more revealing approach lies in a focus on labour market formations and in particular on the nature of persistent labour market segmentation. A body of literature that is particularly relevant to my argument is that which explores the nature of labour market fragmentation in India. Breman, for one, has documented how the rural labour markets of Gujarat are fragmented through caste, gender, patronage and dependency relationships and how this fragmentation effectively excludes some while keeping others in clearly fenced-off segments (1976: 1905–7). In his study of the Coimbatore labour markets during the 1970s and 1980s, Harriss emphasized the rigid segmentation of the urban labour force by permanent workers, short-term workers, casual labourers and petty producers and traders, as well as along different types of employment. The urban labour markets, he concluded, 'appear to be distinctly segmented, and particularistic ties of kinship and caste, and neighbourhood still exercise quite a strong influence upon an individual's employment opportunities' (Harriss 1982: 997; see also Harriss 1986; Harriss, Kannan and Rodgers 1989). Here, a similar focus on labour market segmentation will be used to understand how a particular labour force is generated, why subcontracting is seen by the employers and agents as a lucrative production strategy, and what the drawbacks are of 'putting out' work to rural areas. Moreover, in the process of recruiting labour, a network enterprise such as IKEA is not only faced with localized labour market segmentation but actively contributes to its reproduction in the process of outsourcing.

In what follows, I first look at the way in which IKEA relies heavily on local entrepreneurs who in turn play a central role in recruiting workers from among the rural population.[1] Understanding the strategies pursued by the entrepreneurs and their agents as well as the role played by caste, hereditary occupation and gender, is crucial to gaining an insight into the formation of a particular labour force for the export industry. Second, it will be indicated how the resulting labour force is also the outcome of labourers' own choices, which are shaped by the range of options available, by occupational histories, perceptions of work, caste, gender and skill. In conclusion I will return to the argument that while social constructions of gender and skill help to determine the ways in which the impacts of globalization are transmitted in specific local contexts, they are themselves transformed under the processes of global labour sourcing.

The Location, Company and Products

It is in the town of Bhavani, which is the headquarters of the Bhavani taluk (Erode District, Tamil Nadu), that the main offices of the Sri Murugan Rugs Exports company are situated. The company was started about 25 years ago by Mr Kumarasamy, a member of the local Mudaliyar weaving community. He soon became a major textile trader, selling carpets, handkerchiefs and towels all over India. It was with the saturation of the domestic market in the early 1980s that Mr Kumarasamy got the idea of modifying the traditional *jamakkalam* handloom to manufacture new products that could be exported worldwide. (The *jamakkalam* is a rough carpet of a type that has been woven in the town and taluk for at least 100 years, and weavers from various communities have been involved in its manufacture.) As he had easy access to yarn supplies and had the infrastructure for yarn dyeing, he started weaving yarn mats, which are of popular use in the West as tablemats, and in 1984 he started merchant exports through an exporting house in Cochin, Kerala. At about the same time, he made a trip with his managers to Ludhiana (Punjab, North India) where he saw the manufacturing of *chindi* rugs – rag rugs made on handlooms with the waste materials of the hosiery industry. This prompted Mr Kumarasamy to consider producing similar rugs in Bhavani, and the operation began within a few months' time.

In 1991 Mr Kumarasamy started direct exports, initially through the representatives of an importer in Delhi. In 1993 the Sweden-based chain store IKEA came to know about Bhavani and they themselves approached Mr Kumarasamy, asking whether he could supply rag rugs to them. Over a period of six months they made several visits to Bhavani to research the production capacity and the quality standards of his company. A first trial order soon followed, and because the delivery met the stipulated requirements, more orders were given and the relationship between importer and exporter was firmly established. All IKEA exports are dispatched from the port of Chennai and shipped to various distribution centres of IKEA in Sweden, Germany, the UK, Italy and Singapore. Later, Sri Murugan Rug Exports also started direct sales to an American-based company which has representatives in Delhi. The Sri Murugan company's turnover in 1999 amounted to Rs 35 crore, or nearly £6 million, of which the lion's share is produced for IKEA.

Labour Recruitment and the Strategy of 'Putting Out'

How production is organized in the villages and how labour is recruited to produce such an annual export value are crucial issues for discussion. What we find is a typical variant of a 'subcontracting' or 'putting-out' system – that is, a form of home-based work in which 'raw materials are brought to the home of the producer and finished products are returned to the supplier or his agent' (Breman 1999: 411–12). Currently, work is given to about 7,000 looms in nearly 50 villages, most of which are situated in the Bhavani taluk up to a distance of 70 kilometres (43½ miles) from the town. However, most of the present 7,000 weavers had no experience in weaving at the time exports started. I will therefore describe the ways in which workers were contacted and absorbed in this 'putting out' network and highlight a number of methods which lie at the basis of this specific form of subcontracting work, but which are characteristic of subcontracting and labour recruitment practices in many sectors of India's informal economy. The ethnography is based on a study of six 'weaving villages', a number of production centres and in-depth interviews with workers, agents and managers.

The Initial Stages of 'Putting Out'

It was in the early 1980s that the carpet (*jamakkalam*) looms were transformed into looms on which rugs could be woven and that the Sri Murugan company began its search for workers. While in the past most *jamakkalam* weavers were situated in and around the town of Bhavani, the strategy actively opted for was 'to give work to the villages', as stated by a senior manager. This strategy is unsurprising given the lack of space in town, the active operation of an urban-based weavers' union, and the flow of government regulations which would apply if production was centralized in one factory unit.

A number of basic strategies were deployed to recruit workers in the initial stages. First, weavers were offered loans to purchase their looms. Or rather, looms were given to about 300–400 villagers who were eager to join in, and money was deducted from their first payments to repay the debt. When neighbours and relatives had seen the benefits of weaving for Sri Murugan, they started buying their own looms and took orders. Once there was sufficient local enthusiasm for weaving, the company stopped handing out loans. Second, use was made of commission agents or masterweavers to contact potential weaving candidates. These agents were personally and extremely carefully selected by Mr Kumarasamy and sent to particular areas to recruit new weavers, to train the workforce and to organize the production process.

Commission Agents

About 15 agents were interviewed, and it would seem that although they form a very heterogeneous group, they also have a common profile. First of all, they all have a long and close relationship with Mr Kumarasamy himself. Most of them worked for him as managers, accountants, supervisors or weavers before exports started and therefore have longstanding relationships with him, built on loyalty and mutual trust. They all know the trade and are usually experienced in both the technical aspects of weaving as well as the administrative side of the business. It was from among his most loyal staff and workers that Mr Kumarasamy selected his first agents.

The initial agents were also *sondukaarar* of Mr Kumarasamy – that is, 'relatives', either in the narrow sense of being closely related through blood or marriage, or in the broader sense of belonging to the same Mudaliyar caste of traditional weavers. However, caste also surfaced in a different way. Agents are selected not merely on the basis of how they are related to the owner but also on how they are related to the workers. Mr Kumarasamy selected agents who either belonged to the specific village or area from where workers could be recruited or belonged to the same caste as the workers. Having dealt with the *jamakkalam* weavers in Bhavani before, Mr Kumarasamy knew all too well that labour recruitment and training as well as the generation of trust and loyalty become easier when relationships of kin, caste or neighbourhood can be invoked. Cheating the company becomes more difficult when its agent is also the weaver's neighbour or his fellow caste-member who resides in the same village. To ensure the commitment and cooperation of the agents themselves, the latter are paid on a commission basis. Agents are thus selected on the basis of both meritocratic elements (ability to recruit and control labour) and non-meritocratic elements (links of caste or kinship). Finally, the agents are also appointed as the managers of the production centres from which yarn and rags are distributed to the weavers and where finished products are collected. Each production centre has a manager, who is usually the agent himself, and in the larger centres there may also be manager's assistants and staff.

Let me briefly illustrate the above patterns of putting out with reference to some examples of specific agents and villages. One of the first places where rug weaving was introduced in 1983 was the village of Periyavadamoolapalayam (hereafter PVM), situated about 12 kilometres (7½ miles) from Bhavani. The agent for PVM is Mr Gurunathan. The Mudaliyars are the largest community in this village, where they have a long tradition as weavers of *dhotis* and towels. Born in this village and belonging to the Mudaliyar community, Gurunathan learned to weave towels at home from the age of 12 onwards. As a distant relative of Mr Kumarasamy, he was approached in the early 1980s by the latter to start weaving yarn rugs. Because there were very few orders for towels at that time, he adjusted his two looms and started weaving rugs. It did not take him very long to convince the weavers around him to follow his example, and today, at the age of 39, Gurunathan is the manager of the PVM production centre and the agent for 500 looms in an area covering five villages. It is no coincidence that one of the very first villages selected by Mr Kumarasamy to put out work was a village of Mudaliyars and established weavers, and one of his first agents a fellow caste-member.

It was only a year later, in 1984, that the first rug looms were established in Karukkupalayam, 2 kilometres (1¼ miles) away from PVM. However, the introduction of looms in this village is quite a different story. In 1978, Mr Segar, born in the nearby town of Chennimalai, got married to a girl from Karukkupalayam and after their marriage he moved to that village. He got a job in the company of Mr Kumarasamy in Bhavani, and it was with the latter's financial support and encouragement that he set up a first loom in Karukkupalayam in 1984. While Segar is definitely recognized by everyone as the person who introduced weaving in the village, his role as an agent was only a very brief one. Belonging to a caste of barbers and being an outsider to the village, he was not accepted by the community of Gounders who form the dominant caste in Karukkupalayam. While the Gounders were eager to start weaving, they were less eager to accept Segar's authority as an agent. Or, as a Gounder weaver put it, 'He ordered us to pull a bag with yarn and we could not accept orders from a barber, so we no longer wanted him as an agent.' An agent must get the weavers to work, he must urge them to finish an order in time and must reject pieces that are not up to scratch. For this he might indeed have to shout at times, but most importantly he needs the authority to be accepted in his role as an agent, and this authority tends to be rooted in his social and economic position in the village. Segar was clearly lacking the necessary background in Karukkupalayam to act and speak with authority. His case illustrates the principle not only that kin, caste and locality links facilitate the recruitment and training of labour, but that they constitute the very conditions for the consolidation of the agent's authority. Segar was soon dismissed as an agent and replaced by Gurunathan from nearby PVM.

The story of how Leela became an agent in Punnam, a village 3 kilometres (1 ¾ miles) from PVM, is equally revealing. Leela is the only female agent I met in the taluk. After finishing higher secondary school, she could not find a job and decided to start weaving. For one year she worked as a *kuli* (daily wage labourer) for Gurunathan in PVM, who then encouraged her to start a loom of her own in her native place, Punnam. She installed a loom and within a year's time, Gurunathan suggested that she pass on yarn to other women in her village as well. And so she did. Leela soon became the agent for Punnam and today she gives yarn to about 40 looms and is still recruiting new weavers.

While Gurunathan was aware of the potential female labour force available in Punnam, he did not enter the village himself, but turned to Leela, who was an apprentice of his and belonged to Punnam and its main community of Naickers, and turned her into a sub-agent. Gurunathan was well aware that men were not very likely to take up weaving in this village due to their employment in construction work, and thought it more convenient to employ a woman to recruit female weavers. His strategy proved an immediate success. This case further illustrates how, after the initial stages, the network of agents quickly spread throughout the taluk and how agents themselves started recruiting sub-agents to share their work. In this village, gender and caste proved to be the main obstacle for Gurunathan to recruit workers himself, and it was only with the cooperation of a young, assertive and trustworthy woman that he was able to access the women of Punnam.

Finally, let me tell the story of another production centre, situated just outside the village of Punnam. This is a large production centre that was started in 1987. Today it provides employment for about 400 weavers in eight villages. The first agent, Mr Kumar, was sent here by Mr Kumarasamy himself. He was a man who had been working for many years in the company's office and although he was not from the area he was sent to Punnam because he belonged to the same community as the people of this locality, the Vanniyars.[2] Kumar was asked to tour the area, to persuade people to switch over to rug weaving, and to recruit new weavers from among the agricultural labourers. However, after a few years Kumar was dismissed because of bad management of the centre and replaced by Mr Gopal, also a Vanniyar, who had worked in the Sri Murugan dyeing factory for about six years and who was transferred from Bhavani to run this centre.

Although he was a close and trusted friend of Mr Kumarasamy, Gopal cheated the company of about £20,000 (Rs 12 lakh) during the four years that he was managing the centre. Being well versed in accounting, he altered entries in the account books and drew out sums of money from the head office that far exceeded what was required for the payment of wages. Once caught, Gopal was dismissed on the spot and replaced by Mr Patchimuthu, the current agent, in 1998. Patchimuthu gives the following account of the owner and the area:

> Mr Kumarasamy has a very clever mind and he knows exactly where to place which agent. In this area the Vanniyars are in a majority, and labour-wise this is a very critical point. The workers here often create problems and cannot easily be controlled. I was placed here by the owner because I am also a Vanniyar and he knew that only I would be able to deal with the workers. So, in his office, Mr Kumarasamy has men from all communities and he sends them to those areas where he knows they will be able to keep the workers in hand. For him the most important thing is that production goes on non-stop. There are about 28 agents like me and a large number are Mudaliyar, three are Jangamar, three are Vellala Gounder, four are Vanniyar, and a few are Muslim. The owner cooperates with people from all backgrounds in order to be able to deal with the workers in all areas.

In two places Patchimuthu puts out work himself, but for the other villages he works through ten sub-agents, who are from the individual locality and therefore 'better equipped to give work to their neighbours and relatives and to control the workers', as he says. While the company is predominantly concerned with the recruitment of labour and aims at recruiting widely across castes and occupations, ties of caste and kinship are nevertheless mobilized in the formation of a subcontracting network.

Subcontracting work to home-based weavers has definite benefits for the Sri Murugan company, and by extension for IKEA, yet the system also has its drawbacks, of which the need to rely on a large network of agents and sub-agents is a major one. Even though his agents confirm that Mr Kumarasamy and his managers are extremely careful in selecting agents and sending them to particular villages, the need to rely on agents to recruit and manage labour is itself an unavoidable feature of this mode of production. The pitfalls involved in this are well illustrated by the above case. The managers of the company admitted that they simply have to trust the agents they employ, yet they have now begun to send a production manager from Bhavani to the villages for occasional inspection of the agents.

Labour Control and Discipline

Having recruited workers, the company and the agents then face the issue of how to generate labour commitment, enhance production efficiency and ensure workers' loyalty to the employer and the company. While home-based manufacturing allows for the flexible incorporation of a large labour force, it is less open to smooth labour supervision and quality control. As in so many informal sector industries, piece-rates provide part of the answer, and indeed an important part of it. The home-based weaver is paid according to what she or he produces, and if no rugs are delivered by the end of the week, no *kuli* (piece-rate) is paid to them. While piece-rate payment prevents the company from losing money due to weavers' idleness, it does not in itself guarantee the required production output, quality and speed. For this purpose other measures are applied.

One of these is the close supervision of work in the villages by the agents. Agents visit their villages on a daily basis to ensure that the weavers are working regularly. This is especially crucial when a deadline has to be kept. In those cases, the agents may visit the houses of the weavers two or three times per day to ensure that they are not engaged in any other work. The fact that many weavers continue to combine weaving with other jobs, especially agricultural labour, constitutes a recurrent problem for the agents, who need a stable labour force to guarantee a steady level of production. At the moment, orders for rag rugs are not particularly season-bound and tend to come in throughout the year. Agents are therefore keen to build up a labour force that although not employed on any sort of permanent contract, will nevertheless be available to work for them on a continuous basis.

The main inspection of quality and quantity takes place at the time of piece-checking. All finished rugs are first checked in the production centres and later rechecked in the main office in Bhavani. Each week the weavers take their week's produce to the production centre, where the agent inspects the thickness of the rug, the tightness of the fabric, the straightness of the sides and the colour patterns. Those rugs that do not meet the required quality standards are rejected, and the weaver receives no payment for it. The rejected piece is returned to the weaver, who takes it home, unravels it and reuses the rags to make another rug. Moreover, the carpets carry a label with the weaver's name so that she or he can be traced if a rug is rejected in the second round of piece-checking, which takes place in Bhavani. In this way the loss embodied by a rejected carpet lies wholly with the weaver, and this transfer of risk to the home-based producer acts by itself as a method of quality assurance.

The weekly piece-checking is usually fraught with tensions, and elaborate discussions often arise between agents and weavers as to exactly what constitutes an acceptable rug. While weavers make use of these interactions to try and get their rugs accepted, the agents take advantage of this time not only to check the rugs but also to improve the quality by telling the weavers where they have gone wrong and how their work can be bettered. The workers, on the other hand, remain independent enough to have their own reasons why and when to weave, or not to weave.

To Weave or Not to Weave – the Workers' Perspective

This second part of the chapter attempts to explain why, given the fairly homogeneous employers' strategies throughout the taluk and the steadily growing demand for a stable labour force, some villagers have joined the labour force of export weavers while others have not, and to examine what can account for the wide variations in the composition of the labour force in the six villages studied. In order to question some of the usual assumptions that labour is always readily available to work for the export market and that the export labour force is highly homogeneous, I want to probe into the concrete expectations, alternatives and constraints of the rural population which make them opt for particular forms of employment, while leaving aside others. I am especially interested in the forces that lead to the reproduction of labour market fragmentation as well as in processes by which labour market barriers shift under global sourcing.

The six villages surveyed are situated in the Bhavani taluk, in close proximity of each other and within a distance of 6 to 15 kilometres (3¾ to 9¼ miles) from Bhavani town. I intend to discuss some core factors that seem most evidently to shape the workers' decision or compulsion to weave or not. I will indicate how in each locality these factors combine in a particular manner to generate a specific labour force.

Four villages will be looked at in some detail.

Periyavadamoolapalayam: a Village of Weavers

The village of Periyavadamoolapalayam (PVM) consists of about 80 households, 50 of which are Mudaliyar, 20 Vellalar Gounder and 10 other. The place is generally known as a Mudaliyar village and the people of other communities are believed to have migrated here in more recent times. In PVM, almost all Mudaliyar families weave rugs, and so do a few Gounder families. The Mudaliyars' shift to rug weaving from about 1983 onwards is only a recent variation on a long history of weaving various textile products. The older members of the community vividly remember weaving cotton *veshti* (waist-cloths) and later also saris. When the orders for these products dropped during the 1960s, they began to weave towels for cooperative societies until in the early 1980s these orders also became very erratic, and periods of work were followed by months of idleness. Most weavers recall the period before the arrival of the export rugs as one of severe suffering. As weavers, they had never worked as agricultural labourers for Gounder landlords, to whom they consider themselves of equal status. So they never considered taking up agricultural work, and none of the Mudaliyars in PVM was involved in agriculture when I visited them throughout 1999–2000. Few of the Mudaliyar households own any land beyond the plot on which they live.

They could have shifted to *jamakkalam* carpet-weaving, which was quite popular in several of the surrounding villages, but as one Mudaliyar weaver explained: 'The *jamakkalam* is a rough carpet and we were used to weaving fine textiles such as saris and *veshti*; moreover the weaving of *jamakkalam* carpets is very hard work and only Vanniyars can do it – we are not used to hard physical work.' Their perceptions of what is feasible and appropriate work for them as well as a lack of access to land made the Mudaliyars of this village stick to weaving. Even under rapidly deteriorating conditions in the early 1980s, almost all households continued handloom weaving.

When Gurunathan introduced the export rugs in the village in 1983, it was not long before all weaving households started taking orders from him. Given that almost every Mudaliyar household already had looms at home, the latter merely had to be adjusted for rugs. The new product provided the weavers with an opportunity to pursue their traditional employment and prevented them from having to convert to other types of work that they consider either below their status or physically unsuitable for them. Although the rag rugs are a rough textile product for which few of their more sophisticated weaving skills are required, it is not considered by the Mudaliyar weavers to involve physical work that is harder than they were used to before. On the contrary, as experienced weavers the Mudaliyars feel the rugs are easy to weave, and this sentiment is matched by their large and steady output.

The Mudaliyars' incorporation as workers into this new export labour force has been shaped not only by their occupational history as home-based handloom weavers but also by a sexual division of labour that is based on particular ideologies of gender and skill. Let us first look at the gender composition of the weavers in this village.

Of the 76 weavers in PVM, 46 are men and 30 are women. Before the shift to rugs, the weaving households had a fairly typical intra-household division of labour along gender lines. Usually – but not exclusively – the men did the weaving while the women took care of the preparatory tasks such as yarn reeling and winding. The skills involved in weaving more complicated designs for saris or *dhotis* were usually passed down from father to son or uncle to nephew and only rarely to daughters or sisters. It is not uncommon to hear the men say that women are not capable of weaving saris or *dhotis*, and that only men have the knowledge and patience to weave more intricate designs anyway. Skilled weaving is the well-guarded territory of men.

In her discussion of women workers in the Calcutta jute industry, Samita Sen similarly reiterates how definitions of skill are always 'saturated with social biases' (1999a: 105). Rather than reflecting an objective amount of training, knowledge or competence, particular jobs in the jute mills were defined as unskilled because they were performed by women, children or particular caste minorities. Skill thus acted as 'an ideological category imposed on certain kinds of work by virtue of gender and the power of the workers who under-took these tasks' (ibid.: 105). Sen further explains how these ideologies of skill were constantly drawn on by the employers to justify exploitative wages and the displacement of female and other labour as and when required (1999b: 99–124). Interestingly, however, mill owners were quite willing to abandon these stereotypes in times of labour scarcity or whenever female labour was beneficial to the needs of production. By recognizing the ideological nature of skill definitions we can easily understand shifts in definitions of skill and their malleable use in changing employment contexts. While a similar ideology of skill maintained a rigid gender division of labour among the weavers of PVM and allowed men to shift to rugs in the initial stages, the very definition of skill also changed when a new product was introduced.

Indeed, the introduction of rag rugs brought about two major changes. First, the cutting of rags was far less time-consuming than yarn winding had been in the past, so that the amount of preparatory work was substantially reduced. Second, both agents and weavers agree that little skill is required to weave rag rugs. Because it is a very rough form of weaving it can be learned in a few days' time and is usually taught by a family member, agent or neigh-bour. Fast and informal skill acquisition, however, does not imply that there are no strict quality requirements; it merely implies that basically anyone of minimum height and with minimum strength in arms and legs can weave rag rugs. It also follows that those who opt not to weave do so for reasons other than a lack of skill or training.

Thus, while the earlier sexual division of labour among the weavers of PVM explains the predominantly male workforce in PVM, in that it was ini-tially the men who shifted to rug weaving, the very introduction of this new product rapidly altered the existing division of labour itself. Both the limited skill requirements for weaving rugs and the reduction in preparatory work freed up time for the women in the household, which made it feasible for them to take up weaving too. Moreover, the financial gains from export weaving helped to make it also acceptable for women. This explains the significant and increasing number of women who have taken up rug-weaving over the last few years.

Possibly even more revealing is the fact that today weaving in PVM is no longer considered specifically a man's job. When asked, all men in this village confirmed that 'weaving mats is done equally by men and women!' Following the introduction of a new product in combination with a process of de-skilling, a strongly gendered ideology of skill and a sexual division of labour have been transformed to allow for the incorporation of women in a market segment that was the preserve of men until very recently.

However, mere numbers do not always accurately represent the actual weaving activity within the household, where various loom-sharing arrange-ments can be found. I found in several instances that while the father in the household asserts that he is the one who does the weaving, the loom was used most of the time by his wife or daughter. This undoubtedly leads to an under-estimation of women's share in home-based production for the export market, as well as to an underestimation of the number of household members employed in weaving.

PVM has one of the highest number of looms per household – an average of nearly two looms per household (see Table 1). Again this relates to the facts that looms were already present in most Mudaliyar households, that weaving usually constitutes the sole occupation of male household members, and that women in the household have gradually shifted from preparatory tasks to weaving itself.

Finally, the age composition of the weavers in PVM also differs from that in the other villages: weavers of all ages can be found, from age 11 to age 70, and a substantial number of older men and women are involved in weaving (15 out of 76 are above the age of 50). In the other villages there are few weavers older than 45 (see Tables 2 and 3).

Table 1: Sample of weaving villages (Bhavani Taluk, Erode District, Tamil Nadu, 2000)

	Total number of households	Total number of weaving households	Average number of looms per household
Jambai*		38	1.1
Karukkupalayam	40	30	2
PVM	80	40	1.9
Kamaraj Colony		29	1.5
Naarapalayam	65	43	1.4
Punnam		40	1.1
Total		**220**	**1.5**

Table 2: Weavers according to village and gender

	Men	Women	Total	% Women
Jambai*	8	34	42	81
Karukkupalayam	37	22	59	37
PVM	46	30	76	39
Kamaraj Colony	28	16	44	36
Naarapalayam	22	40	62	65
Punnam	4	41	45	91
Total	**145**	**183**	**328**	**56**

Table 3: Weavers according to village and age

Age	11–15	16–20	21–25	26–30	31–35	36–40	41–45	46–50	51–55	56–60	61–65	66–70
Jambai*	2	8	6	11	5	3	5	1		1		
Karukkupalayam	3	12	10	12	7	5	4	2	2	1	1	
PVM	4	11	6	15	10	8	4	3	5	4	1	5
Kamaraj	1	8	16	9	6	1	2	1				
Naarapalayam	7	17	9	15	9	2	2	1				
Punnam	4	17	8	4	5	4	2	1				
Total	**21**	**73**	**55**	**66**	**42**	**23**	**19**	**9**	**7**	**6**	**2**	**5**
%	6	22	17	20	13	7	6	3	2	2	0.5	1.5

* For Jambai only a sample of weaving households was used; in all other villages all households were questioned.

Karukkupalayam: Agriculturalists Turned Weavers

In Karukkupalayam, situated about 2 kilometres (1¼ miles) away from PVM, the weavers have a very different background: it is special factors that have brought about weaving in this village. The people of Karukkupalayam belong mostly to the Vellala Gounder community and were almost exclusively employed in agriculture until Segar introduced the first looms about 16 years ago. Today, 30 households (out of 40) are weaving for the Sri Murugan company. To understand this significant shift in employment we must comprehend the agricultural background of these households. Before the arrival of the rugs, the people of Karukkupalayam were predominantly employed in agriculture either as landless labourers or as cultivators of small plots of land, varying from 0.2 to 0.8 hectare (half an acre to 2 acres). Over the last few decades the lack of water has become the main drawback for cultivators in the area, and the entire discourse about cultivation, agricultural work, lack of income and poverty in the village is cast in the idiom of water scarcity.

The land around Karukkupalayam is mainly dry and dependent on rain for its cultivation, for there are no rivers or canals near by. Everyone recalls that up to about 20 years ago there was always water in the wells and cultivation was possible throughout the better part of the year. Most cultivators had wells about 12 to 16 metres (40–50 feet) deep and they brought water up in pots with the help of cows. Everyone had fairly equal access to water. This is not simply a romanticisation of the past by older villagers: over at least the last 50 years bore wells have been dug to increasing depths and the use of electric pumps to draw water has proliferated rapidly amongst better-off landowners.[3] The combined use of bore wells and pumps resulted in the intensification of groundwater extraction and a sharp drop in the water table. Access to water has become very unequal as well as uncertain. For the poorer farmers who could not afford to dig a bore well, cultivation became increasingly problematic because the rains proved insufficient to cultivate even dry crops, such as *cholam* (sorghum), groundnut and oilseed. While richer landlords installed bore wells and pumps, smaller cultivators became gradually more dependent on rains as their traditional water-lifts became increasingly inadequate to raise ground water. For landless labourers, agricultural work became progressively more erratic and unpredictable.

It is against this background that both agricultural labourers and small cultivators began their search for alternative employment. But not much was available in the area. Some of the men in the village tried their luck in the power-loom industry of Kumarapalayam, but given the distance they had to cover daily (about 15 kilometres/9¼ miles), the cost of transport (nearly Rs 10) and the timing of shifts in the power-loom factories (from 2am till 2pm and from 2pm till 2am), most of them gave up after a few months. Although the income they earned was good, the men report that they could not adjust to work away from home, because they had always been employed in or around their village, and, on top of that, they felt they could not live with the fixed shifts and the strict supervision, which contrasted so much with the flexible work rhythm they enjoyed in the fields. Not being able to take a break, have tea or smoke a cigarette whenever they liked, proved hard to them – and the dusty and noisy power-loom factories do indeed contrast sharply with the open fields around the village. Essentially the picture they presented was that of 'satanic mills', and their own inability to adapt to a work environment that they experienced as shockingly different.

Whether ultimately they would have adjusted to factory employment had no other opportunities appeared I do not know, but a lack of resources, off-farm skills and outside contacts certainly limited their opportunities in other segments of the regional labour market. The handlooms therefore provided this rural labour force with a very welcome source of employment at home. The agriculturalists-turned-weavers themselves reiterate the advantages of this new occupation. The purchase of a loom is seen as a low-cost and risk-free investment, especially compared to the money that has to be found to start cultivation. Moreover, the ease with which rug-weaving can be learned also made this form of employment instantly attractive. Thirdly, regular employment on the looms can be contrasted with the irregularity of agricultural labour or the unpredictability of cultivation. Fourthly, the *kuli* (piece-rate) from weaving compares favourably with the wages that they earned in the field. And finally, weaving rugs allows the workers to remain independent, to decide their own work rhythm, to work at home as they were used to, and to combine weaving with either domestic work or agricultural work, both paid agricultural labour or work on their own land for those who still have some.

However, this is not the full picture – or at least not the picture that is shared by everyone in the village. Many weavers admit that once they actually started weaving they did not find it all that easy. The weavers in Karukkupalayam complain about pain in all parts of the body, and contrast the unhealthy sitting position with the bodily exercises they did when working in the fields. Some say they would immediately return to work in the field 'if only there was enough water' and thus regular work. Others, however, claim that they have become accustomed to their looms and would no longer be able to go back to agricultural labour.

The perception of weaving is obviously coloured by age differences. Whereas the older weavers vividly remember working in the field, many of the younger ones have never even touched a plough and for them weaving is the only occupation they have experience of. Those Gounders who own land told me that they would never weave 'because it is dirty'. Because the looms are usually set up in front of the house or under a small shed attached to it, rags and dust can be found all over the courtyard, and from the street one can easily identify the houses where rugs are woven. One of the cultivators who had not taken up weaving referred to weaving as 'dirty work', mentioning the pieces of dusty rags and the cotton dust that are spread all over the weavers' houses. However, while discussing this with me, he himself was peeling groundnuts in the courtyard in front of his house and the husks and detritus of the nuts were spread all over the place. This 'dirt' was, however, regarded as 'coming from his own land', and therefore evaluated differently, especially in contrast with 'dirt from elsewhere', as for example from cloth rags. For those without land and without many alternatives, this evaluation changed quickly and made way for a much more positive interpretation of weaving for the export market.

The lack of employment alternatives and the villagers' perceptions about different types of work is closely related to some other features of the workforce in Karukkupalayam: gender and skill. The gender composition of the workforce need not surprise us: 37 men and 22 women weave in this village (Table 2). It was men who started weaving when the looms were introduced, while their wives initially continued sporadic work in the fields combined with the 'cutting' of rags at home. Even though Gounders of this village had never been weavers before, they were quick to reconstruct among themselves the ideology of male and female tasks and to impose a division of labour that allowed men to monopolise the more prestigious job of weaving and to pass on the more demeaning tasks to their wives and daughters. Here as in PVM, however, the weaver's wife or one of his children usually starts weaving once a second loom is purchased, and it is more often a daughter than a son who is set to weaving. The cutting of rags is still predominantly a woman's job, and considered dirty. As a result, several Gounder households employ Harijan women from the nearby Kamaraj Colony to cut the rags.

Although we find weavers of all ages in Karukkupalayam, the majority are young to middle-aged and only six weavers are older than 45. The older people in the village who have spent their entire life in the fields are usually unable and unwilling to make the transition to another occupation. They are either supported by their children or continue to rely on whatever casual employment they can get in agriculture. They are in many ways the poorest group in the countryside.

Punnam: the Formation of a Female Labour Force

Let me now turn to Punnam, situated about 3 kilometres (1 ¾ miles) away from PVM, where Leela is the agent and weaving rugs for the export market is almost exclusively a female activity: 41 out of 45 weavers are women, and most of them are young girls. The vast majority of weavers (32) belong to the Uppiliyar Naicker caste, but no Uppiliyar men weave and the only male weavers are from the Harijan community.[4] Weaving was introduced in this village in 1996 by Leela, and all the women weavers have set up their looms during the last few years. The obvious questions to be addressed here include why men are not weaving and what alternatives are available to women.

Both Uppiliyar Naicker men and women from this village have worked in the construction sector for several generations and they consider construction work to be their hereditary occupation. Boys join from as young as 12 years of age, while girls start construction work when a little older. Women usually continue the work till they give birth and then stay at home for several years because it is impossible to combine child-rearing activities with construction work. During those years at home, they usually do agricultural work in the village itself. Once the children get older, some women join the construction gang again while others continue to work in the village. Construction workers join small gangs of five to ten people, consisting of kin and neighbours, and get their employment in town through contractors who are known to them. Working long days, men and women alike spend most of their time away from the village.

Both men and women say that construction work is tough. While men do the actual building work, women undertake various supporting tasks, such as carrying bricks, sand and water, and cleaning the construction site. There has been a significant occupational continuity among the members of this community, with hardly any Uppiliyar men in the village involved in other employment. In a recent study, Theo van der Loop provides an in-depth insight into the highly fragmented nature of the construction labour markets in Tamil Nadu. Three of his findings are worth mentioning.

First, the labour market for construction work is highly fragmented due to a series of pre-entry factors (such as sex, age, caste, kinship, location and recruitment channels), which keep many out of this occupation and lead others to move out only if better alternatives are available (1996: 271–4). Given the importance of caste- and neighbourhood-based channels of recruitment, neither the Gounders and Mudaliyars nor the Harijans ever stood much chance of entering this occupation.

Second, 'family members of construction workers have only limited access to those fragments of the labour market offering "better" opportunities than construction; a majority thus end up in construction as well' (ibid.: 324). This explains why entire families in Punnam are involved in construction work.

And, thirdly, the wage structure of construction work is most striking. It is tightly related to skill and gender, and therefore reveals a lot about women's recent shift to weaving. A young boy who starts working as an unskilled labourer is paid Rs 40–50 for a day's work. Having become a skilled mason, a man can earn up to Rs 120, while a maistry or mason-contractor can earn up to Rs 150 per day. Women's work is invariably classified as unskilled, for which they are paid a maximum of Rs 40 per day, independent of age or experience. This is less than what a young or unskilled male worker earns and half to one-third of what a skilled male worker gets.

It is this particular wage pattern, in combination with child-rearing concerns and perceptions of tough work, which explain to a significant extent women's recent shift to rug-weaving in Punnam. The Rs 40 *kuli* which women get in construction work is about equal to the *kuli* they receive in agriculture, but as discussed above, agricultural employment is very irregular and does not offer a particularly attractive alternative to construction work. Weaving, however, has much more to offer for women. Because of fixed piece-rate payments for the export rugs, women, as men, can earn up to Rs 70 per day. But what the women weavers emphasize even more are the advantages of home-based work and the way in which they can avoid the hot sun, the daily travel to the construction sites and the harassment from which they suffer while travelling by bus and on the sites itself. The safety of the home is stressed by both adults and young daughters who have recently taken up weaving.

Revealingly, this recent shift in female employment is accompanied by a simultaneous shift in the way the parents of unmarried girls assess what work is suitable for their daughters. Their discourse reflects a remarkably strong ideology – usually typical of the middle-classes – about women's place being at home, where it is safe and where they can work in a protected environment. Several fathers and mothers emphasized to me that construction work is too difficult for their daughters, because it entails heavy physical work without protection from the sun, it requires them to travel outside the village and it exposes them to abuse and harassment on the construction sites. Although their explanation was usually phrased in terms of 'They *can't possibly* do construction work,' it reveals an underlying conviction that they *shouldn't* do this work, which they now perceive as unsuitable for their daughters.

Such a discourse is particularly surprising given the fact that the older adult women who make this statement have themselves worked the better part of their lives on construction sites away from home. It is also a discourse reflecting an ideology of domesticity which I have never heard among those who have no choice other than to send their wives and daughters out for work. The mere availability of new options at home seems to have a direct bearing on how men and women perceive different types of employment and on how they assess what is suitable for whom. Clearly, construction work is increasingly thought of as no longer appropriate for the daughters of the village and as incompatible with their domestic work and child-rearing activities. Or, as soon as material conditions allow, the dominant ideology concerning female roles is shared and replicated, even by those segments of society that are not usually considered the guardians of 'middle-class' morals and ideals.

The men in Punnam say that weaving is a woman's job and that they would not want to shift to weaving because of the poor wages it yields. While this is to some extent true, given what men can earn as construction workers, this picture hides the highly casual and irregular nature of construction work, and therefore the low real income men earn per month. Men can often be found in the village, hanging around without work. Although on most mornings they go to nearby towns to find work, they get on average only two to three days' work per week. The implication of this is twofold. First, the men tend to exaggerate their actual weekly wages to justify their continued employment in construction work *and* their unwillingness to start weaving. Second, the irregularity of employment in construction shows that women opt to weave precisely because it provides them with a *regular* income, given that their father's or husband's wages are highly unpredictable. Women are well aware that they are substantial and regular earners, and they consequently evaluate the earning opportunities offered by export weaving in a positive manner. Vellamani, aged 18, of Punnam told me:

> These looms are a great support for our village. They are a good thing for most households. I did not study and in the past we had to go for agriculture or construction work, while now we can earn actually at home. A woman with two children can easily manage on her own and weave. In the past she could not have managed because there was no work in the village itself and she had to go to Erode or Bhavani for construction work. How could she take care of her children? If work finished at 6pm, they had to wait for the bus till 8pm and would arrive back home by 8.30pm or 9pm. Today we no longer have to go through all that.

In short, the weavers in Punnam can be divided into two groups. The first group of women weavers are those who have been doing construction work before, and they are aged roughly between 20 and 40. The second group of women are the young girls who have never done construction work and who came straight from school into weaving, often having combined weaving with studying for some time. They are all below the age of 20, and the youngest ones are about 14. Girls increasingly stay at home and weave, while boys continue their hereditary occupation as before. In Punnam, a particular combination of occupational histories, gendered ideologies of skill, and employment alternatives has generated a predominantly young and female labour force. Simultaneously, the introduction of these export jobs has itself triggered significant alterations in perceptions of work and values of domesticity.

A Comparison with the Kamaraj Colony

The Kamaraj Colony is the name of a *cheri* (Harijan colony) located just outside PVM and consists entirely of Arunthathiyars, whose traditional occupation is leatherwork and sandal-making. Most of them worked in the past as *pannaiyal*, or bonded agricultural labourers, for the Gounder landlords, and today they are mainly employed as agricultural *kulis* (daily wage labourers). Given the recent history of water scarcity and agricultural decline, employment has been very irregular for them and job alternatives few. As one of the lowest-ranking communities in Tamil society, they are not easily accepted for other occupations such as power-loom or dyeing work. When the agent Segar, and later Gurunathan, approached the colony in the late 1980s, many households were eager to start weaving to bridge periods of unemployment in the fields. Nevertheless, many of them found it difficult to put together Rs 1500 to buy a loom, and even today not all of those who would like to weave can afford a loom, so that many are still forced to rely on whatever work is available in agriculture.

Most households continue to combine weaving with agriculture, but as a result of this they often become the victim of opposing demands on them. Having never been given regular work by the agents in the first place, they immediately exchange the looms for the fields whenever the landowners call on them or when it rains. This, in turn, affects their handloom production and is resisted by the agents who urge them to stick to their looms. As a consequence of their irregular weaving they are now given even fewer orders by the agents and urgent orders are usually not passed on to them. They are certainly not the agents' preferred labour force – preference is given to regular weavers such as the Mudaliyars in PVM, while only extra work during busy times is shared with the people in the colony. In sum, employed as a reserve labour force and on a casual basis by both the Sri Murugan company and the local landlords, the people of the Kamaraj Colony are a prototype example of the increasing casualisation of labour under globalizing conditions (Breman 1999: 407–29). Finding it impossible to serve two masters, they are equally unable to rely on either one of them due to the lack of regular employment. Their caste, class and occupational history combine to act against them and even when new opportunities such as weaving for the export market become available, they are once again stuck at the bottom of the ladder.

Workers' Mobility: Shifting Patterns of Post-Marital Residence

Globalization and in particular the formation of a labour force for the export market is often equated with the increased mobility of people and especially with migration flows to those locations where factory work is concentrated. While such movements certainly do occur to places where production is centralized in clusters of firms and workshops (Parry 2003; De Neve 2003), the subcontracting of work to home-based producers yields a refreshingly different picture of spatial movements. To begin with, the migration of entire households for work is highly limited. Of the 220 households surveyed in six villages, only four households migrated into villages in which neither husband nor wife had been born – but even they had kinship links with local people. All of them were experienced in weaving on arrival, and left their previous 'home' due to a lack of work. Most weaving households, however, have always lived in the villages and are surrounded by many of their close kin.

This picture, however, should not be mistaken for a complete lack of migration. What it does mean is that migration is largely limited to the time of marriage. As has been documented in ethnographies of India, the rule of post-marital residence among patrilineal communities in India is predominantly patrilocal (Sharma 1980: 19; 50; Vatuk 1972: 69–74; 112–48). On marriage, women commonly move to their husband's parents' household, or they set up a new household in his parents' village. While this is also a common pattern in the villages studied, there is a significant shift taking place which I gradually became aware of as I filled in questionnaires but which was also identified and brought to my attention by the villagers themselves. This shift relates to the increasingly popular pattern of uxorilocal residence in the villages where work for IKEA is available: a man moves to his wife's village on marriage, where they usually set up a new nuclear household. In PVM, for example, for 12 out of 40 weaving households the village is the wife's native place, and the husband has migrated there on marriage or soon thereafter. The villagers themselves pointed this out to me by saying: 'Here you will find many households in which men have come from their native place to join their wives' families.' It was clearly a practice which they no longer considered exceptional.

These shifts in post-marital residence were, however, not always to the wife's village but sometimes to the mother's village, where a man may still find connections with maternal kin. For at least two households in PVM, the village was the native place of the husband's mother. The main reason forwarded for these increasing numbers of men migrating to their wife's and/or mother's village after marriage related to a combination of regular weaving opportunities combined with a lack of orders in the men's native place. This was the case in PVM, but a similar pattern began to occur in the other villages too. In Punnam, for example, in seven of the 40 weaving households men had moved in on marriage. Given that it is mainly young women who are weaving here, many of whom are still unmarried, it is highly likely that this trend will continue and that once married, their husbands may move in and take up weaving as well.

The above pattern is also reflected in the household composition. The majority of households are nuclear (180 out of 220 households, or 82 per cent) but they often have parents or siblings living near by, and often share weaving facilities. Of the joint families, most consist of extended nuclear households in which a parent of the husband or of the wife has moved in. Of the joint families that consist of two nuclear households, an almost equal number consist of the wife's parents as of the husband's parents. This reflects again the movement of men on marriage, who often move in with their wife's parents.

The crucial point I want to make here is that these shifts are brought about directly by the availability of work for the export market which is considered to be sufficiently well paid and sufficiently regular for a man to shift to his wife's village on marriage or soon thereafter. Given that the South Indian rules of post-marital residence have always been more flexible and have never been as strict as those found in the north of India, these shifts are easily accommodated among family members and without apparent resistance from husbands (Kolenda 1984). Some men had been weaving before (such as the Mudaliyars in PVM), while others learned it after moving to their wife's village. Many men mentioned that weaving is an attractive job and that the regular orders contrast with the dearth of work in their native place.

However, in a good number of households I found men idling while two or three looms were occupied by their wife and daughters. This was particularly the case with husbands in their fifties and sixties and who had never really taken up weaving themselves. In such households wives and daughters are the main, if not sole, earners, even if their husband and father is the one who collects the raw materials, delivers the finished rugs to the centre and brings the payment home.

Conclusion

As discussed in the first part of this paper, the Sri Murugan Rug Exports Company has been able to enter the international market swiftly and smoothly. There are many reasons for the success of this company, but one of the crucial factors lies in the organization of the production process in which the farming out of work to rural weavers proved a successful strategy. As shown by the comparative study of six villages, the weavers are not a homogeneous and ready-made group of workers, who are, as often assumed, abundantly available, factory-based, young, urban, migrant, female, and waiting at the doors of exporting companies 'to go global'. Rather, they are a mixed group of rural workers. Some are young and others old, some are men and others women, and some belong to the highest rural castes while others are Harijans. The weavers all have diverse occupational histories, different employment opportunities and varying degrees of choice and agency. Their decisions to weave, not to weave or to weave only occasionally are shaped by a variety of factors, of which restricted labour markets, fragmented by caste, gender and skill, and sexual divisions of labour are the most prominent.

I have shown, first, that recruitment and supervision of labour for IKEA requires a network of agents and sub-agents who are themselves recruited on the basis of both meritocratic and non-meritocratic elements. To guarantee steady production outputs, high quality standards and labour commitment, various strategies are deployed of which piece-rate payments, local piece-checking and supervision by the agents are the most effective. Nevertheless, subcontracting also has its drawbacks, from a lack of full commitment by rural weavers to the potential for serious fraud on the part of agents, which in turn obstruct a steady output and limit the possibilities of expansion.

Second, the availability of a labour force at the tail end of the chain is determined by a number of factors of which the regional labour market segmentation and the existing sexual divisions of labour are among the main ones. Labour market segmentation excludes certain castes from agriculture or construction work, and therefore makes the new opportunities to weave for IKEA particularly attractive. This made the Mudaliyars one of the first communities in the area to take up weaving. Particular sexual divisions of labour, on the other hand, prevented women in some localities from weaving in the initial stages, as was the case among the Mudaliyars. The case of the Naicker women in Punnam illustrates that the sexual division of labour in construction work has turned them into the first weavers of the village. As Barrientos reminds us, a gendered perspective on the dynamics of commodity chains reveals how local gender relations and sexual divisions of labour affect the way in which men and women gain access to the chain as workers, agents or entrepreneurs, how the benefits are spread among individuals, and who has the best chance for upgrading within the chain (Barrientos 2001: 85; Ramamurthy 2000: 554).

Third, the comparative ethnography of four villages has demonstrated how, far from being fixed and rigid, these social constructions of gender and skill shift themselves as new opportunities enter the villages. In PVM, Mudaliyar women soon turned from preparatory tasks to weaving; in Punnam Naicker women gradually gave up construction work and began weaving; while in Karukkupalayam both Gounder men and women turned to weaving from agriculture.

Finally, I have indicated that while immigration for work is virtually absent in the villages, revealing shifts have occurred in post-marital patterns of residence, in which patrilocality is increasingly being matched by uxorilocality. A man migrates on marriage to his wife's village because that is where work is available. Although these shifts do not allow me to put forward an argument about the empowerment of women, I have certainly seen a number of strong matri-focal households in which the links between mothers and daughters were particularly strong, especially in cases where the men were without regular employment.

Given the increased importance of global sourcing and international subcontracting in the contemporary world economy, a fast-growing body of literature has emerged which focuses on 'global value chains' (Kaplinsky 2000; Gereffi et al. 2001) and which attempts to say something about how the gains of globalization are distributed across the globe (Humphrey and Schmitz 2001). Global value chain analyses largely converge around the issue of 'who wins and who loses from integration in' the chains and explore how the gains from globalization can be spread more widely (Gereffi 1999; Dolan and Tewari 2001; Humphrey and Schmitz 2000). By focusing on the tail end of one such chain in Tamil Nadu, this study has focused on the processes through which export production is implanted into specific social contexts and is mediated by those contexts. The argument put forward is that while social contexts shape the way in which export companies recruit labour and organize production, the very penetration of export jobs in rural areas has begun to transform the economic and cultural fabric of India's rural society. Whether the changes in ideologies of gender, skill and domesticity, or the new patterns of post-marital residence, will be significant and lasting will in the last instance depend on the durability of these jobs and thus on the permanence of Western consumer preference for cheap rag rugs 'Made in India'.

Notes

1 Fieldwork was conducted from October 1999 till September 2000 in Tamil Nadu, South India, as part of an LSE-based research project on globalization funded by the ESRC, UK. Earlier versions of this chapter were presented at the project workshop in Paris, and at the Universities of Sussex, East Anglia and California, Santa Barbara. I thank the participants for their comments, and also Chris Fuller, Henrike Donner and Ann Whitehead.

2 In the rural areas around Bhavani, the Vanniyars work mainly as agricultural labourers and small landholders. However, over the last decades they have increasingly taken up a variety of other occupations, including the weaving of *jamakkalam* carpets in the villages.

3 Velayutham Saravanan writes that 'in the Bhavani river basin, water extraction from 30–40 feet in the 1950s had gone deeper by 700–1,000 feet in the 1990s' (2001: 293).

4 The Harijan Arunthathiyars live in a separate hamlet outside the village and do not get their yarn from Leela but from Patchimuthu's centre near Punnam. Leela is the agent for the Uppiliyar Naickers and the two Vellala Gounders.

Bibliography

Bagchi, Amiya Kumar, ed. (1999) *Economy and Organization: Indian institutions under the neoliberal regime*. New Delhi: Sage Publications.

Barrientos, S. (2001) 'Gender, flexibility and global value chains', *IDS Bulletin* (3): 83–93.

Breman, Jan (1976) 'A dualistic labour system? A critique of the "informal sector" concept', *Economic and Political Weekly*, 11: 1870–6; 1905–8; 1939–43.

_____ (1996) *Footloose Labour: Working in India's informal economy*. Cambridge: Cambridge University Press.

_____ (1999) 'The study of industrial labour in post-colonial India – the informal sector: a concluding review', in Jonathan P. Parry *et al.*, eds, *The Worlds of Indian Industrial Labour*. New Delhi: Sage Publications.

Cadène, P. and M. Holmström, eds (1998) *Decentralized Production in India: Industrial districts, flexible specialization, and employment*. New Delhi: Sage Publications.

Castells, Manuel (1996) The Information Age: Economy, society and culture, Vol.1: *The Rise of the Network Society*. Cambridge, Massachusetts: Blackwell.

Cox, Kevin R. (1997) 'Introduction: globalization and its politics in question', in Kevin R. Cox, ed., *Spaces of Globalization: Reasserting the power of the local*. New York: The Guilford Press.

De Neve, Geert (1999) 'Tamil warps and wefts: an anthropological study of urban weavers in South India'. PhD Thesis, University of London.

—— (2003) 'Expectations and rewards of modernity: commitment and mobility among rural migrants in Tirupur, Tamil Nadu', *Contributions to Indian Sociology*, 37 (1, 2): 251–80.

Dolan, C. and M. Tewari (2001) 'From what we wear to what we eat: upgrading in global value chains', *IDS Bulletin*, 32 (3): 94–104.

Fernandes, Leela (1997) *Producing Workers: The politics of gender, class and culture in the Calcutta jute mills*. Philadelphia: University of Pennsylvania Press.

Gereffi, G. (1999) 'International trade and industrial upgrading in the apparel commodity chain', *Journal of International Economics*, 48 (1): 37–70.

Gereffi, G., John Humphrey, Hubert Schmitz and others (2001) 'Introduction: globalisation, value chains and development', *IDS Bulletin*, 32 (3): 1–8.

Harriss, John (1982) 'The character of an urban economy: "small-scale" production and labour markets in Coimbatore', *Economic and Political Weekly*, 17 (23): 945–54; (24): 993–1002.

—— (1986) 'The working poor and the labour aristocracy in a South Indian city: a descriptive and analytical account', *Modern Asian Studies*, 20 (2): 231–83.

Harriss, John, K. P. Kannan and G. Rodgers (1989) *Urban Labour Market and Job Access in India: A Study of Coimbatore*. Geneva: International Institute for Labour Studies.

Herod, Andrew (1997) 'Labor as an agent of globalization and as a global agent', in Kevin R. Cox, ed., *Spaces of Globalization: Reasserting the power of the local*. New York: The Guilford Press.

Hoogvelt, Ankie M. M. (2001) *Globalization and the Postcolonial World: The new political economy of development*. Basingstoke: Palgrave.

Humphrey, J. and H. Schmitz (2000) 'Governance and upgrading: linking industrial cluster and global value chain research', IDS Working Paper 120. Brighton: Institute of Development Studies.

—— (2001) 'Governance in global value chains', *IDS Bulletin*, 32 (2): 19–29.

Kaplinsky, R. (2000) 'Globalisation and unequalisation: what can be learned from value-chain analysis?', *Journal of Development Studies*, 37 (2): 117–46.

Kolenda, P. (1984) 'Women as tribute, women as flower: images of "women" in North and South India', *American Ethnologist*, 11: 98–117.

Mies, Maria (1982) *The Lace Makers of Narsapur*. London: Zed Press.

Ong, A. (1987) *Spirits of Resistance and Capitalist Discipline: Factory women in Malaysia*. Albany: SUNY Press.

Parry, Jonathan P. (1999) 'Introduction', in Jonathan P. Parry, Jan Breman and Karin Kapadia., eds, *The Worlds of Indian Industrial Labour*. New Delhi: Sage Publications.

—— (2003) 'Nehru's dream and the village "waiting room": long-distance labour migrants to a central Indian steel town', *Contributions to Indian Sociology*, 37 (1, 2): 217–50.

Piore, Michael J. and Charles F. Sabel (1984) *The Second Industrial Divide: Possibilities for prosperity*. New York: Basic Books.

Ramamurthy, P. (2000) 'The cotton commodity chain, women, work and agency in India and Japan: the case for feminist agro-food systems research', *World Development*, 28 (3): 551–78.

Saravanan, Velayutham (2001) 'Technological transformation and water conflicts in the Bhavani River Basin of Tamil Nadu, 1930–1970', *Environment and History*, 7 (3): 289–334.

Sen, Samita (1999a) 'Beyond the "working class"; women's role in Indian industrialisation', *South Asia*, 22, 2: 95–117.

_____ (1999b) *Women and Labour in Late Colonial India: The Bengal jute industry*. Cambridge: Cambridge University Press.

Sharma, U. (1980) *Women, Work and Property in North West India*. London: Tavistock.

Swaminathan, Padmini and J. Jeyaranjan (1999) 'The knitwear cluster in Tiruppur: an Indian industrial district in the making?', in A. K. Bagchi, ed., *Economy and Organization: Indian institutions under the neoliberal regime*. New Delhi: Sage Publications.

van der Loop, Theo (1996) *Industrial Dynamics and Fragmented Labour Markets: Construction firms and labourers in India*. New Delhi: Sage Publications.

Vatuk, S. (1972) *Kinship and Urbanization: White-collar migrants in North India*. Berkeley: University of California Press.

Wilkinson-Weber, Clare M. (1999) *Embroidering Lives: Women's work and skill in the Lucknow embroidery industry*. New York: State University of New York Press.

Wolf, Diane L. (1992) *Factory Daughters: Gender, household dynamics, and rural industrialization in Java*. Berkeley: University of California Press.

PART TWO:
EDUCATION AND LANGUAGE

6

'CHILDREN ARE CAPITAL, GRANDCHILDREN ARE INTEREST': CHANGING EDUCATIONAL STRATEGIES AND PARENTING IN CALCUTTA'S MIDDLE-CLASS FAMILIES

Henrike Donner

This chapter examines the relationship between gender and globalization.[1] It highlights the way in which education and aspirations for upward mobility, brought about by changing labour markets, have altered understandings of parenting and the division of work among women belonging to middle-class households in two Calcutta neighbourhoods.

Changes related to new forms of employment have influenced formal education in Calcutta and in turn modified the way middle-class women are involved in the daily work of raising children and running a household at different stages. Although mothers have contributed to schooling for generations, the emphasis on employment in multinational companies has brought about a shift in educational strategies towards private English-language education. This is increasingly seen as a precondition for occupational choices offered in the 'global' market, which demands the reorganization of parenting practices and the division of labour in the household.

When globalization is discussed with reference to the middle-class family or the 'domestic sphere', the politics of economic liberalization are held responsible for the widespread emergence of specific types of domestic organization in the context of consumerism and urbanisation among the new middle classes (Jamieson 1998; Giddens 1999). It is assumed that specific notions regarding the separation of a private and a public sphere, the nuclearisation of households, marital relations, and child-rearing practices are adopted in the process. The macro-politics of markets are held responsible for a more homogeneous pattern of household organization worldwide.

With reference to India, the increasing number of nuclear families, love-marriages and divorce in urban contexts is commonly seen as an indication of such changes. Although patrilocal residence, arranged marriages and lifelong unions still constitute the norm, the increased significance of privacy, conjugality and individualism among urbanites is nevertheless interpreted as proof of change (Dwyer 2000). It is by now well established that concepts and practices 'modernise' in accordance with existing notions and modify hegemonic tendencies of global developments (Miller 1995: 8ff; Khilnani 1998: 34ff). With reference to gender relations, the ongoing 'indigenisation' of ideologies of individualism and the family is particularly prominent in representations of the 'new Indian woman', who is middle-class, nationalist, consumption- and family-oriented, and prioritizes motherhood (Fernandes 2000a: 615ff).

However, as Leela Fernandes argues, while the construction of the new middle classes as a cultural ideal is well documented, few empirical studies have been made (Fernandes 2000b: 93). This chapter highlights the impact of globalization from the perspective of the household and women's lives rather than media images and explores ideologies of inter-generational dependence, parenting practices and inter-household relations in respect of changing educational strategies. The effects of education on the domestic sphere and women's roles in raising middle-class children have rarely been addressed, although the representation of motherhood has been studied in the context of recent fundamentalist and nationalist discourses, consumerism and media representations (e.g. Bagchi 1990; Das 1995; Sarkar and Butalia 1995; Sircar 1999; Rajagopal 1999). The lack of an analysis of the domestic organization and women's experiences of changes in this sphere has recently been highlighted by Kumkum Sangari, who called for a study of 'past and present middle-class domesticities' that would provide a basis for a radical 'joint critique of labour, consumption and ideologies' (Sangari 1999: 291). In a different but related argument, Nita Kumar pointed out that where the history of education is concerned, mothers as educators are conspicuously absent from the literature on South Asia (Kumar n.d.). Whether as part of a more generalized critique and social history of the domestic sphere or as a contribution to the study of educational change, this chapter seeks to redress the absence of women as mothers and grandmothers from recent explorations of globalization in India.

The Setting

Whereas it has been asserted that practices common in Indian middle-class households – including child-rearing practices, educational strategies, life-cycle expectations and the management of marital and kin relationships – are transformed in accordance with newly emerging economic patterns, the resulting new formations are rarely studied in much detail. The data presented have been collected in two neighbourhoods of Calcutta through in-depth interviews with members of 32 middle-class households, and more casual conversations with a wide range of people.[2]

The first neighbourhood, located in the centre of the city, developed as early as 1746 into a mixed and densely populated area (Mukherjee 1993: 22–48; Nair 1990: 13ff). The majority of those who were interviewed there are Bengali-speaking Hindus, but a significant number of Bengali-speaking Christians and members of the Marwari business communities are included in the sample. The second neighbourhood is of more recent origin and developed with the influx of refugees from East Bengal, many of whom settled at the fringe of the city in the aftermath of partition (Bose 1968: 33–4). This area is almost exclusively inhabited by middle-class Bengali Hindu families and is, like many other such former 'refugee colonies', characterized by recent affluence.

The definition of 'middle-class' used in this chapter primarily refers to a lifestyle based on male employment in white-collar jobs, oriented towards professional careers or government service, and a shared value system centred on related notions of propriety, a fulfilled life, and an opposition between tradition and modernity. Considerable differences in household expenditure and salary levels exist within this group, but educational achievements are seen by all concerned as a means to enhance upward mobility and are particularly valued amongst the urban Bengali-speaking community. At the heart of this appreciation of formal education lies a tradition of employment in government service, which has from the turn of the last century onwards provided the basis of middle-class identity and domestic organization for this community.[3]

The underlying concept of 'being middle-class' is linked to specific notions of domesticity which emerged during the colonial period, when the modern ideal of the husband in government service and the 'virtuous wife' in the 'well-ordered home' was popularized (Banerjee 1989; Chatterjee 1993; Walsh 1995). The domestic sphere in the households of educated Bengalis became the subject of reform, and motherhood and conjugal roles were redefined in accordance with the needs of 'modern' life. As a growing number of young men entered professional careers or government service, formal education became a major preoccupation of parents, and of mothers in particular. Since independence, middle-class women have themselves entered high-profile positions, and thousands have sought employment in government jobs and professional careers, but in comparison with other developing countries the overall rate of female employment in the service sector has remained low. Furthermore, although the last two decades saw an increase in women's employment in this sector, a decrease in women's participation in the more lucrative and secure positions also took place.

In India, Calcutta is the metropolis with the lowest rate of female employment in the formal sector. Indeed, as economist Nirmala Banerjee points out, while the middle-classes were drawn to new patterns of consumption and upward mobility during the 1990s, the participation of middle-class women in the formal sector diminished (Banerjee 2002). As we will see, the two trends are related in complex ways. Whereas girls' participation in secondary schooling has risen, fewer middle-class women are entering the workforce, and although middle-class families enjoy a much higher standard of living with fewer children to take care of, only a small minority of educated women from such backgrounds joins the labour force. In Calcutta, women's education is seen as a precondition for marriage and motherhood, since in the more competitive and less regulated economy the schooling of children requires new parenting skills.

Among the Bengali-speaking communities of Calcutta, the organization of households and the ideal of the 'Bengali housewife' are cited as reasons for middle-class women not to participate in the labour force – although many had to seek employment in the past and elsewhere in India middle-class women are expected to earn a salary (Debi 1988; Standing 1991). Although more and more young women are in secondary education or enter university, their parents' financial conditions do not force them to seek employment – in fact, parents often discourage young women from 'working outside'. This applies even to those with university degrees, who have usually married upon completion of the course. Thus, the majority of young middle-class women entering paid employment are those who left school early to find work in the service sector because their families depend on their incomes. With the arrival of children, even these young working women, as well as the privileged upper-middle-class graduates who secure positions in teaching or as professionals, are expected to leave or take up more flexible, part-time employment. The majority in fact leave the labour force altogether.

Recent demographic and socio-economic developments have therefore challenged, but not completely changed, the sexual division of labour, and this accounts for the rather straightforward description of the complex relationship between the 'outside' world and the related but subordinate 'inner' or domestic sphere. The marital preference for educated women who will, according to popular views, make good housewives and mothers stems from earlier notions of gendered roles in the family (e.g. Borthwick 1984; Engels 1996). But although the ideology of the ideal homemaker, who guards the education of children, instils moral values in them, and performs these tasks in the spirit of self-sacrifice, is still prevalent, the actual content of this role has undergone changes over the last two decades. These are related to the new demands of schooling and, more specifically, the wide acceptance of English-medium education as necessary for employment in the formal sector.

In Bengali-speaking families, and increasingly among members of other communities as well, the success of children in formal education signifies past values, present status and hopes for future upward mobility. The aspirations resemble those highlighted in work on the 'new' middle classes elsewhere (Varma 1998; Pinches 1999). However, because the majority of those interviewed belong to Bengali Hindu families, the experience of this 'new world' – India after liberalization – is more one of crisis and marginalization than the active pursuit of new opportunities. In addition to the rhetoric about new opportunities in the private sector and IT-related industries, parents and adolescents regard the chances of finding employment in the more accepted traditional occupations as slim, so that thousands have reoriented themselves toward industries that still have to make significant inroads in the state.

For this segment of the population, the solution to the perceived employment crisis has been more and better education for prospective brides and mothers, and for sons, who are expected to enhance their chances for lucrative jobs through more and better qualifications. With reference to schooling, this implies that young married women are crucially involved in the new educational strategies.

The rather conservative middle class of Calcutta has in the last 20 years entered the world of English-medium education, largely because from the mid-1980s education in the vernacular no longer guaranteed a position in government service. Gradually Calcuttans became convinced that what was elsewhere a booming market, with thousands of positions in the software and IT-enabled service industries, would provide new opportunities once the government managed to attract such firms to the region. Whatever the reality, the powerful imagery of new global workplaces and competition led many parents to send their children to English-medium schools, because they believe that new employment prospects will emerge in the city.

Education and Expectations in the Global Economy

The recent economic changes held responsible for these new opportunities form part of the process of globalization, which is perceived ambivalently. While access to consumer goods and new technologies is often highlighted as a positive new indicator of affluence, most of those interviewed agree that among the less desirable outcomes of India's integration into the world market is a marked loss of social security. Within this discourse, economic decline in Calcutta is linked to globalization, Westernization and the decay of 'Indian' or 'Bengali' tradition evident in the decline of family values. Although the reasons for a stagnant economy in the city may be different and the effects of recent economic change on 'traditional' values may be much more diverse, the Bengali middle classes (like other groups) are about to lose many of their privileges and their sense of relative security. The switch to English-medium education was therefore not inspired by opportunities in the city but rather by the lack of alternatives.

The new patterns of education are held responsible for the demands made on parents, who feel they are more preoccupied with their children's education than previous generations were. The demographic profile of the typical middle-class family has changed across communities so that single children – particularly sons – are the norm, but parents – especially mothers – are now involved in school-related tasks around the clock. Among the Bengali-speaking population, nuclear families are rare and since bringing up children has become a more time-consuming and expensive process, few mothers with young children seriously consider moving out of the joint household.

Among the negative assumptions about modern family life, as the well-worn idiom of 'the breakdown of the traditional family' demonstrates, is the idea that parents and grandparents are likely to be abandoned in old age and that more assertive wives break up marriages and are responsible for high divorce rates. Thus the perceived loss of financial security is parallelled by a notion that social relationships have become less reliable, and that 'new women' are responsible for the 'breakdown' of the old order. Such conversations articulate widespread fears about changing forms of reciprocity between the generations and relate to real changes in gender roles, parent-child relationships and the status of ageing people in this environment (Vatuk 1990; Vera-Sanzo 1999; Lamb 2000: 70–111; Parry 2001).[4] Many middle-aged women spoke of their fears that the children they had brought up would ultimately break up the family, move into separate residences, forget about their duties as sons and daughters, and violate the principle of reciprocity between the generations. Familial values guide parents when decisions regarding the choice of a marriage partner are made, but are equally present in decisions regarding 'investment' in a child's education. This is the first reason why sons, and increasingly daughters, are put under immense pressure to succeed at school and in their chosen line of study.

However, although this could – in the view of today's parents – be achieved through hard work by pupils and students themselves, parental involvement has undergone dramatic changes within the last two decades. From the early 1980s Calcutta witnessed extreme competition for admission to English-medium schools, which facilitated the introduction of English pre-school education and the emergence of a veritable industry of coaching centres providing tuition. When it became apparent that in the course of liberalization new IT-based industries were being established in India, computer courses were added to the curriculum of most middle-class students, for which parents paid privately. But although the well-publicised instances of graduates recruited on campus and quickly earning enormous salaries in multinational companies make the front page, they are not relevant for the majority of young job-seekers in Calcutta. For them it was mainly the idea of a clean and respectable industry that transformed educational choices and strategies.

First, formal education starts before children reach the age of three years with the admission to pre-schools and nurseries, which has gradually become a pre-requisite for admission to English-medium schools. In the vast majority of cases, children born in the 1990s were the first generation to be admitted to pre-school or nurseries and to receive formal education in English. Second, after-school activities including tuition and computer education play an important role in preparing children for exams. Finally, the school chosen is no longer the reputed Bengali-medium neighbourhood school, and so the distance between home and school, the time spent travelling and the need to accompany even fairly mature children force mothers to travel within the city on a daily basis.

In spite of their close involvement with schooling and the educational system, parents rarely gave reasons other than that 'It has a good reputation,' 'It is an English-medium school,' and 'It is easy to reach,' when asked why they chose a particular school. All parents I spoke to asserted that they had selected a 'good' school for their children, but few made distinctions based on the content of what was taught, and many emphasized that the choice had been made independent of or in spite of a child's individual development and abilities. It is not uncommon for parents to claim that they would have preferred their son or daughter to be educated in Bengali, mainly because middle-class families generally speak the vernacular at home, and some fear that the younger generation will not be conversant in the mother tongue. However, more important is that they have a good knowledge of English, and none of the families involved arranged for tuition in Bengali, although many children did not acquire literacy skills in the vernacular. On the contrary, most mothers saw their own inability to teach their children English at home as a clear disadvantage for which they had to make up by sending them to pre-schools at an early age. This shift, on the other hand, seems to have given many children from less educated family backgrounds a chance to enter prestigious Anglo-Indian and convent institutions in central Calcutta.

Among parents with children in secondary education, comparable senti-ments prevail. Because secondary schooling is perceived as a precondition for admission to technology-oriented courses – either at university level or in one of the many institutions providing more practical IT training – parents judge successful secondary education largely in terms of the marks necessary to enter IT- or science-related courses.

Generations of young Bengalis were brought up to become government servants – or their wives – and to many this kind of employment promised security, if not a comfortable lifestyle. Students from lower-middle-class families joined government offices or public-sector undertakings at a junior level, and although not paid very well, they could rely on permanent employment, good marriage prospects and a small pension. For this stratum, self-employment and positions in private companies did not hold much promise, and it has only recently become fashionable to talk positively about the career prospects, promotions, perks and higher salaries offered in this sector. With the rising demand for consumer goods and increasingly affluent lifestyle preferred by the middle classes, government service has perhaps become a less attractive option, but although the well-educated elite may not want to apply for 'service' any more, the vast majority has no such choice. In many instances, the rhetoric of individual development and self-realization is used to cover the fact that the reduced number of openings in the public sector has led to the reluctant acceptance of private-sector employment.

Shifts in occupational preference and their effect on households have been analysed in some detail in the case of industrial labour (see Holmström 1999; Parry 2001). In Calcutta, as elsewhere, established strategies are employed to compete in a more flexible labour market. In case of the 'old' middle classes, it is not surprising that education plays a major part. The important role of educational strategies in the life of the middle classes, and the gender-specific meaning education has for the achievement of upward mobility, have been discussed in different contexts (e.g. Béteille 1991; Drury 1992; Scrase 1993; Mukhopadhyay 1994). However, although the views of parents on different types of education have been analysed, the impact of formal education on intra-household relations, apart from the conjugal one, has rarely been explored. In the course of the interviews it became clear that if anything has profoundly altered the way gender roles and ideologies of motherhood are represented among the Bengali middle class – and to an extent other communities in the same setting – it is the orientation of all household efforts towards the children's formal education.

Although only two of the mothers I met on a regular basis were educated in English, none of the children born after 1980 has been admitted to a Bengali-medium school. For some of the vernacular institutions in central Calcutta the situation has become so dire that they recently sought permission from the authorities to switch to Hindi-medium education in order to attract a new clientele.[5] The reason for this complete abandonment of the previously highly-valued education in Bengali – with all its nationalist implications – is simply that parents and children alike assume that the national and multinational companies in which graduates seek employment expect applicants to be fluent in English and to possess IT skills.

The need to compete if not in an international arena then at least in a national market, is acutely present in the accounts of parents and children, and the pressure on households to direct all available resources towards education is interpreted as a result of India's integration into the world market. However, many parents have come to realize that the chances for the majority of young people, who will never leave Calcutta, are limited, and that because the positions available are insecure and comparatively low-paid, the actual relevance of 'computer literacy' has to be doubted. Thus for the younger generation in particular, media images and available consumer goods stand in stark contrast to the limited opportunities to earn high salaries, and the gap between imagery and reality breeds frustration. Moreover, the majority are dissatisfied with their children's schooling even when a son has attended a 'good' school, has gone to college and has completed a degree. Although it may be acceptable for a daughter to be an average student, because she will often not be expected to compete in the job market, she will have to go through English-medium education and is likely to take computer training as well. Campaigns for 'computer literacy' aimed at lower-middle-class students include packages for women, and 'knowing computers' has replaced the familiar 'trained in classical dance/music' in matrimonial advertisements. Such young women could potentially work from home, and this possibility is always mentioned in conversations – but not a single married woman in any of these households was employed in this manner. Instead, IT-training presents an additional advantage in a daughter-in-law as mother, although once married, women rarely use computers for anything other than emails, and virtually none of the families invested in a home computer.

Parenting

In this setting, personhood is crucially constructed in relation to the role played by men and women in reproductive processes, although childlessness does not necessarily lead to any discrimination, and Bengali middle-class families often include unmarried people. Notions of status, individual fulfilment and happiness are, however, inevitably linked to parenthood.[6] To become a parent is considered to be an essential stage in the lifecycle of men and women across classes, and different lifestyles are interpreted accordingly. In Bengali culture, producing and raising children are represented as central determining features of human life itself (Inden and Nicholas 1977; Kotalova 1993: 191ff). It is assumed that marriage and parenthood link social roles with important physical changes and character traits, which are acquired through 'making a human' (*manush kora*) by bringing up a child. Although parents from a wide range of backgrounds can have children, and love them and bring them up, it is widely assumed that the generalized concepts and values inherent in the parent-child relationship are reproduced most successfully in middle-class households.

This view is most apparent in the discussion of parental roles, and particularly motherhood, which were subjected to intense scrutiny during the colonial period when the art of being a good daughter and daughter-in-law, and good citizen and mother, was defined in terms of a set of new domestic skills (Sangari 1999: 305ff; Borthwick 1984: 151; Bose 1996: 118). Such notions have been institutionalized in many contexts, and dominate the way local versions of contemporary middle-class motherhood are represented (e.g. Mascarenhas-Keyes 1990; Ram 1998; Stivens 1998).[7] Here as elsewhere, many parents contrast the wish to have children with the skills necessary to bring them up in the right manner, and the ideal of parenting as a 'modern' practice requires the assistance of a growing number of experts like teachers, doctors, journalists and public figures like actors or politicians. Increasingly, bad parenting has become a matter of public debate and is associated with localized practices and negative notions of 'tradition'. More and more experts are available to guide parents on how to enhance their offspring's educational success and reliability.

With the introduction of formal education for a wide range of middle-class boys during the colonial period, within which education was linked more closely to employment opportunities, Western-style schooling began to affect family life. Gradually the role of mothers as facilitators of formal education took shape with the introduction of housekeeping skills and literacy among women. Many of these changes emerged slowly, and most mothers inter-viewed pointed out that the preference for English-medium education brought about new challenges. For them, formal schooling in English repre-sents a moral dilemma, and mothers, who are responsible for providing the child with love and support as well as the close supervision needed to succeed in school, are often extremely anxious about this aspect of education.

The world of the home with its emphasis on relatedness among relatives, reciprocity between generations, and adequate consumption patterns, is con-trasted with the undesirable temptations and dangers present in the world outside. These are governed by the power a mother can exercise over her child's thoughts, movements and socialising, and in order to do so she has to be a 'friend'. This notion of intimacy with control is, of course, a hallmark of 'modern' parenting. But in this setting, unlike in the West, the notion is devoid of any focus on character formation aimed at the child's independence.[8]

On the contrary, children of both sexes are often discouraged from forming lasting bonds with their peers, and are confined to the house as much as pos-sible. This tendency is particularly strong with girls, who are left to spend their leisure time watching TV and making phone calls to family and friends. Most importantly, with the decline in the birth rate, the rise in living standards and the modification of residential patterns, children are reminded that they are their parents' future source of support. Such developments are acknowledged in family histories that very often centre around issues of childcare, parenting and motherhood, within which the emphasis is on hardship, sacrifice and the heavy responsibility carried by parents (Drury 1992: 64). People aged above fifty can easily identify major changes: most of them grew up in collaterally extended households, they always had more than two siblings, and married women were expected to give birth to more than one child. Among people in their forties, today only a minority live with the husband's brothers' families, and women have had two children only where the first-born was a girl. In the age group below thirty, none of the women has had two children, and not a single mother planned to have a second child in the future, even in the rare cases where the first child was female.

Apart from the moral concerns schooling raises, fathers and mothers alike reflect upon the changing role played by parents in their children's education. In many instances their own mother's involvement was depicted as, casual and relaxed, and fathers acted as (often distant) mediators between the outside world of school and the home. Today the everyday tasks are mainly carried out by mothers and grandmothers, who, as we will see, mediate between the house and the school by performing a wide range of tasks derived from new educational strategies.

In the families we are concerned with, schooling dominates family life around the clock, and mothers are involved with school-related activities almost all day. Thus their view on motherhood and 'parenting' is defined by their experience of formal education and their children's success in English-medium schools. Unlike earlier generations, who largely saw female education as providing 'proficient' domestic labour, mothers today must effectively manage and organize the school careers of their children (Sangari 1999: 308).

Among the most drastic changes was the introduction of pre-school education from the middle of the 1980s, since when middle-class children as young as eighteen months old have been admitted to English-medium nursery schools. For their mothers, apart from accompanying children to and from school, compiling useful information about admission to 'secondary' schools has became a major task. The admission process for most English-medium schools is highly formalized, and parents spend endless mornings queuing for documentation, as well as organizing the necessary coaching for interviews and admission tests before their children reach four years of age. Once a child has been admitted, the mother will have to learn how the school functions, which tests, exams and events take place, and what kind of tuition is required to gain good marks. In more than one way these new generations of mothers go through a phase of on-the-job-training and become responsible adults only once their children enter formal schooling.

But mothering also means the creation of a favourable environment for 'study' at home, which many describe as 'giving the children peace of mind'. This expression is particularly significant for women in lower-middle-class families, who are generally less well educated and often feel that they cannot contribute a lot to English-medium schooling. Because children constantly involved in studying are exempted from domestic responsibilities, their mothers' role is to facilitate study at home, provide them with special meals, encourage them and remind them of their duties, and organize their leisure time for them. So although children may spend most of their time away from home and receive tuition in their 'spare' time, they return to the house and are expected to revise and prepare for their lessons and do their homework. As one mother put it, 'There is always something to do – they can always study' – which is particularly true in the case of girls, who are, under the pretext of studies, discouraged from socialising. For many children, successful schooling also implies that their mothers organize extracurricular activities that may enhance their children's performance at school – for instance, computer classes, writing and art competitions.

Not surprisingly, mothers say that to make children successfully complete their formal education is the most challenging aspect of their lives, and it causes serious anxiety. But because most children are raised as single children in an 'extended family' that includes their grandparents as well as their parents, their mothers can, unlike their Western counterparts, rely on grandparents to support them.

Shared Parenting

Parents in these households have almost inevitably been brought up in collaterally extended units in which more than two married couples and their children have shared the same residence. Shared parenting is characteristic in these households, and although such large families are rare among those interviewed, children are still inevitably brought up by more than one carer. Multiple-care or shared parenting has been studied in considerable detail by psychologists and anthropologists working in South Asia (Kurtz 1992: 104ff; Seymour 1999: 77ff; Trawick 1990: 218ff).

The pattern of shared parenting, described in seminal accounts of family and childcare in Indian middle-class families such as Seymour's study of two neighbourhoods of Bhubaneswar, or Trawick's analysis of relatedness in a lower-middle-class Tamil family (Seymour 1999; Trawick 1990), corresponds to the sharing of responsibility among patrilineally-related kinsfolk. Analysing urban lifestyles, Seymour argues that shared parenting is disappearing among the middle-class residents of 'New town', who are largely in government service and live in nuclear families (Seymour 1999: 14). This is not a dominant trend in the two neighbourhoods of Calcutta I am concerned with, although it may become more prominent in the future.

In Calcutta, middle-class mothers explain that the continuous need for shared parenting is caused by the cost and length of formal education in private English-medium schools. Furthermore, many emphasized that the demand for shared parenting counteracts the trend towards nuclearisation of households. I therefore suggest that the new patterns of schooling, which imply the extension of maternal involvement in formal education, make shared parenting mandatory and do in fact prevent the early separation of households.

Although this may seem like a 'traditional' pattern, the involvement of grandparents in the raising of their grandchildren has recently been found to be on the rise in industrialized societies with a high rate of working women. In Bengali middle-class families, however, it is rarely paid work that keeps the daughter-in-law preoccupied. It became obvious in the course of this research that with the more elaborate demands of formal schooling, young mothers spent a considerable amount of time outside the house, and therefore depended more heavily on the support of female relatives, notably their mothers-in-law. Today, just as a daughter-in-law in employment leaves most of the housework to her mother-in-law – one of the reasons given for the professed preference for a non-working daughter-in-law – a young mother whose child attends a distant English-medium school will rely on servants and her mother-in-law to look after the household.

Paternal Grandmothers

In contrast to parenting practices among the majority in industrialized societies, motherhood in Calcutta is here not primarily experienced as an extension or realization of 'coupledom' but in terms of the relationship between the mother and her mother-in-law. With the new focus on extended English-medium education, the way in which mothers and paternal grandmothers are involved in raising children has undergone considerable changes.

The actual relationship between mother-in-law and daughter-in-law can vary considerably according to class and context (cf Vera-Sanso 1999; Lamb 2000: 71ff), but the two roles are structurally posed against each other, since they compete for the attention and resources of the same male breadwinner in the household. Ray among others has argued that intra-household relations have been modified by 'modern' conjugal relations which emphasized the bond between husband and wife and granted the in-married daughter-in-law some legitimate space of her own (Ray 1995). The rise in marriage age and spread of ideals of individualism are held responsible for this strengthened position of the young woman in the house, and the imagery of the 'modern' daughter-in-law who is unable or unwilling to 'adjust' is a common cliché in popular culture. But conjugal relations have changed partly because of demands for progressive parenting, and the extensive new schooling contributed to the transformations in the extended household.

In the past, married women fortunate enough to spend many years with their husband and sons looked forward to their sons' marriages because although they remained involved in housework, they could delegate many tasks to their sons' wives. Many chose to 'retire' once these wives had been trained. Although daughters-in-law were dominated by their mothers-in-law for most of their married lives, the relationship shifted gradually as the younger woman became middle-aged and able to run the household. Young married women generally worked hard, even when servants were employed, while many elderly women depicted the period after the marriage of sons as the best part of a woman's life. Within this framework the arrival of grandchildren signalled a new and very desirable phase in the lifecycle – a state within which a woman was allowed more leisure time and a wider range of individualistic pursuits, mostly of a religious nature. Although widowhood was a perpetual threat to old women in these households, grandparents experienced their involvement with grandchildren as largely fulfilling and special. As their direct responsibilities for bringing up their grandchildren diminished, becoming a grandparent was associated with 'a carefree life' and characterized by a phase of detachment from social obligations. Grandchildren, as Tagore's poem *Grandfather's Holiday* suggests, were there to teach their grandparents to let go: [9]

> Hurricane of freedom in my heart as you jump.
> Who has taught you, how he does it, I shall never know –
> You're the one who teaches me to let myself go.

In the contemporary urban middle-class family, a retired grandfather may in fact spend hours playing with his grandchildren before he retires to his study or joins his friends for extended *adda* sessions. Yet paternal grandmothers rarely gain much leisure time and cannot devote themselves exclusively to play, religious activities and extended socialising. In the smaller joint families, because the only daughter-in-law is increasingly involved in the activities related to her child's formal education and future employment, her mother-in-law remains the most important woman in charge of the housework. In this setting, the involvement of the paternal grandmother in daily chores is therefore prolonged and many elderly women are well aware of the changes the role has undergone. This is most evident when a daughter-in-law continues with outside employment after giving birth, in which case her mother-in-law may find herself home alone with a young grandchild. But even where the daughter-in-law is a house-wife, the grandmother's involvement with the household actually increases once her grandchildren grow older and enter formal education. Not surprisingly, this pattern is perceived as a threat to the established intra-household hierarchy.

The transformation in these Bengali middle-class households – and partly those of Marwaris as well – cannot be interpreted only as a result of a new emphasis on conjugality, because it probably results more from the new priorities of formal education and employment. It has been described here with reference to those settled in Calcutta but is even more obvious in the case of migrants' families. Where the whole nuclear family has migrated – usually in the case of well-educated upper-middle-class professionals – it has been guided not only by the 'natural' wish of husbands and wives to be together but also by considera-tions regarding the education of children. In many cases, married women did not join their husbands on an assignment and continued to live with their in-laws, whether in other instances a mother would return to Calcutta after trying to live with her husband elsewhere, only to find that bringing up children was much more difficult away from the joint-family setting.

Even when the whole family has settled elsewhere, shared parenting and the increased involvement of grandmothers in the raising of grandchildren does not always cease with migration. An increasing number of elderly women spend the better part of the year in Mumbai, Singapore or the United States with their only sons, partly providing assistance for their daughters-in-law. In the case of migration to the Gulf, which is very common among Bengali Christians in the central Calcutta neighbourhood, young children are regularly brought up in their grandparents' house, while their fathers may return only upon retirement.

Among the grandmothers' generation, individual reactions to this new pattern vary. Whereas some enjoy the feeling that they are needed and indeed manage to extend their influence over their sons, and most feel obliged to offer care for their grandchildren, many older women clearly see that this type of obligation goes beyond what is considered to be the 'traditional' duty. They are aware that these new responsibilities comprise tasks with little status, and contest the hierarchies between the women in the house. Furthermore, their expectations of this particular stage in the lifecycle are different from what they experience. Not surprisingly, childcare and housework have to be constantly negotiated, and even grandmothers who take full responsibility for grandchildren while their mothers are working are prone to display signs of resistance, such as the development of chronic illnesses and the manipulation of social relations with extended kin. Whereas some grandmothers are filled with pride and are energetic enough to continue with their responsibilities at the same rate as before, others feel weighed down by the emotional, physical and financial constraints of this continuous commitment. Most are critical of this 'modern' version of grandparenthood and feel exploited, which they express in the time-worn idiom of expectations of reciprocity between the generations. Describing the new regime, one elderly lady resident in central Calcutta stated that grandmothers increasingly feel that they are deprived of their rights as grandmothers and are forced into parenting a second time round.

Mothers and Networks

A further significant change is related to the increase in young married women's mobility, which in turn has enhanced their capacity to maintain social relations individually. Among the communities represented here, only Marwaris adhered to the strict rules of avoidance between affines commonly associated with north Indian kinship in the past, whereas among Bengali-speakers hierarchies between the two groups of affines have always been less pronounced. Nonetheless, urbanisation enhanced a 'bilateral tendency' in all communities. Migrants to the city, regardless of where they came from, used extended kinship networks during formal education and to find employment, and the significance of the resulting transformation of affinal ties – the bilateral tendency – was first mentioned by Vatuk (1972: 140–8).

A second factor in the emergence of mothers as independent agents in social relations is the decrease of long-distance marriages over the last two decades. For 20 years, brides in arranged matches have almost inevitably been chosen from families living in Calcutta, and love marriages, often within the same neighbourhood, have been common (Donner 2002). Proximity and existing social relations allow daughters to maintain close links with their natal homes and it is not unusual for a married daughter to visit her parent's house a couple of times each week.

Qualitative changes occur as the middle classes realize strategies aimed at upward mobility, since parents assume that children need more and broader supportive networks to succeed in the new market-driven economy. So although a daughter may have received a dowry, she may depend on further financial, emotional and ritual support. The parents of a daughter may even be expected to contribute to the cost of bringing up their grandchildren.

For young married women with children, formal education and the mobility necessitated by schooling legitimise comparatively independent networks which have been notoriously restricted, controlled and marginalized in north Indian kinship (Vatuk 1975: 181–6; Raheja and Gold 1994: 73–120). For older women sharing their residence with a son and his family, this independence implies less authority in the house and the need to adjust.

Conclusion: Educational Strategies and Intra-Household Relations

The new educational strategies employed by Bengali middle-class households and the related modification of shared parenting provide the framework within which women's changing work patterns and expectations towards old age have been explored.

It appears that the conditions brought about by economic change are class-specific, so that they are not confined to the Bengali or even Indian context (see Ram and Jolly 1998), but the homogenising tendency implicit in processes of globalization is still limited by local preconditions. In this context, parents' notions about their children's chances of gaining employment in particular industries signify a 'glocal' perspective that is partly shaped by perceptions of global markets and worldwide middle-class lifestyles (Robertson 1995). This global orientation is part of a context in which residential patterns and the local construction of gender and inter-generational obligations powerfully determine the effects of new educational choices. As the preferred type of employment as well as the notions of security attributed to it change, relationships in the household and women's experience of different stages in the lifecycle are also transformed.

Women as mothers have partly new obligations, notably the management of schooling and inter-household links. These links, including a married woman's relationship with her natal home and friends, are important, because middle-class parents rely on multiple contacts to enhance the chances for their own children, given the loss of secure employment. The flexible job market depends on 'knowledge, contacts and networks', as Holmström has argued, and it is not surprising that in their search for security households should draw on already existing relationships with others (Holmström 1999: 175). But the 'bilateral tendency' (Vatuk 1972) associated with urbanisation, which constructs the couple and their children as a unit to which the grandparents are attached, is counter-balanced by the increased dependency of mothers on their mothers-in-law, because their activities keep them away from home so much.

This changing scenario has gradually strengthened the position of daughters-in-law. As mothers they can act in the best interest of the household when they increase their mobility and with it the range of relationships they actively maintain. Consequently, the status of in-marrying women, traditionally placed in an inferior position, is changing. Senior women as grandmothers, moreover, can no longer expect to withdraw from daily chores as paternal grandmothers become increasingly involved in childcare and household activities. Unlike their daughters-in-law they tend to lose control over their own lives, and many are aware of the increasing social competence their daughters-in-law have developed.

The new economic conditions supported by the discourse on 'progressive' motherhood force women to cooperate more closely and at the same time divide them more profoundly. While mothers-in-law experience the new work patterns as a frustrated lifecycle expectation, their daughters-in-law express increased security, control and relatedness, which they derive from the mobility, socializing patterns and command over consumer goods related to their role as mothers with children in formal education.[10] The emerging maternal identities and 'parenting' practices can be interpreted as a further example of 'Indianisation' in the context of globalization, whereby institutions and practices rather than becoming homogenised are adapted and take on new meanings in a local context.

Notes

1 The main title translates the Bengali saying *Putra muldhan, praputra tar sud*, except that the latter actually refers to sons and grandsons only.
2 Fieldwork was conducted from September 1995 to April 1997, and from October 1999 to August 2000, and was supported by the ESRC and the Research Fund of the University of London. Earlier versions of this chapter have been presented at the project workshop in Paris, seminars in the LSE and the University of Oxford, and the annual meeting of the South Asia Anthropologists Group. I am grateful for comments made by participants on all these occasions and suggestions by Chris Fuller, Jackie Assayag, Hendrik Wittkopf, Geert De Neve, Barbara Harriss-White and Jonathan Spencer.
3 This orientation emerged during the late colonial period, and although this largely urban community cannot be described as belonging to the 'new' middle-classes, the implications of new economic opportunities shaping educational priorities, and the impact of consumerism described as part of middle-class lifestyles elsewhere, apply (McCarthy 1994; Varma 1998; Pinches 1999).
4 These themes are depicted in the popular soap operas, which contrast 'the traditional' world, normally represented by a devoted maternal figure whose efforts and inborn strength make the constant recreation of valuable family bonds a source of pride and economic success, with the materialism put forward by her children.
5 The majority of pupils attending these schools today are from upwardly mobile working-class backgrounds and belong to families originally from Bihar and Uttar Pradesh.
6 No contemporary form of a celibate lifestyle – e.g. joining an enclosed religious order – is available to women. Although a gradual withdrawal from sexual relationships with age is expected, this occurs after the reproductive roles have been fulfilled.

7 Stivens's work on Malaysia provides a comparative perspective on such discourses (Stivens 1998).
8 The main fear is that children may fall in love.
9 See the volume of selected poems edited by W. Radice (Tagore 1985).
10 This is not to suggest that the romanticised image of old age guided by religious calendars and rituals denotes a life less troublesome and safer, or more satisfying.

Bibliography

Bagchi, J. (1990) 'Representing nationalism: ideology of motherhood in colonial Bengal', *Economic and Political Weekly*, 42/43, 20–27 October 1990: WS 95–71.

Banerjee, N. (2002) 'Between the Devil and the deep sea : shrinking options for women in contemporary India', in K. Kapadia, ed., *The Violence of Development: The politics of identity, gender and social inequalities in India*. Delhi: Kali for Women; 43–68.

Banerjee, S. (1989) 'Marginalization of women's popular culture in nineteenth-century Bengal', in K. Sangari and S. Vaid, eds, *Recasting Women: Essays in Indian colonial history*. New Brunswick: Rutgers University Press; 127–79.

Béteille, A. (1991) 'The reproduction of inequality: occupation, caste and family', *Contributions to Indian Sociology*, (n.s.) 25: 1, 3–28.

Borthwick, M. (1984) *The Reluctant Debutante: The changing role of women in Bengal 1875–1927*. Princeton: Princeton University Press.

Bose, N. K. (1968) *Calcutta 1964: A social survey*. Bombay: Lalvani.

Bose, P. K. (1996) 'Sons of the nation: child rearing in the new family', in P. Chatterjee, ed., *Texts of Power: Emerging disciplines in colonial Bengal*. Calcutta: Samya; 118–44.

Chatterjee, P. (1993) *The Nation and its Fragments: Colonial and postcolonial histories*. Princeton: Princeton University Press.

Das, V. (1995) 'On soap operas: what kind of anthropological object is it?', in D. Miller, ed., *Worlds Apart: Modernity through the prism of the local*. London: Routledge; 169–89.

Debi, B. (1988) *Middle-Class Working Women of Calcutta: A Study in continuity and change*. Calcutta: Anthropological Survey of India.

Dickey, S. (2000) 'Permeable homes: domestic service, household space, and the vulnerability of class boundaries in urban India', *American Ethnologist*, 27 (2): 462–89.

Donner, H. (2002) 'One's own marriage: love marriages in a Calcutta neighbourhood', *South Asia Research*, 22: 79–94.

Drury, D. (1992) *The Iron Schoolmaster: Education, employment and the family in India*. Berkeley: University of California Press.

Dwyer, R. (2000) *All You Want is Money, All you Need is Love: Sexuality and romance in modern India*. London: Cassel.

Engels, D. (1996) *Beyond Purdah? Women in Bengal 1890–1939*. Delhi: Oxford University Press.

Fernandes, L. (2000a) 'Nationalising "the global": media images, cultural politics and the middle-class in India', *Media, Culture and Society*, 22: 611–28.

—— (2000b) 'Restructuring the new middle class in liberalizing India', *Comparative Studies of South Asia, Africa, and the Middle East*, 20, 1/2: 88–111.

—— (2002) 'Rethinking globalization: gender and the nation in India', in M. de Koven, ed., *Feminist Locations: Global/local/theory/practice in the twenty-first century*. New Brunswick: Rutgers University Press, pp. 147–167.

Giddens, A. (1990) *The Consequences of Modernity*. London: Polity Press.

—— (1999) *Runaway World: How globalization is reshaping our lives*. London: Profile Books.

Holmström, M. (1999) 'A new map of Indian industrial society: the cartographer at sea', *Oxford Development Studies*, 27: 165–86.

Inden, R. B. and R. W. Nicholas (1977) *Kinship in Bengali Culture*. Chicago: University of Chicago Press.

Jamieson, L. (1998) *Intimacy: Personal relationships in modern societies*. Cambridge: Polity Press.

Khilnani, S. (1998) *The Idea of India*. Delhi: Penguin.

Kotalova, J. (1993) *Belonging to Others: Cultural construction of womanhood among Muslims in village Bangladesh*. Doctoral Thesis, University of Uppsala.

Kumar, N. (n.d.) *Mothers and Non-Mothers: expanding the discourse of education in South Asia*.

Kurtz, S. N. (1992) *All the Mothers are One: Hindu India and the cultural reshaping of psychoanalysis*. New York: Columbia University Press.

Lamb, S. (2000) *White Saris and Sweet Mangoes: Aging, gender, and body in North India*. Chicago: University of Chicago Press.

Mascarenhas-Keyes, S. (1990) 'Migration, progressive motherhood and female autonomy: Catholic women in Goa' in L. Dube and R. Palriwalla, eds, *Structures and Strategies: Women, work and the family*. Delhi: Sage Publications; 103–27.

McCarthy, P. (1994) *Postmodern Desire: Learning from India*. Delhi: Promilla.

Miller, D. (1995) 'Introduction: anthropology, modernity and consumption', in D. Miller, ed., *Worlds Apart: Modernity through the prism of the local*. London: Routledge; 1–22.

Mukherjee, S. A. (1993) *Calcutta: Essays in urban history*. Calcutta: Subarnarekha.

Mukhopadhyay, C. C. (1994) 'Family structure and women's participation in science and engineering', in C. C. Mukhopadhyay and S. C. Seymour, eds, *Women, Education and Family Structure in India*. Boulder: Westview Press; 103–32.

Nair, P. T. (1990) 'The growth and development of Old Calcutta', in S. Chaudhuri, ed., *Calcutta: The living city*. Vol. I. Delhi: Oxford University Press; 10–23.

Papanek, H. (1989) 'Family status – production work: women's contribution to social mobility and class differentiation', in M. Krishnaraj and K. Chanana, eds, *Gender and the Household Domain: Social and cultural dimensions*. Delhi; 97–116.

Parry, J. P. (2001) 'Ankalu's errant wife: sex, marriage, and industry in contemporary Chhattisgarh', *Modern Asian Studies*, 35: 783–820.

Pinches, M. (1999) 'Cultural relations, class and the new rich of Asia', in M. Pinches, ed., *Culture and Privilege in Capitalist Asia*. London: Routledge; 1–51.

Raheja, G. G. and A. Gold (1994) *Listen to the Heron's Word: Reimagining gender and kinship in North India*. Berkeley: University of California Press.

Rajagopal, A. (1999) 'Thinking about the new Indian middle class: gender, advertising and politics in the age of globalization', in S. Sunder Rajan, ed., *Signposts: Gender issues in post-independence India*. Delhi: Kali for Women; 57–100.

Ram, K. (1998) 'Maternity and the story of enlightenment in the colonies: Tamil coastal women: South India', in K. Ram and M. Jolly, eds, *Maternities and Modernities: Colonial and postcolonial experiences in Asia and the Pacific*. Cambridge: Cambridge University Press; 114–43.

Ray, B. (1995) 'The three generations: female rivalries and the joint family in Bengal 1900–1947', in R. K. Ray, ed., *Mind and Body: Life and mentality in Bengal*. Calcutta: Oxford University Press; 364–90.

Robertson, R. (1995) 'Globalization: time-space and homogeneity-heterogeneity', in M. Featherstone, S. Lash and R. Robertson, eds, *Global Modernities*. London: Sage Publications; 25–44.

Roy, M. (1975) *Bengali Women*. Chicago: University of Chicago Press.

Sangari, K. (1999) *Politics of the Possible: Essays on gender, history, narratives, colonial English*. New Delhi: Tulika.

Sarkar, T. and S. Butalia, eds (1995) *Women and Right-Wing Movements: Indian experiences*. London: Zed Books.

Scrase, T. J. (1993) *Image, Ideology and Inequality: Cultural domination, hegemony and schooling in India*. New Delhi: Sage.

Seymour, S. C. (1999) *Women, Family and Childcare in India: A world in transition*. Cambridge: Cambridge University Press.

Sircar, A. (1999) 'Love in the time of liberalization: qayamat se qayamat tak', *Journal of Arts and Ideas*, 32–33: 35–59.

Srilata, K. (1999) 'The story of the "up-market" reader: Femina's "new woman" and the normative feminist subject', *Journal of Arts and Ideas*, 32–33: 61–72.

Standing, H. (1991) *Dependence and Autonomy: Women's employment and the family in Calcutta*. London: Routledge.

Stivens, M. (1998) 'Modernizing the Malay mother', in K. Ram and M. Jolly, eds, *Maternities and Modernities: Colonial and postcolonial experiences in Asia and the Pacific*. Cambridge: Cambridge University Press; 50–80.

Tagore, R. (1985) *Selected Poems*. London: Penguin Books.

Trawick, M. (1990) *Notes on Love in a Tamil Family*. Berkeley: University of California Press.

Varma, P. K. (1998) *The Great Indian Middle Class*. Delhi: Penguin.

Vatuk, S. (1972) *Kinship and Urbanization: White-collar migrants in North India*. Berkeley: University of California Press.

—— (1975) 'Gifts and affines in North India', *Contributions to Indian Sociology*, (n.s.) 9: 155–96.

—— (1990) '"To be a burden on others": dependency anxiety among elderly in India', in O. Lynch, ed., *Divine Passions: The social construction of emotion in India*. Berkeley: University of California Press; 64–88.

Vera-Sanso, P. (1999) 'Dominant daughters-in-law and submissive mothers-in-law? Cooperation and conflict in South India', *Journal of the Royal Anthropological Society*, 5: 577–93.

Walsh, J. (1995) 'The virtuous wife and the well-ordered home: the re-conceptualisation of Bengali women and their worlds', in R. K. Ray, ed., *Mind, Body and Society: Life and mentality in colonial Bengal*. Calcutta: Oxford University Press; 331–59.

7

OF LANGUAGES, PASSIONS AND INTERESTS: EDUCATION, REGIONALISM AND GLOBALIZATION IN MAHARASHTRA, 1800–2000

Véronique Bénéï

The passions are not to be counted out in situations where interest-motivated behaviour is considered to be the rule.

Cardinal de Retz (Hirschman 1977: 135)

March 2000, Kolhapur, Maharashtra, western India. It is noon on Saturday and the school day has just ended at the Vidyapeeth Marathi Shakha primary school, one of the oldest and most reputable Marathi-medium institutions in this southern town.[1] We are in the teachers' room. The new Congress government in the regional state has just announced its decision to introduce compulsory English from Class I onwards. Ms Kalloli, the school principal, who has always publicly expressed her pride in her 'Indian culture' (*Bhartiya sanskruti*), is strongly opposed to such a measure. She is vehemently discussing the government's intention with her staff. I have known Kalloli Bai well for over two years. She is a strong-willed lady in her early fifties and is often rather outspoken. Yet never have I seen her behave so passionately. Her face is red with anger, her hair flying loose as she gestures forcefully in the course of her diatribe vituperating against what she sees as the new government's 'populist policy'.

A few days later, when we meet again, Kalloli Bai takes up the topic afresh on her own initiative. Although she has cooled down by now, she makes no secret of how dear to her heart the issue of language is, shaking her head in negation: 'No, it is definitely not good. It should not be done.'

'Why not?', I prompt her.

Pat comes her answer. 'Before, we had the Moghuls, in the times of the Muslims, and we had to learn the Farsi language. Then with the advent of Shivaji the Marathi language was successfully imposed. But then, later on, the English came and forced their English language on us. Then we got our independence, and our Marathi, our own language [*swabhasha*] back again. Now what is the point of imposing the "firangi" [foreigners', i.e. English] language on us again?'

Introduction: 'Globalization' in Maharashtra

It is often said today that English has become a global language in the 'new era of globalization'. On a world scale, financial and economic transactions are increasingly conducted, and technological and cultural transformations effected, in this language. Its mastery is consequently considered a prerequisite for taking advantage of the new opportunities the worldwide phenomenon is purported to offer locally. In India, new economic opportunities have been created since economic liberalization began in the 1980s. Of all the states in India, Maharashtra is among the most developed, both industrially and technologically. The state government's decision in March 2000 to introduce basic English from Class I onwards has therefore to be understood in this socio-economic context.[2] Furthermore, regional politics play a considerable part in educational matters at the state level. It is no coincidence that this measure was taken at that particular moment in history. That the government had been in power for only a few months when it made this announcement is important on two counts: first, the new political configuration put a halt to four years of aggressive 'sons-of-the-soil', Hindu right-wing regionalist and nationalist (BJP/Shiv Sena) policy; and second, the policy went hand in hand with a strong emphasis on the Marathi language as one of the key elements defining a 'true (Hindu) Maharashtrian and Indian identity'. The new government also had to appeal to the electorate that had voted in this new version of the Congress, playing to what it perceived to be its demands. This electorate was far from homogeneous: it included members of the 'middle classes', as well as 'lower classes' and less advantaged socio-economic groups, and people of different faiths, some of them more secular-minded than others. The one common denominator linking these otherwise highly diverse social and political actors was perceived to be their desire to get a share of the economic manna, which could more easily be secured by the acquisition of English language skills. And so the new government decided to facilitate it.

Some socio-economic background is in order here.

A large majority of the jobs newly made available at the time of economic liberalization were initially held by those who 'traditionally' had a command of the former colonial tongue: the elite and, to some extent, the so-called middle classes. Today, the middle classes represent a much larger part, almost a third, of the Indian population. A growing number of social actors have made inroads into these former job preserves, while also gaining access to other economic niches, including IT services. More recently, even the lower rungs of Indian society have entered the race to 'globalization'. As a result, the English media and English-educated circles have been increasingly worried about the linguistic craze that is said to have befallen the entire population. Members of the economically privileged sections of the population already possessing a social and linguistic capital in English proffer diverse examples of the phenomenon. The craze has reached such a proportion that a majority of vernacular speakers may send their children *en masse* to English-medium schooling. The case of an old, illiterate female Maratha servant sending her grandchild to an English-medium nursery school has become an exemplar. So has that of a Marathi-medium-educated neighbour putting her four-year-old into an English-medium nursery school and then imposing extra language tuition on her to improve her proficiency.

It is true that an increasing number of English-medium institutions have seen the light of day throughout India, and the state of Maharashtra is no exception. The aim in this chapter is to put this fact into a wider, more complex context and contribute to the dossier of languages as total social phenomena. The purpose is not to conduct a theoretical or empirical discussion of the concept of 'globalization', nor to specifically evaluate its empirical novelty.[3] Rather, I shall resort to several levels of analysis to produce various *effets de connaissance* (Revel 1996: 19) so as to uncover layers of historical and social meaning associated with English and vernacular languages (here, Marathi) in this part of India.

Three levels can be distinguished: national and international economics, regional and imperial history, and micro-sociology. Lack of space prevents dwelling on the first level at length. The question is whether a renewed interest in the English language in India is linked to, or even largely derived from, recent 'globalization'. First, evidence from Maharashtra suggests a more elaborate process at work, indicating that internal and local economic trends, related to international agribusiness, played a significant part even before the advent of this new 'globalization'. Second, such a renewal of linguistic interest begs the question of whether English as a 'global' language is a new phenomenon at all. Arguably, what is happening today is not dissimilar from processes associated with the heyday of the British Empire. Third, the view that Indian middle classes are seizing on English-medium instruction *en masse* as an opportunity for gaining socio-economic advantage needs qualification. Not only does such a situation show interesting similarities with developments in the later nineteenth century; it also reveals complex tensions between educational and professional choices, usually associated with middle-class aspirations and expectations on the one hand, and patriotism and local or regional attachments on the other.

In a nutshell, this chapter seeks to identify mediations between 'individual rational and collective identity' (Revel 1996: 24) by providing an understanding of the choices social actors make, and the consequent tensions, in relation to the perception of key components of their identities in the face of global constraints. The chapter consequently highlights the need to consider local manifestations, both real and imagined, of the phenomenon of globalization. Rather than arguing along the lines of 'rational choice strategy', I show how languages may be fundamental vehicles of identity and, as such, sites of considerable emotional investment and deep-seated attachment potentially in conflict with socio-economic interests. By looking at case studies of members of various communities, ranging from dominant Hindu Maratha to Brahmin to minority Jain, the chapter also sheds light on how different communities negotiate their relationship to language and how families engage with the dialectics of language as passion, and socio-economic opportunities as interest.

Linguistic Globalism in the Region

The issue of language has been crucial in post-colonial India. Regional states were carved out of the new national territory on vernacular linguistic bases. Numerous debates and controversies ensued, ranging from linguistic delimitation to the medium of instruction to be preferred in each state (vernacular over English, one vernacular versus another vernacular), to the strong antagonism between the Dravidian languages, such as Tamil, and the now 'official', 'Sanskritic' language, Hindi. The southern states, favouring English as a lingua franca (see Ramaswamy 1997), have vehemently resisted the attempt by northern nationalists since independence to impose Hindi upon them. Today, however, Hindi has succeeded in securing an increasingly dominant position across the country for inter-state communication in administrative and political matters.

These developments have gone hand in hand with the spread throughout India since independence of the educational model of the 'three-language formula'. This model is particularly apposite for reflecting on issues of locality, nation and globalization. It ensures that education is provided in a given state's official language (e.g. Marathi in Maharashtra, Kannada in Karnataka, and so on) *or* a child's native tongue for the first ten years of primary and secondary schooling, from Class I onwards.[4] In addition, both the 'official' language (i.e. Hindi) plus a third language are taught from Class V onwards. In Maharashtra, almost since the creation of the state in 1960, this third language may be English.

For Marathi-speaking children in Maharashtra, the pattern is therefore as follows: they begin their education, aged six, in Marathi, then start learning Hindi and English from Class V (aged 10) onwards. As indicated above, children belonging to linguistic/religious minorities are entitled to attend school in their native medium. The only additional requirement in this case is that the educational institution teaches Marathi together with Hindi and English from Class V onwards. Such a three- or even four-tier linguistic scheme is crucial to the creation of an integrated Indian nation with a lingua franca, whether Hindi or English. Yet this model also reflects tensions between local or regional and national identities, and opportunities brought about by economic liberalization and globalization. The renewed interest in the English language, even in Maharashtra where the gradual replacement of English by the regional vernacular had taken place for administrative purposes, is fraught with tensions.[5]

Some socio-cultural and historical background is in order here.

With a total literacy rate of 77.27 per cent, Maharashtra comes second only to Kerala, and the rate greatly increased between 1991 and 2001 (Biswas and Raju 2002). As well as Brahmans and other upper castes, Marathas and so-called 'allied castes' and, to a lesser extent, ex-Untouchables, whether Dalit or not, have also received public instruction. This is largely the result of educational policies started long ago, which gradually opened up education for the majority. The publicly-funded state educational system, started after the creation of Maharashtra state, provided the basis for homogeneous primary and secondary schooling throughout the state. The state system was partly built on the variety of state institutions set up as early as the British Raj, and partly on the large network of privately-run institutions that were started in western and southern Maharashtra throughout the twentieth century. These institutions had been founded by various agents, not only missionaries but also freedom fighters, peasant communities (such as the Rayat Shikshan Samstha in Satara, founded by 'Karmaveer' Bhaurao Patil; see Matthew 1988), non-Brahman organizations, including Jain sectarian communities (for instance in Sangli) and so on (see also Bénéï 1997). They were taken over and funded by the state, even while retaining their private status and management, and were made to comply with the official curriculum that was evolving at the time. Even today they constitute a fundamental part of the educational system in southern and western Maharashtra (Bénéï 2001).

Of all the private institutions existing at the primary level, an infinitesimal proportion has been promoting English (almost exclusively those started by missionaries), while the overwhelming majority impart instruction in Marathi. A few figures will suffice. In Kolhapur, Marathi-medium schools in 2000 still catered for over 84 per cent of the primary school population, whereas English-medium schools catered for less than 12 per cent. The increase in the number of English-medium schools was marginal compared with the general increase in educational facilities. Thus the parents sending their children to English-medium schools in Maharashtra, and particularly in southern Maharashtra, still accounted for a small minority.

Imperial and Global Idioms, and Economic Privileges

> It is obvious that we never had it so good up until the 1980s and 1990s. Until then we were very privileged – we had tremendously high standards of living compared with the rest of the population. Today, things are changing fast, and it is also very obvious that we are going to enter competition with other classes who never occupied such privileged positions before.

So in 2000 spoke Prakash Mankekar, a Brahman from Pune in his mid-forties, one of those who have benefited the most from English education and who now see the craze for this language endangering their long-standing socio-economic and cultural dominance. Interestingly, this purported craze for English bears striking similarities to the colonial situation in the nineteenth century in the Bombay Presidency, as do the implications of choosing between a 'post-colonial, imperial and global' language and an indigenous one as a medium of instruction. That the English language enjoys a dominant position in the financial, economic and technological domains in India today is by no means a recent phenomenon. Rather, it goes back to colonial times and the construction of the British Empire, with which English was closely associated from the early nineteenth century.[6] English then was not only the language of the British, as we all know, but also that of the British *Empire*: it was in English that colonial orders were carried out, particularly after the transfer of power from the East India Company to the Crown following the events of 1857.[7] Consequently, acquisition of the language was also a gateway to local administrative positions for some sections of the indigenous population. By mastering the imperial language, members of the Indian elite were able to access high-ranking positions in the administrative services of the Raj (see Breckenridge and van der Veer 1993; Cohn 1997; Metcalf 1995; Stokes 1989). Thus they were also able to participate in the 'global civil society' that emerged during this period and 'carried the imprint of the nationality that propelled it' (Hopkins 2002b: 31). The English language had become the 'indispensable common currency of what might be called national globalization, whether for commercial or for cultural exchanges' (ibid.: 32).

The notion of English as an imperial and global language was therefore already in place in the nineteenth century. What is occurring today is reminiscent of a phenomenon that took place over two centuries ago within India, albeit on a more limited scale, being largely confined to the imperial administrative bureaucracy. From being a predominantly imperial language (as well as a global one for an elite minority), English has now become properly 'global' *within* India. An increasing number of Indian citizens now partake of a polyglot environment in which the English language is synonymous with economic dominance and cultural primacy, at the same time enabling them to participate in a wider community worldwide (Harper 2002).[8]

The linguistic situation in Maharashtra today has striking resonances with the 'great debate' between vernacular and English-medium instruction raging in India throughout the nineteenth century. This debate has been popularized for generations of Indian and English schoolchildren by repeated reference to the declaration made in 1835 by Lord Macaulay, then a member of the Executive Council for the East India Company: 'We must at present do our best to form a class who may be interpreters between us and the millions whom we govern – a class of persons Indian in blood and colour, but English in tastes, in opinions, in morals and in intellect.'

Macaulay's declaration has often been singled out to illustrate the ravages of cultural colonisation mediated by the imposition of the English language on indigenous populations. Yet, as noted by Zastoupil and Moir (1999), such a view fails to capture the complexities of the colonial experience regarding linguistic matters.

Macaulay's statement is often quoted within a theoretical framework reinforced by the assumption of a logical, coherently articulated and homogeneous 'imperial project', the problematic character of which has already been much discussed by students of colonialism. With respect to education, such emphasis on an imperial will does not do justice to the agency of the indigenous population who in many respects played an active part in the educational process of the nineteenth and subsequent centuries.[9] Among the British, there were also deep conflicts between Orientalists favouring the teaching of 'classical' languages (such as Arabic or Sanskrit) and 'vernacularists' and Anglicists. Such conflicts were reflected in the variations in policy on education in different presidencies. Whereas the Bengal Presidency strongly favoured English-medium education (epitomised by the institution of Fort Williams), the Madras Presidency was in favour of a mix of English and vernacular languages, and the Bombay Presidency, part of which is now Maharashtra, gave much more prominence to vernacular languages.

The figures nevertheless reveal that the overwhelming majority of pupils attended vernacular schools. It can be surmised that the people who had received any kind of instruction in 1845 accounted for hardly 1 per cent.[10] Out of these, ten years later, the number of pupils in English-medium schools was hardly 8 per cent of the total number of pupils.[11] (In comparison, over 70 per cent of students were studying in English-medium schools in the Bengal Presidency at the same period.) Yet a craze for English instruction (the term here could have meant either the language of instruction or the type and contents of instruction imparted as opposed to those in traditional 'indigenous education') was also repeatedly reported from the 1840s onwards by self-congratulating British educational inspectors.[12] The craze was, however, exaggerated. It is true that a number of public petitions asking for the opening of an English school were sent to the educational department of the Presidency at the time; they were carefully kept in the departmental records as 'native evidence' and justified inspectors' perception of an overall craze among the whole population. But what neither petitions nor inspectors emphasized was that such petitions were more often than not initiated by influential people belonging to already privileged sections of the population.[13] This in turn fed into the misgivings entertained by some British administrators and educationalists about the spread of English instruction and its economic consequences, because they feared encroachment on their own lucrative activities. Thus an editorial in the *Bombay Saturday Review of Politics, Literature and Commerce* of 1861 judged English-educated natives 'conceited in claiming employment'.[14] With respect to the contemporary context, an important difference therefore lies in the respective positions and interests of the speakers; in the mid-nineteenth century, it was British educational inspectors who either deplored the alleged public craze for English or congratulated themselves upon it, whereas today it is the privileged sections of the Indian population that bemoan it.

Empirical evidence suggests, however, that notwithstanding their awareness of the potential for economic mobility furthered by English education, there is still widespread and strong reluctance among Marathi-speaking people to send their offspring to English-medium institutions. This is true of both parents and teachers, although the teachers are usually most likely to avail themselves of any existing educational opportunities. Remember Kalloli Bai's comment at the beginning. Although people like her are generally among the best informed about career opportunities and the most astute in terms of educational strategies, they share the common reluctance, and only recently have a very few of them started to send their children or grandchildren to English-medium schools. The rest of this chapter examines this reluctance and the tensions involved in more detail.

Regional Identities and Nation-Building

English and Marathi: Lingering Colonialism versus Regional and National Patriotism

The reluctance to embrace English-medium instruction unreservedly at the expense of the linguistic attachment to their vernacular language is largely premised on the enduring perception among many ordinary Marathi speakers that English is the language of their 'colonial masters'. English, indeed, continues to have strong colonial overtones and sensitive connotations in many parts of India, and English is often referred to as the 'firangi' language.[15] The enduring potency of such a representation is reflected in the debates about how the use of English is (in)authentic and (un)justifiable, which appear time and again in the Indian press, both English and vernacular. The reluctance shown by Marathi-speaking parents to send their offspring to English-medium education is linked to Marathi's prominence in the definition of what it means to be a Maharashtrian today, as I have shown elsewhere (Bénéï 2001).

Many studies of nationalism have stressed linguistic factors as particularly prominent in nation-building, whether at a national or a regional level (Anderson 1983; Gellner 1983; Hastings 1999; Hobsbawm 1997). This certainly obtains in India, where regional nationalisms have often been intricately associated with regional languages (cf Cohn 1998), and Maharashtra and Marathi are a case in point. To be sure, Marathi's normalization and homogenization into a fully-fledged language (as opposed to a dialect) was enabled by the philological explorations of British linguists and educationalists working closely with local Sanskrit pundits in the nineteenth century (Nemade 1990; Bénéï 2001b; Naregal 2001). As such, the official Marathi of today is largely a modern creation. So, too, is the powerful notion, and the complex bundle of emotions associated with it, that Marathi is the Maharashtrians' 'mother tongue' – a concept largely alien to Indian vernacular speakers prior to the advent of European philological influences in the nineteenth century (Ramaswamy 1997).[16] Yet none of these historical facts prevents the vernacular language from mediating a deeply-felt sense of belonging today, whether articulated at a national or a regional level. The regional language, the idea and feeling of belonging, is no less real and authentic for its speakers, who have developed strong feelings and emotions about it. Marathi's clear association with the assertion and defence of a sense of regional and national belonging is widespread among members of the public, whether parents or teachers. In Kolhapur, Marathi-medium teachers were often very vocal about the necessity to teach in Marathi as against the 'firangi' language. The very wording of Kalloli Bai's statement was itself illuminating: as we shall see, it revealed conceptual connections between language and the construction, or rather, maintenance of a sense of belonging incarnated in the regional warrior-hero Shivaji as the guarantor of *swabhasha*.

The concept of *swabhasha*, 'one's own language', testifies to the importance of language in the regional construction of a sense of belonging in Maharashtra and also has ideological and emotional implications. It was often used by Marathi parents of both English- and Marathi-educated children to express their attachment to Marathi. A popular expression was in the form *swataci bhasha* – as in *Amci bhasha 'he, swataci* ('This is our language, our own') – often in association with the notion of *matru bhasha*, 'mother tongue'. As in northern India (Kumar 1992), in Maharashtra the notion of *swabhasha* is intricately associated with *swadesh* and *swadharma*, 'one's own country' and 'one's own religion' respectively.

Furthermore, all three notions are themselves closely linked together in a long-standing tradition of regional patriotism (Bayly 1998) in which pride of place is given today to the seventeenth-century Maratha warrior-hero Shivaji. 'Shivaji Maharaj', as many Marathi-speaking Maharashtrians fondly and respectfully call him, epitomises Maratha martial bravery and strategic political skill. He is also considered the founder of the Maratha nation and as such, he is the central pivot around which all regional history is taught in schools in Maharashtra. Shivaji is portrayed as the promoter and defender of the three notions in Class IV history textbook. This mantra is endlessly drummed into pupils' heads.

From a very early age, therefore, children are forcefully exposed by their teachers and other adults to the conceptual conflation of country, religion and language embodied in Shivaji, just as the goddess Tamilttay embodies the Tamil language in Tamil Nadu (Ramaswamy 1997). This ingraining in turn has an emotional power that accounts for the fear of identity loss experienced by Marathi-educated Hindu Maharashtrians faced with the possibility of English teaching, as indicated by Kalloli Bai's reaction. Furthermore, favouring Marathi-medium instruction on identity grounds is not confined to teachers sympathetic to Hindutva but is widespread, even when it is also supported for other reasons.

Thus for someone like Khandekar Sir, the head teacher of the most progressive school that I visited in Kolhapur, Pratapsinh Vidhya Mandir (PVM), it goes without saying that education should be provided in Marathi. And when his wife started her own private primary and secondary school on their home premises over ten years ago, the medium of instruction was not at issue: it was *of course* to be Marathi. Since its inception the school has been doing well, and counted a roll of 1,000 pupils by the end of 2000, testifying to high demand for private instruction. And as evidence that this is no cynical move on their part to educate others in Marathi while securing English instruction for their own children, their two sons, after studying up until Class V at another private Marathi-medium school, joined the familial school.

To be sure, some teachers teaching in Marathi do send their children (or some of them) to English-medium institutions, as do some parents not belonging to the most privileged sections of the population. But even today they do not account for the majority – far from it. In most of these cases such choices seem to be made within families with a long-standing tradition of education, and with overt aspirations to upward social mobility. Thus Ms Shinde, a Maratha whose *mama* (mother's brother) was one of the founders of the educational society running PVM, comes from such a family. All her relatives on her mother's side studied in one of the prestigious Marathi institutions of Kolhapur, but the males pursued their studies at the famous state-run English-medium Rajaram College. She herself studied in the Marathi medium, but she made sure that both her son and daughter received some education in English, although in her daughter's case it was in her final years of schooling. Her son married a Marathi-educated girl, Sushila, who was a high-achiever and now teaches in a college. Whereas Sushila initially wanted to get her daughter into a Marathi school, it was her mother-in-law who insisted that the girl should be sent to the poshest and costliest of English-medium institutions in town, Shahu Chhatrapati Vidhyalay. Located north of Kolhapur in the former palace stables, this school was founded a decade ago by a descendant of Shahu Maharaj, who had initiated educational and social reforms at the turn of the century in his then princely state.

English Medium, Social Mobility and Integration

Clearly, whether Marathi-speaking Maharashtrians adopt English *en masse* is a much more complex question than is often suggested. If some parents are aware of the need for embracing a modernized type of education to provide better opportunities for their offspring's economic future (including computer studies), such awareness does not necessarily translate into abandoning education in the vernacular language altogether, which they still regard as key to Maharashtrian identity. This certainly begs for a reappraisal of the allegedly popular craze for English-medium instruction. Marathi-speakers belonging to the main Maharashtrian communities have still not opted in large numbers for such a type of instruction. Yet the number of English-medium educational institutions, including primary-level ones, has risen in Maharashtra too. How is one to interpret this development? Which members of the public avail themselves of this facility?

Apart from the upper castes and classes who have 'traditionally' availed themselves of English-medium instruction, the parents presently opting for this type of education belong either to the Marathas or 'allied castes' or to minority communities – whether Brahman, Muslim, Jain or others – at either extreme of the class ladder. Parents of Maratha and 'allied castes' belonging to lower socio-economic backgrounds, for instance, have often been in close contact through their jobs, or sometimes in their capacity as servants, with upper-middle-class benevolent families who may have encouraged them in their aspirations.

Such was the case of Subhedabai, a Maratha lady who had been a servant within the Borgaonkar family for over 40 years. Subhedabai was illiterate and had six children. Her husband died while the children were still very young and she, with emotional, material and financial support from her Brahmin employers, raised her six children as best she could, sending them to Marathi state schools. All her children got married, the daughters at an early age (15 or 16), and the sons after they had managed to secure stable positions as either petty clerks, peons or bus drivers. The youngest was married in 1990. Although all Subhedabai's grandchildren had till then been sent to Marathi-medium schools, she insisted that her last grandchild be sent into English-medium education. The boy, Sunil, was born in 1993 and sent to an English nursery at the age of four. However, he was later withdrawn from the nursery and put back into the Marathi medium when the parents became aware of the child's difficulty in coping with a totally alien linguistic environment. The end of this story is common to many Marathi-speaking families, whether literate or not, who at some point have experimented with English-language instruction. It also points to the 'naturalness' associated with the notion of mother tongue for vernacular speakers, something which was often very explicitly expressed by parents:

> He [their son, for instance] wouldn't get it. Learning in English did him no good – he could not learn anything. It is so unnatural. Learning in a foreign language is not right; it hinders the child's development. It is more natural to learn in one's mother tongue.

Interestingly, the tensions caused by this choice of language were no less salient in cases of successful exposure to English-language instruction, as is exemplified by Baba Pundat, the head of a Bhangi (ex-Untouchable) family. At the beginning of my research, this family had 16 members spread across three generations and living together.[17] Two of the sons ran the prosperous spare-part workshops started by their father decades earlier. Baba, in his early seventies, recalled the early days when he had to follow his caste's calling (scavenging) and had to struggle hard through the educational system, paying for his studies by working as a mechanic. His educational beginnings were harsh; he remembered not being allowed to sit within the classroom at the primary school because of his 'caste untouchability'. He was allowed to follow the class only from beyond the threshold of the classroom. Baba managed to study up to Class VII in the Marathi medium at Kolhapur New High School before switching to English Class V. He left school after Class VI. In the next two generations, those who could handle studying in English were sent to English-medium institutions, regardless of gender, while the less academically able ones went to Marathi-medium ones. Some of the English-educated children went for higher education and later on secured middle-ranking jobs in a company and the local administration. In spite of this, Baba, for whom (particularly English) education was a precious asset and represented a means of escaping the socio-economic status ascribed to him by his caste, as well as the stigma attached to it, often expressed a sense of unresolved tension between the desirability of learning in one's 'mother tongue' and that of acquiring the linguistic proficiency necessary to achieve a higher socio-economic status. Baba, who had consciously pushed the ablest among his offspring into English-medium instruction, would sometimes confide that he had 'made a mistake' (*majhe cukle*), because 'one should definitely learn in one's mother tongue' (*matru bhashemadhyec shiklec pahije*).

In stark contrast to this attachment to the Marathi language found even among Marathi speakers who have recently opted for English education, language does not seem to be of such absolute value among parents belonging to minority communities. For them, rather, it is a relative matter: language is not specifically associated with a sense of belonging to a particular community and the choice of a medium of instruction is dependent on its immediate value for enabling communication in business situations, especially among merchant families.

Many examples of this pattern were to be found among Jains, who were concerned with educating their offspring not so much in English as in a 'commerce-friendly' medium congenial for conducting business. Among the first generation of migrants (from nearby Kannada-speaking Karnataka), when linguistic and social integration into Maharashtra had not yet been fully effected, the choice of instruction medium was not between Marathi and English but between the state and community languages (Marathi or Kannada). In the next generation, this strategic choice would be reproduced, but between Marathi and English. As one of the elderly female members, Sunila Shaha, said, the family needed at least one son to be educated in English for the purpose of joining the family business, although this had hitherto been conducted in Kannada. In this example, educational choices were not significantly determined by a sense of belonging to an original linguistic community. Rather, what was at stake was economic and social integration within the regional, and later on, wider, network. Similar strategies were found among Muslim merchant families. In these cases, then, language *per se* does not matter, and Marathi serves a purpose similar to English in the next generation.

Interestingly, Sunila's daughter Sucheta, who had been educated in Marathi and whose son and daughter were then studying in Marathi as well, also seemed critical of those allegedly embracing English-medium instruction *en masse*, in a way very similar to some affluent families in Bombay and Pune. Sucheta's socio-economic status was partly dependent on the acquisition of English education by some prominent members in her family a generation earlier, and she felt that her family's status was potentially threatened if English education was to become available to other sections of the population.

Being Indian the Global Way: Speaking Regional, National and Cosmopolitan Languages

Even among privileged sections of the population who have had long-standing access to English-medium instruction, however, language may still be tied up with issues of identity in a variety of ways, some less predictable than others. At issue here is whether the tensions between dominant regional identities largely premised on linguistic factors, and economic and financial constraints are irresolvable, or whether a *modus vivendi* can be found to reconcile them in the construction of a new, or different, Indian identity. In some cases, at least, it seems that English instruction is not necessarily antithetical to the transmission of regional and national linguistic identities, as illustrated by the case of Prakash Mankekar and his wife, Raminder Gotra Singh, who were introduced earlier. Let me return to them, because their case provides an interesting contrast with that of the headmistress, Kalloli Bai.

Prakash and Raminder, like their parents, were both educated in English. Their eight-year old son Gautam has always been taught in an English-medium educational environment. Interestingly, however, there was a marked change in the way Prakash and Raminder apprehended the issue of language after their son's birth. Before, Prakash used to publicly claim a lack of proficiency in Marathi in spite of being a totally fluent 'native speaker', as I had realized during conversations with monolingual Marathi speakers. Raminder, whose (Punjabi) family is based in Delhi, has a very similar linguistic history, and the couple never interacted in any other language but English. After Gautam's birth, they started speaking Marathi (Prakash) and Hindi (Raminder) at home, so as to ensure their son's proficiency in both languages. When I first met Prakash and Raminder again after their son's birth, they explained how it had been difficult to switch back into their 'first' languages owing to lack of practice, but they had consciously and deliberately endeavoured to regain verbal proficiency. They explained their reasons as follows.

Although Gautam's English education was not at issue, it also had become extremely important for Prakash and Raminder that he should not only feel at home in English in India and abroad (where part of both families have migrated), but also that their son should acquire the linguistic skills to enable him to interact and feel at ease with *all* Indians anywhere in India. (They assumed that Hindi had now become reasonably acceptable in the central and southern states.) This was what being Indian today meant to them. Such a linguistic definition of 'Indianness' of course depends upon ideological choices as much as on available linguistic resources. In his parents' decision to choose to bring up Gautam speaking Marathi and Hindi as fluently as English, it is important that he is a Maharashtrian on his father's side and lives in Maharashtra, but also regularly visits his mother's family in Delhi. This kind of linguistic definition of Indianness is still limited to rather privileged sections of the population. But it may also become more widespread in the years to come along with, or rather in competition with, the increasing prominence of a *swadeshi* definition of Indianness largely associated with Hindu markers of political identity, as in the brand packaged by Hindutva politicians and some government officials today.

Conclusion: Globalization at the Grassroots Level

The issues of language and education are complex ones in Maharashtra today inasmuch as attachment to a regional or national language is increasingly negotiated by parents in relation to strategies and economic opportunities furthered by the phenomenon of 'globalization'. An exploration of parental choices of medium for primary instruction in Kolhapur has helped to unravel some of the tensions involved in such negotiation. Social agents' strategies vis-à-vis educational institutions and linguistic systems may vary according to how they construct their identities in terms of a compromise between love of language and strategic interest.

Although some parents are seizing on private English-medium instruction, the same is true of private Marathi-medium education. As became clear in the course of research, demographic factors have to be taken into account in this context. It is no secret to anybody that the population in India has risen steadily since independence, but state educational facilities, like other types of facilities, have not improved accordingly (Biswas and Raju 2002). Primary education has suffered the most, continuing a tradition dating back to colonial times that has favoured secondary and university education at the expense of a mass education system (cf Basu 1974; Naik and Nurullah 1988;

Viswanathan 1998). As a result, almost 60 years after independence the average literacy level in India is a mere 65.38 per cent (Census 2001) – much lower than in other non-European countries of comparable economic development. Moreover, the general public holds ordinary state schools in low esteem. Teachers are often accused of lack of commitment and interest in their jobs (high rates of absenteeism are often mentioned), and facilities are often said to be poor. As a consequence, even state-school-educated people tend to send their children to privately-run schools which, although not always offering better teaching conditions, are reputed to be run seriously and with dedicated teachers. In itself, however, this is not evidence that English-medium instruction, at least at the primary level, is gaining significant ground at the expense of the vernacular, and in fact vernacular education has expanded at the same or an even higher rate. Where there have been significant changes, it is, on the whole, at either extreme: among the very well off or among the traditionally downtrodden who have risen up the social ladder under particular circumstances.

Lastly, the linguistic question also brings home considerations of more general importance regarding 'globalization'. The phenomenon should be studied not only in relation to its presumed effects on local situations, as reported by the media and expressed by some anxious elite circles, but also by examining variations at intermediary levels – whether local (Kolhapur), regional (Maharashtra) or national (India) – and within various social and cultural groups. Only then can we gain some precise documentation and real understanding of the globalization that is purportedly occurring today.

To return to the beginning of this chapter, we may interpret the Maharashtra state government's decision to introduce English basics to Marathi primary schools as a cunning political move, which both serves to preserve the interests of the upper classes, reassured in their monopoly over English education, and fulfils a populist, demagogic purpose for those members of less advantaged classes tempted by English-medium instruction. Yet we may also want to see this policy as aimed at placating a majority of Marathi-speaking middle classes who, as we have seen, are still torn between an education they see as crucially relevant to their linguistic, cultural and political identity, and a more strategically useful, 'globalization-oriented' instruction.

Even in an epoch of globalization, language use reflects rational choices (economic, political, ideological and so on) and acutely crystallizes senses of belonging, serving as a vehicle for the expression of passionate attachment linked to the affirmation of regional and national identities. But these identities are also fragmented ones, split between and overlapping regional, national and global dimensions. Interestingly, such a situation is to some extent resonant with that prevailing in some parts of nineteenth-century colonial India. In this respect, Revel's discussion of micro-history in which he seeks to identify the mediations existing between 'individual rational and collective identity' (Revel 1996: 24) is particularly apposite here. According to Revel, in 'global history' each actor undergoes various processes at various levels, from the most local to the most global (ibid.: 26). And it is at various levels and playing with scales of analysis (economic, historical, sociological, anthropological) that we can identify crucial moments and processes at play in linguistic situations and in the construction of senses of belonging. Only then can we begin to understand the myriad ways in which these individual and familial lives so dear to anthropological scrutiny actually articulate with larger processes of local, national and global history.

Epilogue: of Passions and Interests

According to Albert Hirschman, capitalism in the seventeenth and eighteenth centuries was invented as the panacea for preserving society, inasmuch as it was a means of quelling the religious and other passions that had proved so destructive to British and European society (1977). To Hirschman it is no exaggeration to see capitalism as being part of a 'civilizing mission', in which economic and religious or social goals are reconciled. It is noteworthy that such a view legitimized the colonial mission associated with the development of capitalism outside Europe – for instance, in other parts of the former British Empire. Even the Utilitarian doctrine was imbued with civilizing ideals wherein 'the ideals of altruism and the strongest claims of self-interest coincided' (Stokes 1989: 46). Taking such a reconciliatory perspective between capitalist and social objectives may help to shed light on the complex and often apparently contradictory arguments put forward by social actors (administrators, traders, missionaries, and so on) who laid claim to local resources, human or material.

In this respect, it is important that English was one of the European languages associated from the very beginning with capitalist enterprise. Acquisition of the English language opened up economic avenues whereby the rewards of capitalism reached local (often elite) people, but in keeping with the ethos of a civilizing mission, the language also has a divine aspect, at least in the eyes of eighteenth- and nineteenth-century philologists.[18] In colonial India English was perceived by some educationalists, both British and to some extent Indian, as the means to rescue some sections of the local population from ignorance and obscurantism, providing them with entry into the realm of Christian morality (Bénéï 2001b).

In some ways, then, the passions elicited by religion in Europe, and Britain in particular, were quelled by bringing modern capitalism to the colonies in association with languages deemed to be endowed with an inherently Christian quality. Ironically, such divine essence never fully transcended existing religious antagonisms within the European world. What is also noteworthy is that by shifting the locus of passion from religion to capitalism and exporting the latter to the colonies, Europeans also brought with them their passion for their own languages. These were part and parcel of the colonial encounter, and were matched by strong linguistic attachments on the part of the local populations. It is also likely that the passionate dimension of Indian languages, which has been documented for certain parts of India (cf Ramaswamy 1997 for Tamil Nadu), was heightened in the course of a renewed linguistic awareness brought about by negotiations between various groups of social actors, both British (administrators, traders, educationalists, missionaries) and Indian (Sanskrit pundits, speakers of Hindi, Urdu or Marathi, social reformers and freedom fighters). As we have seen, vernacular linguistic passions remain very much alive and Cardinal de Retz's statement still holds good.

Notes

1 The data for this chapter were collected in the course of fieldwork conducted from 1998 to end of 2000 in primary schools in Kolhapur, southern Maharashtra, thanks to a generous grant from ESRC. In addition to observation in schools, interviews were also carried out with children, parents and teachers. This chapter was presented in different versions at the Globalization workshop, LSE, September 2001 and at Columbia University, February 2004. Thanks are due to all those present who helped to refine the argument.

2 The official objective was to give children the opportunity to acquaint themselves with this foreign language so that learning it becomes easier for them in Class V. This policy took effect in the academic year starting in July 2000. In all the schools that I visited in Kolhapur city and district in the following months, its implementation had actually been effective. Children were taught songs with mimes from Class I onwards.

3 See in this respect A. G. Hopkins's illuminating collective volume (2002a) and in particular, the chapters by Hopkins and by C. A. Bayly for a discussion and categorization of the different phases of globalization in world history. Briefly, these authors distinguish between 'archaic', 'proto-', 'modern' and 'post-colonial' globalization. What they also emphasize is that globalization has never been a continuous linear process but that different forms of globalization have been ruptured by phases of 'deglobalization', the last of them persisting from World War I until the mid-1970s.

4 Six languages are thus officially recognized as 'native tongues' in Maharashtra, namely Marathi, Hindi, Urdu, English, Gujarati, and Sindhi. In some areas of southern Maharashtra bordering Karnataka, an allowance is made for Kannada.

5 The latest illustration of vernacular dominance was the translation in the 1980s of the whole series of the Gazetteers pertaining to the former Bombay Presidency from English into Marathi, which was instigated by the then Congress state government. On this reappropriation of colonial documents by local, regional and national imaginings, see Bénéï (1999).

6 On European attempts to vernacularize the concept of a universal language and to impose English as an international language of discovery from the early seventeenth to the mid-nineteenth centuries, see Mikosz (1998). Mikosz also brings to light the influence of non-English and non-European languages upon an understanding of language by English theorists.

7 In the first decades of the British Raj, Urdu was favoured by the East India Company as the administrative and commercial language (Cohn 1997; King 1992).

8 That this is no longer due to the economic dominance of British interests, which have long been superseded by American ones, is in this respect irrelevant.

9 As shown by the setting up of the education department in the Bombay Presidency from the 1840s onwards (Bénéï 2001b; 2002). See also Naregal (2001).

10 *Report of the Board of Education of the Bombay Presidency* of 1845.

11 *Report of the Board of Education of the Bombay Presidency* of 1855.

12 In this respect, one might note an ironic twist to the linguistic trend towards the use of English as a 'cosmopolitan language', inasmuch as this trend is renewing a phenomenon of linguistic cosmopolitanism attested in the form of Sanskrit on the South Asian subcontinent before the first millennium (Pollock 1998). Cosmopolitan Sanskrit steadily waned from about the late tenth century onwards, as it was gradually replaced by emerging distinctive vernacular literatures and court cultures. (The recent repeated moves by the Hindutva-dominated central government to assert that Sanskrit is *the* unifying national language may be read as a counter-move towards recovering something of an indigenous cosmopolitan culture; see Ramaswamy [1999].) Throughout the nineteenth century, learning was epitomised by the mastery of English, becoming 'a social substitute for the ancient system of learning the Sanskrit language' (Nemade 1990: 3). The 'transition from Sanskrit bilingualism to English bilingualism', started in the first two decades of the nineteenth century, was completed in its last quarter (ibid.: 5). The Sanskrit superlanguage thus gave way to the English superlanguage, with the added consequence of enabling links with literary and cultural forms beyond Asia. On discussions about the adoption of English as lingua franca in India, see *The Journal of the Bombay Branch of the Royal Asiatic Society*, Vol. IV, 1853, p. 289, 'On the geographical distribution of the principal languages of India, and the feasibility of introducing English as a lingua franca', by Sir Erskine Perry, President of the Society, as well as *Bombay Quarterly Magazine and Review, 1852-1853*, Vol. III, pp. 230–1. On hierarchies of language and their subversion by speakers in general, see Burke and Porter (1991: Part II).

13 Lack of space permits no further details. See, for instance, *Report of the Board of Education for the year 1846*, no. VI, 1847, Bombay, American Mission Press, pp. 7–8; *Board of Education, Superintendent, Presidency Division. Bombay*, 1850, Henry Green's report on vernacular education, no. 2 of 1850, dated 19 February; and *Education Department, Bombay*, Vol. II, no. 610, p. 9. It is worth comparing these with reports bemoaning the overt resistance expressed by some local populations against British education on grounds of poverty and limited trade within the locality. See, for instance, *General Department, Bombay*, Vol. 27, no. 1077 of 1853, sections 12–14.

14 *Bombay Saturday Review of Politics, Literature and Commerce* of 1861, Vol. II, April to Sept. Bombay, Exchange Press: 234–5.

15 The Marathi term 'firangi' stems from the English word 'foreigner' and although it means more generally a European, it carries an implicit reference to the colonial period and British power. Today, it is commonly used in a slightly derogatory way.

16 The notion of 'mother tongue' is closely articulated with notions of motherly love and sense of belonging to a common *ethnos* and territory, both aspects being examined at length in a book in preparation.

17 The patriarch, fondly named Baba by the family members, his wife, their eldest 'widowed' daughter with one of her two children, as well as their three sons with their respective wives and two children each.

18 Thus wrote an anonymous author in *Blackwood's Magazine* about 'Grimm's Teutonic Grammar' (47, May 1840: 216): English is 'the noblest language Divine goodness has instituted for the use of man'.

Bibliography

Aarsleff, Hans (1983) *The Study of Language in England, 1780–1860*. London: Athlone Press.

Basu, Aparna (1974) *The Growth of Education and Political Development in India, 1898–1920*. Delhi: Oxford University Press.

Bayly, C. A. (2002) '"Archaic" and "modern" globalization in the Eurasian and African arena, *c*.1750–1850', in A.G. Hopkins, ed., *Globalization in World History*. London, Pimlico; 47–73.

Bénéï, Véronique (1997) 'Education, industrialization and socio-economic development: some reflections for further sociological research in western India', in Véronique Bénéï and Loraine Kennedy, eds, *Industrial Decentralization and Urban Development*. Pondicherry: French Institute, Pondy Papers in Social Sciences, 23: 101–8.

—— (1999) 'Reappropriating colonial documents in Kolhapur (Maharashtra): variations on a nationalist theme', *Modern Asian Studies*, 33 (4): 913–50.

—— (2001a) 'Teaching nationalism in Maharashtra schools', in C. J. Fuller and Véronique Bénéï, eds, *The Everyday State and Society in Modern India*. London: Hurst & Co.; 194–221.

—— (2001b) 'A passion for order: vernacular languages in the nineteenth-century Bombay Presidency', paper presented at the South Asian Studies Programme, Asian Studies Centre, St Antony's College, Oxford, 23 January.

—— (2002) 'Missing indigenous bodies: educational enterprise and Victorian morality in the mid-nineteenth century Bombay Presidency', *Economic and Political Weekly*, 37 (17): 1647–54.

Biswas, Barnali and Saraswati Raju (2002) 'Maharashtra: a socio-special analysis of literacy trends with special reference to the 2001 census', paper presented at the Seminar on Progress of Literacy in India: *What the 2001 census reveals*, NIEPA, New Delhi, 5 October.

Bourdieu, Pierre (1985 [1977]) *Outline of a Theory of Practice*. Cambridge: Cambridge University Press.

—— (2003 [1984]) *Distinction: A social critique of the judgement of taste*. New York/ London: Routledge.

Brass, Paul (1997 [1990]) *The Politics of India Since Independence*. Cambridge: Cambridge University Press.

Breckenridge, Carol and Peter van der Veer, eds (1993) *Orientalism and the Postcolonial Predicament: Perspectives on South Asia*. Philadelphia: University of Pennsylvania Press.

Burke, Peter and Roy Porter, eds (1991) *Language, Self and Society: A social history of language*. Cambridge: Polity Press.

Carrithers, Michael and Caroline Humphrey, eds (1991) *The Assembly of Listeners: Jains in society*. Cambridge: Cambridge University Press.

Carter, Anthony T. (1974) *Elite Politics in Rural India: Political Stratification and Alliances in Western Maharashtra*. London: Cambridge University Press.

Cohn, Bernard S. (1997 [1996]) 'The command of language and the language of command', in *Colonialism and Its Forms of Knowledge: The British in India*. Princeton: Princeton University Press; 16–56.

—— (1998 [1987]) 'Regions subjective and objective: their relation to the study of modern Indian history and society', in *An Anthropologist Among the Historians and Other Essays*. Delhi: Oxford University Press; 100–35.

Cooper, Frederick and Ann Laura Stoler, eds (1997) *Tensions of Empire: Colonial Cultures in a bourgeois world*. California/ London: University of California Press.

Crystal, David (1997) *English as a Global Language*. Cambridge: Cambridge University Press.

Gellner, Ernest (1983) *Nations and Nationalism*. Oxford: Oxford University Press.

Harper, T. N. (2002) 'Empire, diaspora and the languages of globalism, 1850–1914', in A.G. Hopkins, ed., *Globalization in World History*. London: Pimlico; 141–66.

Hastings, Adrian (1999 [1997]) *The Construction of Nationhood: Ethnicity, religion and nationalism*. Cambridge: Cambridge University Press.

Hirschman, Albert (1977) *The Passions and the Interests: Political arguments for capitalism before its triumph*. Princeton: Princeton University Press.

Hobsbawm, Eric J. (1997 [1990]) *Nations and Nationalism Since 1780: Programme, myth, reality*. Cambridge: Cambridge University Press.

Hopkins, A. G., ed. (2002a) *Globalization in World History*. London: Pimlico.

Hopkins, A. G. (2002b) 'Introduction: globalization – an agenda for historians', in A. G. Hopkins, ed., *Globalization in World History*. London: Pimlico; 1–10.

Hopkins, A. G. (2002c) 'The history of globalization – and the globalization of history?', in A. G. Hopkins, ed., *Globalization in World History*. London: Pimlico; 11–46.

Kaviraj, Sudipta (1992) 'Writing, speaking, being: language and the historical formation of identities in India', in D. Hellman, Rajanayagam and D. Rothermund, eds, *Nationalstaat und Sprachkonflikte in Süd- und Südostasien*. Stuttgart: Steiner; 28–65.

Khilnani, Sunil (1998) *The Idea of India*. New Delhi: Penguin Books.

King, Christopher R. (1992) 'Images of virtue and vice: the Hindi-Urdu controversy in two nineteenth-century Hindi plays', in Kenneth W. Jones, ed., *Religious Controversy in British India: Dialogues in South-Asian languages*: 123–48.

Kumar, Krishna (1992) 'Hindu revivalism and education in north-central India', in M. Marty and S. Appleby, eds, *Fundamentalisms and Society*. Chicago: University of Chicago Press; 536–57.

—— (1994) *Learning from Conflict*. Delhi: Orient Longman.

Matthew, Anjilvel V. (1988 [1957]) *Karmaveer Bhaurao Patil*. Satara: Rayat Shikshan Samstha.

Metcalf, Thomas R. (1995) *Ideologies of the Raj*. Cambridge: Cambridge University Press.

Mikosz, David (1998) 'Eurocentric views of universal languages from 1605 to 1828', *Itinerario*, 22 (2): 103–15.

Naik, J. P. and Syed Nurullah (1995 [1945]) *A Students' History of Education in India, 1800–1973*. Delhi: Macmillan.

Naregal, Veena (2001) *Language Politics, Elites and the Public Sphere: Western India under Colonialism*. Delhi: Permanent Black.

Nemade, Bhalchandra (1990) *The Influence of English on Marathi: A sociolinguistic study*. Kolhapur: Rajhans.

Pollock, Sheldon (1998) 'India in the vernacular millennium: literary culture and polity, 1000–1500', *Daedalus*, 127 (3): 41–74.

162   GLOBALIZING INDIA

Ramaswamy, Sumathi (1997) *Passions of the Tongue: Language devotion in Tamil India, 1891–1970.* Berkeley: University of California Press.
—— (1999) 'Sanskrit for the nation', *Modern Asian Studies*, Vol. 33, No. 2: 339–82.
Revel, Jacques, ed. (1996) *Jeux d'échelles, La micro-analyse à l'expérience.* Paris: Gallimard/Le Seuil, Coll. Hautes Etudes.
Stokes, Eric (1989 [1959]) *The English Utilitarians and India.* Delhi: Oxford University Press.
Varma, Pavan K. (1998) *The Great Indian Middle Class.* New Delhi: Viking.
Viswanathan, Gauri (1998 [1989]) *Masks of Conquest: Literary study and British rule in India.* Delhi: Oxford University Press.
Zastoupil, Lynn and Martin Moir, eds (1999) *The Great Indian Education Debate: Documents relating to the Orientalist-Anglicist controversy, 1781–1843.* London: Curzon Press.

Archival Documents

Blackwood's Magazine, 47, May 1840.
Board of Education, Superintendent, Presidency Division, Bombay, 1850.
Bombay Quarterly Magazine and Review, 1852–1853, Vol. III.
Bombay Saturday Review of Politics, Literature and Commerce of 1861 (Vol. II, April to Sept), Bombay, Exchange Press.
Education Department, Bombay, Vol. II, no. 610 of 1851, p. 9, Maharashtra State Archives.
General Department, Bombay, Vol. 27, no. 1077 of 1853, sections 12–14, Maharashtra State Archives.
Journal of the Bombay Branch of the Royal Asiatic Society, Vol. IV, 1853.
Report of the Board of Education of the Bombay Presidency of 1845, Bombay.
Report of the Board of Education for the year 1846, no. VI, 1847, Bombay, American Mission Press.

Government Publication (Marathi)

Shivaji Chhatrapati, iyatta cauthi, Itihas, nagarikashastra ani prashasan (1995 [1992]) Pune: Maharashtra Rajya Patthyapustak nirmiti va abhyaskram sanshodhan mandal.

PART THREE:
CULTURE AND RELIGION

MAPS OF AUDIENCES: BOMBAY FILMS, THE FRENCH TERRITORY AND THE MAKING OF AN 'OBLIQUE' MARKET

Emmanuel Grimaud

For the film producers and distributors of Bombay (Mumbai), the foreign territories (or 'the Overseas') are not an abstract entity but an active field of transactions made up of unequally profitable areas. Called 'the sixth territory' on the distribution map, the Overseas are in fact a conglomerate of distant and fragmented spaces.[1] If the Middle East, Africa and the traditional locations of the Indian diaspora have been among the privileged destinations for Indian film prints for many years, it seems that several elements altered the film production game significantly at the turn of the twenty-first century and considerably modified the status of the Overseas in the minds of Indian producers.

After the debacle of his film *Trimurti* (1995), the film director Subhash Ghai declared that he was making his next film *Pardesh* (shot partly in the United States, partly in Mysore) for the diaspora and that the latter was a more secure market than India itself. In spite of a more limited audience, the diaspora was offering incomparable profits and paradoxically seemed, to many filmmakers, to be more receptive and easier to reach than the local audience. The producers often used the rhetoric of globalization to justify strategic attempts to redirect their efforts towards this distant public, presented in the film press as an Eldorado to escape the crisis of local taste variability. This reorientation also seemed quite safe for many film professionals because it did not imply a major redefinition of their narrative conventions. In their fluctuating search for an all-India audience, Bombay filmmakers have been exploiting for a long time the cinematic potential of Overseas locations and diasporic settings and resources.[2] However, in the 1990s the diaspora was promoted as an essential but ambiguous partner of a bigger conquest that compelled the filmmakers to invent new devices of relocalization at both the shooting and post-production stages.[3] A multitude of dubbing experiments were conducted by Bombay film distributors playing with the Overseas in order to multiply their chances of good financial returns. Supported in their quest for new territories by a diffuse network of film exhibition that is also difficult to control, the Indian distributors rarely tried to reach traditional western audiences head-on. Countering a preconceived (and inoperative) idea of the 'global market' as a unified entity, many believed in gradual distribution, hoping that through the diaspora the Overseas circuit would open itself up progressively .

Searching for a larger public on the map, the distributors often encountered partial audiences, but some of them had wider scope than others. A good example that provides a starting-point for an analysis of strategies carried out under the label of 'globalization' is that of the home-made dubbing of a popular Hindi film for the French-speaking territories.

Instead of trying to address the entire French market, the distributor chose to reach a highly localized point on the planet, to intrigue a strategic set of spectators (located somewhere on a French-speaking island) who had never been exploited, intended to give him access to a larger audience (the French public). I will describe how this curious experiment with geography took place and how the dubbing-room gave rise to a surprising product that referred to a potential but uncertain 'proto-public' (an imagined audience-in-the-making). I will also show how unintended viewing circuits had already emerged far from the dubbing-room and were almost ignored by the distributors. Combining these elements together will help us to understand how an 'oblique' market was formed or produced in different ways and how distance itself was a productive agent in this process.[4] I use the term 'oblique' to designate the alternative route taken by the distributors to approach the French territory. The ambivalent status of the dubbing room in which they could perform their lip-synch experiment will be analysed in this chapter. If a screening can be seen as an encounter between an imaginary audience and a real one who have to be convinced, in this case the dubbing surgery added a new layer to the encounter and gave rise to a productive clash.

The Globe as an Experimental Field

'Do you know that today the distribution of Bombay films has gone global?'

In 1998 Yashraj Films decided to dub one of their most popular films, *Dil to Pagal Hai* (hereafter DTPH; informally known in English as *The Heart is Crazy*), into French. Why did Yashraj choose a territory on the map which was at that time more or less ignoring Hindi movies? Another well-known production house, Rajshri Pictures, had made a similar attempt a few years earlier with their film *Maine Pyaar Kiya*, but the endeavour failed. The film producer and distributor Yash Chopra (Yashji) was actually encouraged to explore the possibility of a new market by film importers in Mauritius, who were convinced that a French version would appeal to French-speaking Indians and thereby give new life to the original film.

Yashji gave the project to an important dubbing director in Bombay, Lila Ghosh (Lilaji). She delegated the dubbing direction to her daughter Mona, who asked me if I might work for her as a language supervisor. At the first meeting Yashji told us that the distribution of Hindi films had gone global and that new markets and new audiences were emerging. This worldwide movement was an opportunity that should be seized.

'We have decided to undertake an experiment,' Yashji said. 'If the French version of DTPH works in Mauritius, we will be the first to do it and we will send it to other French territories – and maybe even to your native country.' The dubbing was to be done in Yashraj Film Studio with the company's own sound recordist. It would be a truly home-made product.

A student from the Alliance Française had written a translation, but with little thought for words or expressions. The noble language of the original was replaced by a pale dialogue with no poetic sentiment. The theme 'What is love?' (*mohabbat kya hai?*) was established by Yashji's voiceover at the beginning of the film and reinforced by the interaction between the characters, played by the actors Madhuri Dixit (as Pooja) and Shahrukh Khan (as Rahul). Pooja believed an external force would lead her to her beloved, but Rahul was more sceptical. 'Someone … somewhere … is made for you', declared the trailer. The film was based on a quadrilateral relationship: Nisha (played by Karisma Kapoor) was in love with her childhood friend, Rahul, who was more attracted to Pooja, who was loved by her old friend Ajay (played by Akshay Kumar).

At our second meeting, Yashji wanted to know whether such a quadrilateral relationship would interest a French audience, beyond the Indian diaspora.

'The film is about characters who can't control their destiny and struggle to discover and reveal what is inside them. Is there enough psychology for a French audience?', he asked.

And Mona added: 'I love the film because it is true. There is always somebody made for us in this world!'

I was sceptical about the acceptability to a French audience of the over-emotionalised romanticism of certain scenes and the naivety of some of the dialogue, especially the scene in which Pooja explains the significance of

Valentine's Day to her friend Anjali in a big shopping centre. Contrary to other films that could be categorized as 'exotic' products, DTPH at first glance was not exotic at all. This was definitely not an image of India that the French public would be expecting. How it might appeal to them was a question that would come up again and again during the dubbing process. The dubbed version of DTPH had to reach two audiences instead of one: a public familiar with Hindi films who had seen the original version many times, and another, new public. According to the distributors' plan, this second audience would have to be approached slowly, with the support of the first one.

When a Dubbing-Room Becomes a Language Laboratory

This was not the right moment to solve the problem of French perceptions of Hindi films, however, because the French audience was not the main target. The distributors depended on a strategy designed to appeal first to the French diaspora and then through it, by degrees, to reach the French public. Another factor reinforced their confidence in these tactics. French-speaking Indian dubbing artists were rare in Bombay and they had to be trained on the spot. Yashji rejected my suggestion that he should send the film to a French dubbing studio in Paris. He wanted it to be dubbed in Bombay with local artists. If the experiment was to be repeated, they would have created a stock of available French-speaking artists. Not only were the costs of a move to Paris too high but he also preferred to create a trained and visible network close to home.

'I want Indian dubbing artists with an Indian accent,' Yashji added. 'People must see that it is an Indian film and an Indian story!' He charged the dubbing director with creating a 'diaspora-oriented' French, declaring, 'I don't want any dialect in my film. I want a French language with an Indian accent that can be exported everywhere in the French territories!' He was convinced that a film in an exportable Indianized French was the best way to attract not only the diaspora but other viewers, since the dialogue itself would convey a kind of exoticism.

We were helped by being able to make use of the original film sets (a futuristic dance theatre, ultra-modernist interiors, an urban landscape, a modern shopping centre), which were so generic that the story might be taking place in Bombay, London or Beverly Hills. Although the original characters were from Bombay, they could as well have been from London or New York.

'If the story can happen anywhere, why not Paris?', said Mona.

Scenes were shot both in Bombay and foreign settings. Most of the time, the spectator did not need to know where the story was precisely located to appreciate it. One scene in an airport merely suggested that a character was going to London, and another that someone had come from Khandala (near Bombay). Locational vagueness is a basic essential that makes future relocations easier. At the same time, many of the modernist locations used in a Hindi film shot in foreign cities or reconstructed inside a studio (such as a Beverly Hills interior) become generically identified on screen as 'Bombay places'. The dubbing of DTPH added another layer to these already existing ambiguities.

Yashji had transformed a constraint (the impossibility of sending his film for dubbing in France) into an advantage by asking the dubbing director to use a language that could not be identified with any of the existing French-speaking Indian communities, but that would be a generalized hybrid Indo-French. The characters would have a strong Indian accent and they would not be asked to play native French people, but Indian migrants settled in France. For two months Yashraj Studio became a curious laboratory experimenting with words and overseas communities. The sound recordist sardonically called it 'the French dubbing laboratory'.

Uncertain Locations, or How to Create a New Contrast of Voices Inside a Dubbing-Room

The studio process not only played with words but also recreated human emotions, constructing a new list of players different from the original community of actors. Mona and I gathered the only French-speaking actors we could find in Bombay, but there were not enough to complete the full DTPH cast, so to make up the numbers we had to choose either French-speaking Indians with no training in acting or Indian actors with no experience of French. We selected a few actors who had learned French in childhood. Girls from the Alliance Française came with their mothers, hoping for a glamorous contract. An Anglo-Indian girl with a Quebec accent phoned Yashji every day, hoping for a break in Hindi films.

Yashji brought some Mauritian film importers along to the dubbing-room, with the idea of selling at least a part of the product in advance. 'None of these voices is any good,' one of them said to me during the test. 'Don't waste time trying to get them to express emotions!'

However the ultimate decision was Yashji's: it was for him to approve the final panel of voices. He repeated again what he had told us before. 'My distributors want *Indian flavour*.' A Marathi actress, Iravati Harshe, dubbed Madhuri Dixit's voice, and a Bengali assistant director, Mritika Mukherjee, dubbed Karisma Kapoor. Devan Varma, who played the role of Madhuri's father in the original, was a personal friend of Yashji and wanted to dub his own voice. 'Let me try. I know Marathi, Gujarati, Malayalam, Tamil, English, German and French,' he said proudly. A well-known actress of the Marathi screen, Nina Kulkarni, dubbed Madhuri's mother. Atul Kumar, a brilliant theatre actor from Delhi, played the role of Akshay Kumar. Arguing that French and Bengali tones were not very different from one another, Mona herself dubbed several female voices without knowing a single word of French. She worked on the basis of a Devanagari transcription. Yashji approved all the voices except the substitute Shahrukh's, and asked me to try. I had no experience in dubbing, but to my surprise he found my performance artistically credible.

If a French-speaking Indian could easily identify the origin of each actor through his accent, a French native could perceive other differences. Devan Varma sounded like a Polish migrant, Karisma was shifting between German and North African tonal values, and Madhuri's French accent was closer to Eastern European. In their variability, the voices suggested other locations. This diversity was accidental, but the importer noticed it. 'Good contrast!', he said. Before leaving the studio, he looked at the translation and advised: 'Be collo-quial and romantic as well. The Mauritian people are our target. They will come and hear the songs, and they will enjoy the scenes in French, especially Shahrukh's voice!'

Once the casting was completed, Yashji and the importer disappeared, and Lilaji (via her daughter Mona) was in charge inside the dubbing-room.

'Whose Language Is It?', or The Birth of a Home-made Alien

Yashji remained invisible during the dubbing process and delegated to Lilaji the responsibility for recreating a family of Indians who had recently migrated to France. Whereas the conventional dubbing director replaces one language with another, Lilaji was asked to use two languages to construct a third one. She considered the French language dull and unemotional, whereas Hindi qualified as 'a highly emotional language'. Mona therefore urged us to let 'the Indian emotions come through'. Taking responsibility for the transfer of emotions from one language to the other, Lilaji sometimes distorted the French dialogue to such an extent that it sounded violently overdramatic.

The dubbing artiste had first to listen to the original sound track and then work out the tone and emotional values. What Mona had meant by 'Indian emo-tions' became clear when she compared the performance of two female dubbing artistes, Nina and Aban. The first was playing the role of Madhuri's dance teacher in the film. Her French was not very good, but she was originally a the-atre actress, whereas Aban was a teacher from the Alliance Française with no experience of acting. Of Nina's performance Mona said, 'She gives much more variation than the original. It has nothing to do with language, but I think she understands emotions very well.' As the days passed, Mona gained experience in judging the emotional content of a dialogue in French. She frequently asked the dubbing artiste to place the emphases exactly as they were in the original dialogue. When she found the original sound track too dull, however, she would invite the dubbing artiste to add tonal differences that were not in the original, 'to bring out the colour', as Lilaji had said.

Each dubbing artiste was taking part in a bizarre game, playing with a language that was not his or her mother tongue. Yashji was not the only one to explore such unfamiliar territory. Devan Varma, the old actor who was playing his own role, took one full day to dub only two scenes and ultimately tore the script into pieces, saying exasperatedly that it had been 40 years since he had learned French. The language supervisor made him repeat each line a hundred times before it became usable, writing the dialogue in Devanagari script. Rehearsal stopped when the actor became tired and sometimes the dialogue was impossible to understand. But later during the screening, the importers were impressed with Devan Varma's stagecraft. 'His performance is the best!', said one of them. Devan Varma had managed to incorporate his own linguistic inability into the role he was playing, making it part of his own character. 'He quite definitely sounds like a Mauritian grandfather,' commented the importer.

And so the purely linguistic mistakes were forgiven, but no emotional underplaying was permitted. Mona and Joshi, the sound recordist, were forever giving the artistes the same instructions, 'More energy!', 'Put more force into it!', 'Project more!', 'It's dull! – Make it more lively!', and so on. The sound recordist demanded even more intensity than in the original or than the dubbing director wanted. The dubbed dialogue was considered as good as the original only if it projected at least the same power (*josh*).

At the end of the dubbing, Lilaji declared that she had created another kind of French, which she called *Frenchi Filmi*. One example will illustrate this weird hybrid. The dubbing director realized that the synchronization with the lip movements was perfect when we chose to keep some of the original Hindi words in the French version. '*Are ja ja*, you'll never find another dancer like me!', says Karisma to Shahrukh in one scene. A satisfying equivalent in French could not be found, so the dubbing director suggested keeping the original *Are ja ja* for its 'Indian flavour'. 'An Indian character might easily use such an expression,' said Lilaji. After a few days, she became extraordinarily confident in judging the emotional quality of a line dubbed in French, without knowing the language. The *Frenchi Filmi* did not simply mix Hindi and French or give rise to new colloquial lines. The dubbing director had

managed to reproduce in another language the tonal differences between one
Hindi word and another, and between the various Indian accents.

Playing with Distance: 'We Have Such Empathy w ith the Original!'

The importers of the French DTPH, convinced by the extract that Yashji had
shown them, were worried about the translation of the title: *Dil to Pagal Hai*.
They wanted it to be like the entire dubbed version: displaying the right
balance, a certain distance from the original – not too far but not too close. *Le
cœur a sa folie* ('The Heart Has Its Own Madness') was proposed as a near-
literal translation.

A new meeting was organized in Yashji's office. 'We have such empathy
with the original,' said the importer. Yashji rejected my suggestion, *L'un pour
l'autre* (*Made For Each Other*). 'It sounds too much Art Cinema or French New
Wave,' he said. Once again, the distributor had to trust somebody else or rely
on his own intuition. He could not blindly accept a proposal without testing it.
He decided to send the titles to Mauritius and wait for feedback. *Mon cœur est
fou* (*My Heart Is Mad*) and *Je les rends folles* (*I Send Them Mad*) were rejected. *Le
coeur rend fou* (*Love Sends You Mad*) was adopted after being tested by the
importers in Mauritius, who extolled this new title's resonance. According to
them, 'It is closer to the original,' and 'People love it very much here in
Mauritius.'

Looking at the final poster, on which the only modification was the title,
was a strange experience. *Le cœur rend fou* appeared to me a little out of place
alongside the actor Shahrukh, looking like John Travolta in *Saturday Night
Fever*, between both the female stars, Madhuri and Karisma. The disparity
between the title and the image, between a poetic language and a brash
modernity, was exactly the kind of outlandish fusion that many film critics
were criticising in the original Hindi films, and especially in relation to the
songs, in which poetic lyrics were often accompanied by sexually suggestive
images. This usually results from an unintentional overlap of input by two
mediators, the lyric writer and the choreographer, each following the dictates
of their art in relative isolation from one another.

Comparing the original poster with the new one, it was as if certain structural aspects of the first had managed to transfer and be affixed to the second.
But there was something else that this new poster was carrying, a new feature
that was not there in the original: the image was the same, but the title was
implicitly a double one, waiting for bilingual deconstruction by the audience.
This laboratory (re)creation, however, was designed only to move the original
to a territory that had never been explored. The distributor and his importer

would now have to wait for the moment of truth, when their distant audience would acclaim or rubbish this supposedly authentic remake.

'Dubbing Is Recreation', or The Philosophy of a Hybrid-Maker

Now that DTPH was almost ready for export, a voice test would help us to identify the precise difference between Lilaji's method, which I shall call a *recreative* mode of dubbing, and a more conventional, transparent dubbing that simply substitutes one version for another without adding any local flavour to it. Of course, a recreative dubbing director like Lilaji also substitutes a second version for a previous one and, conversely, the substitutive dubbing director who believes in fidelity to the original is also recreative, despite pretending that his work is surgically transparent.

A few days after the end of the dubbing of DTPH, Lilaji was looking for a voice with a French accent to dub Jean Reno in *Godzilla*. She gave me a few lines in Hindi as a voice test. After 20 minutes, she said, 'You are a natural artiste, but I am looking for a parody of French, not for a natural French accent.'

How could I imitate my own accent? Lilaji wanted 'French emotion' in the way Yashji wanted 'Indian flavour'. My voice test was used later as a reference point for the dubbing artist to develop a French Hindi to be imitated.

'People must be able to imitate your voice in their everyday lives!', said Lilaji. Dubbed by an Indian dubbing artist, Jean Reno's voice became an exotic variant easily reproducible by the audience.

The voice test was supposed to be sent to Rome, where a supervisor from Columbia was checking the tests of Columbia pictures from all over the world. In the studio, Lilaji was carrying two files – one the translation in Hindi (called 'the Script') and the other the Post-production Book sent by Columbia, in which the dialogue in English was time-coded with a commentary. 'It helps me a lot,' she said. 'This is the Bible of dubbing. You find all the time-codes, the pauses, the spellings, the actions. They send such things because they don't want the dialogue to stray from the original.'

The Post-production Book generated another recreation scenario, describing American behaviour for the dubbing director, who retranslated the Script as she and the artistes worked through it together and modified the instructions given in the book. Dubbing was not in this case a simple 'translation' or 'adaptation'; it was a creative repositioning of words and actions – a means of making them reproducible by others. In making available the Post-production Book, American distributors assume that every foreign-language variant will be identical with the original, but it is an assumption that is not always shared by dubbing companies. Lilaji treated dubbing as a process of generating another form, consciously creating composite versions.

Film distribution is full of recreative networks like the one we have observed. Officially, Hollywood tries to avoid them as much as possible, but cannot do so in practice. Most of Lilaji's contracts came from US distribution companies, but they, of course, had no idea of how she made use of the Post-production Book.

Overlapping Audiences: Someone, Somewhere is More Recreative Than You!

At the time of my enquiry, there were a number of different networks in France for the exhibition of Indian movies. The big cinemas, which showed Asian films and also screened a few selected and commercially successful blockbusters, and the cinemas hired by Tamil film associations to screen Indian films for Indian people, most of the time without subtitles, more or less ignored each other. At the end of the 1990s, many French distribution houses started looking for Hindi films that could be dubbed, rather than subtitled, and shown on TV to a wider audience. Several French distribution houses tried to build up their own network in Bombay, dealing directly with Indian distributors. They considered shortening the films to make them watchable for a French audience, or organizing their own dubbing in a French studio.

One of these companies arranged a big demonstration during the Cannes Film Festival for the local cinema owners to show them the glamour of Bombay film, with their songs and dance sequences. No dialogue was used, but the dance sequences were used as an appetiser – and that was enough to convince many cinema owners. But the Indian distributors sitting in their offices back in Bombay knew nothing about this. Although Yashji was certainly not alone in trying to penetrate a market that might at a distance be regarded as hermetically sealed, his strategy was different from other producers, who tended to trust remote agents and to allow local distribution companies to re-edit their films or dub them as they wanted.

Back in Paris I tried to work out the itinerary of the French version of DTPH. The traditional stores in which Bombay and Tamil films were sold (mostly illegal copies from London and Dubai) had heard of it. The Mauritian shopkeeper said, 'My children don't speak Hindi so I give them this to watch.' But the French distributors specializing in Asian films did not know about DTPH. One of them laughed at me, 'A Bollywood film dubbed into French by an Indian Company? We would have never taken such a risk!' The same distributors had no idea of the existence of alternative theatres in Paris, showing films for the Indian population. Living in the same world, they did not share the same outlook on the world market.

Later, Yashji's assistant sent me the reviews written in Mauritius and given to the importer. He wanted a translation. Surprisingly, these reviews were good – so much so that Yashraj Films was already trying to arrange the dubbing into French of another film. This second initiative by Yashraj Films meant that a market for dubbed versions had evidently come into being. Clearly, the French DTPH had been well received, at least in Mauritius. But who had ensured that it would be so well-received, and how? I was not naive enough to believe that the producer alone was able to create such a market at a distance with a single test product.

The last part of this chapter explores the conditions which enabled such a product to be accepted. These could have been carefully studied by the overseas film importers before a single screening generated any such positive response, but the distributors in Bombay were not aware of this when they decided to start their experiment.

Several film journals published in Mauritius and sold by the Indian stores and video-club complexes surrounding the Gare du Nord in Paris showed me that a pre-existing set of critical tools for appreciating a Hindi film, *and* its dubbed version as an associated product, were already circulating in the Mauritian film press.[5] The *Frenchi Filmi* was nothing compared to the populist, but creative, tone used by these amateur journals, which were reforming the rules of the critical genre, perhaps finding their inspiration in Bombay film reviews rather than in French ones, and thereby unintentionally inventing a new style quite different from the Bollywood Internet websites designed by French amateurs. Whereas these new French Bollywood filmgoers, giving their opinion of their first Bollywood film screening, were using such adjectives as 'fantastic', 'traumatic' and 'dynamic' to speak about Hindi movies, the Mauritian press was less emphatic and more precise, discussing the films in detail.

The physical appearance of a major female star, for instance, generated the following comments:

Rani Mukherjee must beware of the corpulence that seems to be overwhelming her frame. Her largish face has become positively moonlike. Her legs are plump, as indeed is her rump. An actress must be able to keep in shape. The face and the general outline must be pleasing to all. In spite of her serious weight problem, Rani has done well. She acts naturally. Her dances are beautiful. She must just improve her diction.

Whereas Yashji's project gave rise to an ambiguous hybrid – difficult to locate, and open to the public to simply accept or ignore – the Mauritian journal *Film Star Magazine* shows that a long time before a Bombay dubbing-room was

experimenting with *Frenchi Filmi*, a Mauritian team was writing distinctive
Franco-Indian criticism in its own way, although it was largely ignored by the
mainstream French film journals. The question remains whether the
Mauritian film reviewer was sticking to the kind of criticism practised in
popular film magazines of Bombay.

In the following extract, the actor Bobby Deol is compared to a good horse,
only needing encouragement.

> In the role of a man who is haunted by suffering, despair, revenge, Bobby
> Deol seems very convincing. He doesn't speak much. His face expresses
> his anger. He keeps the same dark face all through the film. With this
> role, Bobby becomes an inevitable choice for future action films. One
> day he could well replace his brother, the actor Sunny. Since *Barsaat*, his
> first film, we have believed he would be a promising actor. He needs only
> a good film director to give him the appropriate role – and to apply the
> whip accordingly!

The Mauritian journal also translated literally some remarkable quotes from
dialogue into French, such as some by Johnny Lever, a well-known comic
actor:

> Playing a recently-married Sikh departing on his honeymoon, Johnny
> leaves a good impression. Some of his dialogue is amazing. It includes:
>
> 1 (to his wife) You are stronger than me. Let's go to a hotel and I will
>   show you my courage!
> 2 I have been on honeymoon for four years and I have found neither
>   honey nor moon!
> 3 Beaten up by a man, Johnny replies: 'Does my face like your father's
>   now?'
> 4 'Do you see me as a horse or a donkey?'

The style of the Mauritian *Film Star Magazine* was so close to Bombay film
mag criticism that the journal was accused of plagiarism by its readers. Here
is the journal's reply in English (*Star Magazine*, vol. 20, no, 26, 26 February
2000):

> We get all the news from India. We are in constant communication with our
> friends, journalists in Bombay. We talk to film stars and film people all the
> time. These relationships have existed for 25 years. You could not publish a
> film magazine without experience or contacts in the field. You could not

copy the opinion of a film from an Indian paper and give it to the people here. We go to see pictures in cinemas and make our own comments.

The problems faced by the Mauritian journal are not very different from the ones encountered inside the dubbing-room: how to stay close to the original and also be unique; how to be re-creative *and* substitutive at the same time; how to find the right equilibrium between them. The journal had to spend a lot of energy proving its authenticity and its uniqueness. 'We are not a second-class journal. Our criticism is not copied from others!' says the Mauritian critic. 'But people like to read the Bombay press *and* our journal!' In its own way, the interplay between the press and its audience was therefore continuing the dubbing process. The journal itself was treated by its readership as a dubbed version of an original, carrying the same ambiguities.

Viewing as Dubbing, or How Dubbing Treatment Became the Target of Many Comments

From an observer's point of view, the progress of a dubbed version is in many ways more complex to follow, because of the multiplicity of its layers, than that of an original. Mauritian people came to see not only the film itself but also the way it had been dubbed. The dubbing treatment added another level of reading, an integral part of the pleasure of viewing.[6] According to a Mauritian film importer, several theatre owners advertised the film release in Mauritius as follows: 'Come and see Shahrukh, Madhuri and Karisma speaking French!' '*Les folies de l'Amour à l'indienne pour la première fois en français!*' (*The Madness of Love Indian-style for the first time in French!*), '*Quelqu'un quelque part est fait pour vous – venez voir Le Cœur qui rend fou!*' (*Someone somewhere is made for you – come and see Love Sends You Mad!*).

In a Mauritian video club in Paris, I had the opportunity to attend a screening of DTPH. Here is an extract from a conversation I heard between three young men and the club owner:

'It's funny, how Shahrukh plays the French actor,' says one man.
'Where did they get the voices? Is it Mauritian creole?', asks the other.
'Are these perhaps the original actors' voices?', asks the third.
'No, no, it was made in Bombay,' says the club owner.
'It's the first time I've heard them speaking French,' says the first.
'Karisma and Madhuri are educated girls – they are bound to have gone to a French school,' adds the second.
'No, they must have got people in Mauritius itself to do it. Look, Shahrukh has no accent and it's not his original voice,' says the third.

'They've kept the songs in Hindi. Imagine these songs in French,' says the club owner.
'But French people don't know how to sing!', comments the first man, and laughs.

During the screening, the men kept imitating the French voices, laughing, and trying to remember the original dialogue. They were constantly shifting from Hindi to French and vice versa. It was as if they were trying to make the *Frenchi Filmi* their own and at the same time seize the opportunity of this screening to replay not the original film but the more complex dubbed one made from one audible sound track and another implicit one that they were making explicit. Everyone was aware of the non-professional quality of the dubbing, but it did not seem to matter. This dubbed version was a pretext for being both *filmi* and *frenchi* at the same time.

Alongside the previous invitation to appreciate the dubbing as an extra component, the spectators' reactions added yet another layer of meaning. In a constant interplay of dissociation and reassociation of voices and image (or dubbing and original), as the exhibitors anticipated, the viewers were also reproducing the dubbing room and its debate, continuously commenting on the transformation and how the actors were modified, the dialogues changed and the image itself affected by this language 'surgery'. Whereas the French amateurs considered the dubbing a 'curiosity', judging it to be a technically inferior, semi-professional product – although they were not really capable of gauging the transformation – the Mauritian spectators were too familiar with their actors and their mannerisms not to try to guess and reproduce the entire process in their own way. I am not saying that every Mauritian spectator saw the film in this way, but their pleasure was certainly entirely different from the recently converted French Bombay film-lover for whom a dubbing had to serve a more transparent viewing experience.

The French amateurs, who could not have access to the original without translation, were not expecting an alternative product in which another stratum of differentiation (some local colour) had been added. Nevertheless this blurred object, not exactly made for them but targeting them, was appreciated as a strange but enjoyable variant. The dubbing treatment itself was analysed by a French amateur who was very fond of Hong Kong Films and had recently shifted to Bollywood, sharing his new passion on the net:

The dubbing artistes have accents you can cut with a knife – but for those who don't know English or don't like subtitles or for perverted minds like mine who want to have three hours of hilarity, it is a good way to experience the film. Compared to the dubbing of the Hong Kong films of the early 1980s, it is very fine work, du *travail d'orfèvre!*'

Another short review, published for the increasing numbers of French admirers of Bollywood films, also mentioned the existence of this unusual product, full of humour and informality, not to be taken seriously:

> For masochists, there is another sound track in VF 2.0 – quite unexpected and hilarious. The characters speak with a very strong accent. Lots of fun!

DTPH revealed that Hindi movies did not need to have exotic locales and scenes to find room in the French market. Indian modernism could also draw and retain the attention. The dilemma of the dubbing-room was suddenly solved. On the way from Bombay to Paris (via Mauritius), a new form of relationship between a film and an audience had emerged, which the distributor sitting in his office in Bombay could not have anticipated and which many Indian films released in France after DTPH reinforced incidentally. This relationship was based on a geographical, as well as a conceptual *distance*, an unexpected two-way participation that enabled the Mauritian audience to see the same film again, but modified and judged as a double film, and the French public to appreciate the same product, but with another degree of empathy.

The World Market, or How to Make Many Films into One and Split One Audience into Many

The 'world market', as Indian distributors like to call the Overseas circuit, is far from being a homogeneous entity. Although it remains much smaller than the indigenous market, it continues to transform, fragment and reassemble itself into unexpected units. Moreover, it has provided Indian producers with opportunities to put into practice unusual film-making strategies. The purpose of this chapter was less to trace the transformation of this market in historical terms than to understand through ethnographic methods the course of an experiment, starting at its design stage in the distributor's office in Bombay and ending with analysis of overseas audience reactions. My aim was to explore through a case study the heterogeneous (and sometimes conflicting) elements that have amalgamated to form a film market. The creation of a market is not a linear process and many experiments are necessary before the producers can say that a film market actually exists.

At first, the strategy of the distributor was oriented towards French-speaking Indians who knew the original version, rather than towards a French audience in general. This type of audience is a distinctive feature of the Indian diaspora all over the world; it is an Overseas continuation of what the Bombay distributors and producers call locally the 'repetitive audience', which comes back to the cinema to watch the same film several times.[7] The Mauritian audience was no more than a repetitive audience which spoke another language, becoming for the Indian distributor a *cumulative* audience.

Secondly, the dubbing itself had to become a component of the film appreciated as such by the distributors and exhibitors. This task could not have been accomplished without the complicity of the public and critical media. Jumping from one language to another, the Mauritian press was already making this kind of circulation commonplace and, as we have seen, the Mauritian audience was looking for other ways to renew its pleasure. Contemplating the transformation of an original into a double – sometimes laughing at it, criticising it or re-enacting it – was a way to give it new life.

Let us look back from the public's unexpected reactions to Yashji's primary tactics. If his (not so) secret desire was to reach tentatively beyond the Indian diaspora, to the French public, his experiment was far from a failure – but nor was it a definite success. Targeting a global market, the producer who wanted to conquer the French territories found a much more limited, but also more enigmatic, audience: a market of unknown and changing requirements among the diaspora, in which Mauritian Indians coexisted with French amateurs looking for a parallel experience. Unlike *Lagaan* and *Devdas*, the successful careers of which started the burst of amateur viewing of Bollywood films in France, the French version of DTPH could not reach the French screen. No screening was organized in a big cinema in Paris, but many small private screenings took place in Mauritian households and in French circles of film-lovers.

When Yashji said that 'Indian distribution had gone global', he had probably no answer or analysis to give – only the intuition that shifting to new audiences through the diaspora itself was the most secure way to explore the commercial possibilities of Overseas territories. In retrospect it is easy to criticise Yashraj's rustic strategy, because we know today that the French audience (as distinct from the Francophone African territories already penetrated) is without doubt a potentially lucrative market, but this was by no means certain at the time of the first dubbing of DTPH. No one can say whether the film would have reached the French public directly if it had been sent to a French dubbing company and if, thanks to its producer, the dubbed version had simply substituted a standard sound track for the original, without preserving the 'Indian flavour'. There was only the one alternative: to call in an Overseas-dubbing expert, a hybridizer like Lilaji who treated foreign languages like regional dialects and created an enigmatic but powerful mix that did not exist in the recipe-book.

The usual priority in the dubbing process is to make the dubbing itself discreet enough to be ignored by the viewer, but Lilaji's method was different. She was interested in carrying out non-transparent dubbing and creating colourfully hybridized elaborations inside an entirely Indianized world. In the final dubbed sound track, signs of Indianness, far from being erased, were cultivated, added and cherished. This kind of subtlety which may or may not really be appreciated only by the French-speaking diaspora and possibly the 'masochist amateurs' (as our Internet Bollywood filmgoer puts it), coupled with what the Indian distributors called 'global distribution' at the turn of the twenty-first century, has nonetheless given rise to plenty of such experimental assemblages. 'Selling two films into one' or 'doubling one film into two' was common practice among Indian distributors and Overseas exhibitors. It required the support of local and solid recreative networks like the one we have described. Such strategies are not only playing with captive audiences that are suddenly promoted to a privileged position in the distribution game, in spite of being officially considered minorities on the world market. They also affect the film content itself, adding a new layer of reworkings and differences inside the film scenario, and new sounds and lip-synchs, which were not in the original.

Conclusion

A movie is rarely made once and for all. It leads an unpredictable life long after its release, duplicating itself and encountering new audiences that juxtapose in time and space. By accident I attended a screening of the well-known Hindi film *Sholay* in a small city in Rajasthan 25 years after its first release. The film had been entirely re-edited by the cinema owner (scenes were back-to-front) to attract the audience again. 'I wanted to give the audience the same movie but *different*,' he said. Of course it does not happen every day, but methodologically speaking such experiments are significant and show why it is difficult to close biographies of films and film-making processes, except arbitrarily.[8] Films are screened, rescreened, dubbed, re-edited, shortened or extended sometimes many years after their first screening and far away from their original place of production. A film is always a proliferation of versions, a world of modified objects. These assemblages are not exactly comparable to the famous 'fractals' which are based on the principle of identical repetition, looking the same on any scale (Mandelbrot, 1977). It seems that the more a film circulates, the more it is in fact unlike its original. If you do not see exactly the same film in Mexico, Timbuctoo or Jaipur, it is because there are many intermediaries playing with real and virtual audiences, trying to add new territories to the distributor's map.

Because it is difficult to see all prints in circulation and all audiences who watch a film, a true world 'biography' of a film seems to be an impossible task. The only thing the researcher can do is to point out the local mechanisms that contribute to making the various versions, for in order to find a new audience, or release a film in a distant territory or adapt it to a new medium, the film usually comes back to the distributor who decides to make changes, additions or cuts. These adaptations, carried out locally, are part of the post-(re)production life of films.

On the other hand, it also happens that films (like other works of art) may circulate without any change. Until recently, many prints of Bombay films were sent to the Middle East, Africa or South America without dubbing or subtitles. It was said in Bombay that these audiences were not paying very much attention to the dialogue, and even without it, they could still more or less understand what was happening on screen. This situation was quite comfortable for Indian film distributors. But this does not mean that local inputs and accompaniments were not sometimes made later in the chain by intermediaries or theatre owners, who had to employ translators and organize for themselves the conditions to produce a new viewing context and yet another standard for reception on the audience map.

Notes

1 Officially, the Indian distribution map is made of six main circuits: West (Bombay), East (Calcutta), North (Delhi), North East, South (Madras) and Overseas. But as a distributor puts it, there are many parallel maps: 'The World for us has six circuits. The Overseas are one of them. Then there are many sub-circuits. And every distributor has his own circuit.'

2 A growing literature about the diaspora and Indian cinema has appeared in recent years (Mishra 1996; Sahai 1998; Desai 2004).

3 Elsewhere, I have given a detailed account of the film-making process in the Bombay film studios in the 1990s (Grimaud 2004).

4 On the ethnography of disseminated networks, see Miller (1975) and Marcus (1997); on the notion of 'parallel modernity', see Larkin (1997; 2003).

5 At the time of my enquiry, several journals published by French-speaking Tamils were circulating in the Paris stores: *Film Star Magazine*, *Ciné-Inde*, etc.

6 Whereas Georges Melies did not want to reveal his special effects trick to the public because he was afraid that people would not come to the theatre any more, Dadasaheb Phalke, who was one of the pioneers of Indian mythological cinema at the beginning of the twentieth century, thought on the contrary that people must understand how films and special effects tricks are made, so that they will enjoy them more. A comparable device is at work here, where the dubbing process was considered by the exhibitors as a way to increase the audience's pleasure.

7 A good film is said to attract a repetitive audience. Some songs are very often added to a previous version of a film to attract the public again and again (Grimaud, 2002).

8 The notion of a 'biography of things' has become a fruitful paradigm in anthropology (Kopytoff 1986; Bromberger and Chevallier 1999). On the need to consider the 'work of art' as a multiplicity of versions, see Becker (2001).

Bibliography

Becker, Howard (2001) 'The work itself/L'Oeuvre elle-même', in Jean-Olivier Majastre and Alain Pessin, eds, *Vers une sociologie des Œuvres*. Paris: L'Harmattan; 449–63.

Bromberger, Christian and Denis Chevallier (1999) *Carrières d'objets: Innovation et relances*. Paris: Maison des Sciences de l'Homme.

Desai, Jigna (2004) *Beyond Bollywood: The cultural politics of South Asian diasporic film*. New York: Routledge.

Grimaud, Emmanuel (2002) 'Reshaping the vision: film scraps, middlemen and the public in a Bombay motion-picture theater', *L'Homme*, 164: 81–104.

—— (2004) *Bollywood Film Studio ou comment les films se font à Bombay*. Paris: CNRS Editions.

Kopytoff, Igor (1986) 'The cultural biography of things. Commodization as process', in Arjun Appadurai, ed., *The Social Life of Things*. Cambridge: Cambridge University Press; 64–91.

Larkin, Brian (1997) 'Indian films and Nigerian lovers: media and the creation of parallel modernities', *Revue de l'Institut Africain International*, 67 (3): 406–40.

—— (2003) 'Itineraries of Indian cinema. African videos, Bollywood and global media', in Ella Shohat and Robert Stam, eds, *Multiculturalism, Postcolonialism and Transnational Media*. New Brunswick: Rutgers University Press; 170–92.

Mandelbrot, Benoît (1977) *Fractals: Form, Chance and Dimension*. San Francisco: W. H. Freeman.

Marcus, George E. (1995) 'Ethnography in/of the world system. The emergence of multi-sited ethnography', *Annual Review of Anthropology*, 24: 95–117.

Miller, Daniel (1995) *Worlds Apart: Modernity through the prism of the local*. London, Routledge; 169–89.

Mishra, Vijay (1996) 'The diasporic imaginary : theorizing the Indian diaspora', *Textual Practice*, 10 (2): 421–47.

Sahai, Malti (1998) *Relocating Indian Cinema*. New Delhi: Oxford University Press.

9

MALABAR GODS, NATION-BUILDING AND WORLD CULTURE: ON PERCEPTIONS OF THE LOCAL AND THE GLOBAL

Gilles Tarabout

The term 'globalization' resists attempts at narrow definition. Although discourses on the subject appear to relate to something 'happening out there' (Harriss 2001), its meanings are so diverse that a single definition proves elusive. However Baricco (2002) suggests that despite problems both of definition and understanding, we nevertheless have little difficulty in being for it or against it.

This can generate strange worlds. Ulf Hannerz cites the example of the winning song in a 1987 national song contest in Sweden, which excited strong protests not because it was a calypso sung by a Finn but because for some people its refrain, 'Four Bugg [a brand of chewing-gum] and a Coca-Cola', represented 'cultural imperialism', a 'cocacolonization of the world' (Hannerz 1989). Thus globalization may be understood as a euphemism for US imperialism (Harriss 2001), while various cultural hybrids might go unnoticed. This aspect of globalization is generally condemned. Other aspects – for instance, the need for universal cultural values – are often seen as desirable without a contradiction being perceived. Thus in the issue of *Economic and Political Weekly* containing Harriss's critique of the effects of economic globalization, we also find a debate about the right to disregard national sovereignty in order to safeguard monuments which 'are part of a cultural heritage of humankind as a whole' – in this case, the Bamiyan Buddhas (Hensman 2001). Reactions therefore vary according to what is globalized.

In a recent survey, Bengalis condemned policies of economic liberalization which were felt in India to be the effects of globalization, but at the same time positively evaluated 'the free flow of information engendered through global media, albeit taking a critical view of the culturally inappropriate foreign influences' (Ganguly-Scrase and Scrase 2001, p.141).

Discourses on 'globalization' rely implicitly on various dichotomies: us and them (Toufique 2001), centre(s) and periphery(ies) (Hannerz 1989), and, of course, global and local (with a possible mid-term like 'the nation'). Arjun Appadurai has proposed a more subtle model for the 'deterritorialized' world we are supposed to live in. He interprets locality as a 'phenomenological quality', a 'structure of feeling' resulting from a teleology and an ethos (Appadurai 1996, p.181), and distinct from 'neighbourhoods'. Nevertheless, in this model and in less sophisticated ones, there are at least two recurrent risks. The first is to regard 'modernization' as the inevitable result of globalization, which would make theories of globalization the descendants of diffusionism (Barnard 2000: 168). The second, related risk, with which we are more concerned here, is the perception of relations between the global world and localities as unidirectional, the local being either passively modelled by the global or perceived in terms of its resistance to it. This view has been opposed by scholars of various intellectual traditions for obscuring the dialogic quality of world exchanges that lead to complex and changing forms of cultural hybridization.[1]

Within the general frame of this discussion, this chapter aims at illustrating how cultural interactions at the local level have a longstanding history in which local actors are precisely that: actors.[2] My case study of a village cult in South India, now also presented as theatre performance in the West, is an example of a passage to the global market resulting from a historically complex process where different mediations are required at different social levels. In such a process, the motivations and perspectives of the people concerned may continue to differ according to their respective social and cultural interests.[3] Moreover, individual experience at the village level may include representations of global values, giving rise to specific complexities and sometimes tensions.

More precisely, this study is focused on what Appadurai called 'the work of the imagination', that 'is neither purely emancipatory nor entirely disciplined but is a space of contestation in which individuals and groups seek to annex the global into their own practices of the modern' (Appadurai 1996: 4). My analysis will develop and illustrate this argument, by systematically linking representations and discourses to agencies. However, contrary to Appadurai's main argument, my emphasis will bear on historical continuities rather than discontinuities. I argue that cultural globalization as a representation has grown out of ideas about development, progress, modernity, and former universalisms that provoked in their time similar tensions about annexing 'the global' into individual and local groups' practices.

Teyyam as a Cult of and for Localities

My case study is about a ritual known by the name Teyyam (or Theyyam).[4] *Teyyam* ('deity') is a village, family or caste cult celebrating localized deities. It is also called *teyyattam* ('dance of the deity') or *kaliyattam* ('play-dance'), as well as other names.[5] As part of the ceremonies, the god or goddess is incorporated temporarily in a male specialist who is said to be possessed and who speaks as the deity itself. Such deities are often, but not always, former human beings whose exceptional deeds, and typically an exceptionally violent death, have raised them to divinity.[6] They may be linked to a living lineage or caste, and usually have a territorial jurisdiction. Their cult can be patronised by any caste from Brahmans to ex-Untouchables. The deities can become incarnate in two kinds of specialists. During the year they may possess the regular priests of their shrines, often of the same or of a slightly different status from the patrons. At festivals (not necessarily the annual one), they become incarnate in specialized dancers, usually of a much lower status than the patrons. This latter manifestation, called also Teyyam, will be considered here.

At festival times the deity comes in its 'full form' – that is, its incarnation in the dancer will take an impressively spectacular form, involving elaborate make-up and costume, loud drumming, ritual recitation of divine deeds, various dance steps and sometimes a demonstration of fighting abilities. These are a public manifestation of the power of the divine presence, further demonstrated by the performance of superhuman feats. Some of the Teyyams, for example, roll on glowing embers, drink incredibly large quantities of alcohol, or tear apart with their teeth the dozens of live chickens offered to satisfy the god's hunger. The ritual violence of these cults is indicative of the kind of power that these gods are deemed to possess. They are highly dangerous, and all kinds of misfortune are attributed to their punishment or their desire to be recognized and thereby 'seated' in a shrine. But properly placated, the deities wield a highly protective power, so that people can ask them for favours, such as health, fertility, success and prosperity. Teyyams may also act as arbitrators in local disputes (land disputes, accusations of theft, etc.), and their judgements uphold the moral order.[7] All in all, teyyams are seen to provide their devotees with superhuman means to influence events.

These cults are still central to the religious and social life of millions of people in northern Malabar, the northernmost region of Kerala, mostly but not only in rural areas. They give meaning to the daily lives of their devotees and they are crucial in producing and reproducing 'locality' itself – lineages, castes, villages, groups of devotees – in the sense of a 'structure of feeling' developed, to quote Appadurai again, 'under conditions of anxiety and entropy, social wear and flux, ecological uncertainty and cosmic volatility, and the always present quirkiness of kinsmen, enemies, spirits and quarks of all sorts' (Appadurai 1996: 181). In a way, Teyyams are the incarnation of 'localities' at different social levels.

In the course of history, these cults have met with contrasting responses from different outside observers, commentators and mediators, representing, in retrospect, one form or other of 'the global'. As a starting-point, let us look at some comments written at the beginning of the twentieth century.[8]

Meeting with the Colonial West

The Teyyam ceremony was first described in 1901 by Fred Fawcett, then Superintendent of Government Railway Police, Madras, and Local Correspondent of the Anthropological Institute of Great Britain and Ireland. He spent some three and a half years in Malabar, now the northern part of Kerala. Fawcett's description is part of his well-known account of the 'Nayars of Malabar', published in the *Bulletin of the Madras Government Museum* and regularly cited by later compilers. His writings in general show a keen sense of observation and a constant preoccupation with accurate ethnographic detail, typical of his explicit aim to be 'objective'.[9] As he put it, 'neither fancy nor beauty shall allure us from the dull path of precision' (Fawcett 1901: 265). This was coupled at times with the somewhat condescending attitude characteristic of other writings of the enlightened colonial elite. An example is his description of a Teyyam dancer after his performance, although he does not morally condemn the ceremonies he describes (p.261):

> The poor old man who represented this fearful being, grotesquely terrible in his wonderful metamorphosis, must have been extremely glad when his three minutes' dance, preparation for which occupied all the afternoon, was concluded, for the mere weight and uncomfortable arrangement of his paraphernalia must have been extremely exhausting.

The comment is far from innocuous. Behind the concern for 'the poor old man' is a radical negation, bearing not so much on the religious dimension of the ceremony as on the 'irrationality' of the practice. The paraphernalia becomes an 'uncomfortable arrangement', and the spending of a full afternoon for 'three minutes' dance', a mere folly. The term that could best sum up Fawcett's impression, despite the claim to objectivity, would perhaps be *weirdness*, a word that appears in his text to qualify the 'human tumult busy in its religious effusion' (p. 265). This weirdness is attached, in his eyes, not only to the aspect of the divine figures he sees but also more generally to the conduct of the people following irrational religious practices. Speaking about religion among castes considered to be of low status in Malabar ('the more uncultivated, the wilder races') he finds that 'this is almost entirely primitive in character; no more the cult of Siva or Vishnu than of Sqaktktquaclt' (p. 254). The 'weirdness' and 'primitive character' of Teyyam and related practices are explicitly described as part of a worldwide phenomenon, which the coloniser alone can embrace in his global and 'rational' eye, record in its details and eventually assign to his own world as exotic curios or weird tales.

Meeting with Christianity

Fawcett's condescending detachment was not shared by all. Colonial officials' representations and values were not necessarily the same as those of evangelists, with their (global) missionary agenda. As late as 1944, V. William, a student of the United Theological College, Bangalore, wrote about Teyyam with the explicit aim 'to furnish the Christian Evangelists [...] adequate materials to start their reform in the light of the Christian Gospel' (William 1944, Preface: 30–1):

> This is only a survival of the most primitive animistic belief in religion which Hinduism does not desire to see any more. There is no art or anything of cultural value in this cult appealing to the modern mind. The practices adopted in this cultus are hideous, monstrous, demonic and frightful when compared to the Bhakti cult of popular religion. Fear dominates in this cult and there is no place for love or personal devotion. Psychologically it does more harm than good to the worshippers. [...] Those who conduct the Theyyam are seeking more for their profit than for any religious good. The ignorant and the poor are made by this cult to keep themselves in their blindness. This is dehumanization and flagrant exploitation of human personality. These subhuman practices stunted the growth of personality to have any philosophical outlook. Morality and ethics which are the highest values in religion are not to be found in any of these cults. Thus these animistic primitive cults act as a break to the forward movement of culture or civilization or religion which become static and stagnant.

Apart from the anthem on primitive irrationality, a few themes appear in William's text which were not present in Fawcett's and which correspond to often expressed criticisms of local cults the world over: that they are superstitious, a cynical exploitation of poor ignorant people, devoid of any morality and ethics (which define religion according to an evolutionist, universalist view), and an obstacle to civilization, to the very notion of progress.

Such a charge should not be summarily dismissed as the mere expression of a Christian evangelist who assumes the burden of global morality and the 'forward movement of culture'. Besides the fact that Christians in general (an important minority in Kerala), and evangelists in particular, did exert some influence over the evolution of cults in India, directly or indirectly (Frykenberg 1988), it is worth remarking that William formulated his judgement after quoting 'Hindu' opinions. One, for instance, comes from a Mr. K. Kunhikannan, who wrote in April 1912 in the *Madras Christian College Magazine* about Malabar village gods (quoted in William 1944, pp. 28–9):

Probably few nations in the world ancient or modern, have been more superstitious, more credulous, more gullible than the hindus. It is a most significant and noteworthy fact that even at this distance of time, even in this budding 20th century, in an age of triumphant intellectual and scientific advance unparalleled in the history of the human race, many things which have been burned to ashes under the all-embracing fire of modern science and thought are still piously retained by the vast majority of hindus. [...] It is a very sorry spectacle to witness the hindus still worshipping the village gods and goddesses in the most hideous and superstitious manner. In my own place there is a 'Kavu' [shrine] where thousands of fowls and sheep are every year butchered for the propitiation of the supposed god or goddess. The sacred temple is literally transformed into a slaughter-house. Can any man conceive a more horrible and degrading way of worshipping the supreme Father of the Universe?

This is a local author who confesses with dramatic effect that in his 'own place', 'village gods' receive horrible cults in contrast to appropriate worship directed to 'the Father of the Universe' (the 'global' and the 'local' are also articulated in terms of divine figures!). While a Christian influence can be detected in these last words, the overall perspective is informed by ideas about modernity found everywhere at this time. But there is also a regional dimension, as the author implicitly relies on the longstanding Brahmanical aversion to animal sacrifice, which had found historical expression in various Indian religious movements, and was also emphasized in the reformist agenda of socio-religious and caste organizations from the early nineteenth century.

Reformists in Action

Unlike other parts of India like Bengal or neighbouring Tamil Nadu (Frykenberg 1989), Hindu socio-religious reformers appeared in Kerala only in the late nineteenth century, with the exception of a few isolated figures like Sri Vaikunda Swamikal (1803–51). Although the latter's activities were restricted to the southern districts of Travancore (Sarveswaran 1980), his advocacy of both social equality and religious reforms, such as the suppression of animal sacrifice, was already indicative of developments to come. From the 1860s, various caste organizations were founded in Kerala. One of their main aims was the consolidation and social 'uplift' of the community concerned, but they also promoted religious reform, and their own 'new elite' of journalists, advocates and medical doctors operated as social activists under the spiritual authority of a saintly figure.[10]

Mr P. N. Damodaran, a source quoted by William, was probably a member of this elite. He wrote in *Matrbhumi Weekly* of 15 March 1937 (quoted in William 1944, pp. 27–8):

> Thirayattam or Theyyam is a cult found only in North Malabar. In English this can be called Devil Dance. [...] Thirayattam is destructive and is worth to be destroyed. The rowdyisms, inhuman and barbarous behaviours and immoral actions that are in and near the Kavus [shrines] and which are prevalent at the time of these festivals are innumerable and beyond description. When we understand that animal sacrifices, immorality and drunkenness are indispensable elements in this cult, this should not be suffered to continue even for a moment.

William considered this 'the opinion of every educated Hindu who only anticipated an extinction of this cult in the near future' (ibid.: 28). That he was misled in this particular conclusion is another matter. The fact remains that Teyyam, like other cults using animal sacrifice and alcohol, was the target not only of Christian evangelists but of Hindu reformers as well as new urban elites, including elites from communities practising these cults. This implied tensions at the local level about the kind of 'locality' sustainable in the face of a 'modernity' perceived as rational, moral and global.

The most important among these reformers, for this chapter, was Sri Narayana Guru (1856–1928). An exponent of spiritual wisdom advocating equality and tolerance, he summed up his message in the motto 'one caste, one creed, one god for man'. But in spite of the universalist tone of his philosophy, and of the general respect which he commanded even in far-away circles (he was well known to people like Rabindranath Tagore, Mahatma Gandhi and Romain Rolland), his activity was in fact restricted to uplifting the specific, local community into which he was born, the toddy-tappers. Toddy-tappers – Izhavas or Tiyyas – were at the time below the untouchability line, and were divided into many status groups. Through their capacity to make use of new economic opportunities, their influential position in electoral politics, and the militancy of their leaders, the toddy-tappers were eventually able to gain increased social respect and, at the same time, became more united as a social group. The role of Sri Narayana Guru was decisive in this shift in public estimation. The suppression of animal sacrifice and the cult of deified human beings, such as Teyyam, were among the many reforms he advocated. As one of his hagiographers explains in a chapter entitled 'The Electric Shock' (Kunhappa 1982: 27):

> In more than a hundred places, he unseated the gods whose names had associations with the killing of birds and consumption of liquor, replacing them by idols of Siva, Subramania and Ganesa and instituted *poojas* of the type performed in temples dedicated to them.

Similar 'universalising' processes (in terms of pan-Indian cults) were still taking place among the toddy-tappers long after the demise of the Guru (Osella 1993). Suppression was more radically, though never totally, enforced in the south of the State than the north, where Teyyam is practised, but the reform movement was also influential there. Since the local toddy-tappers, the Tiyyas, were and still are central to the practice of Teyyam, one of the aims of the movement was reform of such cults. The Tiyya elite began to organize itself in 1906 by founding the Sri Gnanodaya Yogam, 'Society for the Awakening of Knowledge' (Menon 1994 : 67). Soon after, Sri Narayana Guru himself came to lay the foundations of a Tiyya temple in which only 'pure' ritual would be followed. Prayer societies were also developed. As historian Dilip Menon puts it, 'The complex pantheon of shrine worship was in the process of reinterpretation, and a sharp division emerged between "brah-manical" and "non-brahmanical" deities, at least within the discourse of reform' (ibid.: 70).

The apparent unanimity in condemning Teyyam for its 'primitivity', voiced with various nuances by Christian evangelists, Hindu reformers and local elites, masked quite different purposes. For missionaries, what was at stake was conversion to the only rational and universal faith, Christianity. For Hindu socio-religious reformers, what was involved was the elaboration of purified forms of Hinduism, thought to correspond to universal values of the time (although their language was one of return to the origins). Members of the new local elite, on the other hand, while genuinely partaking of the ideals of religious reform, had their own, more immediate agenda, and saw universal progress with reference to a localized socio-political arena. What was at stake was the progress of their own community, and ultimately their own position as an elite.

In this interplay of global references and local relations of power, Teyyam cults did not do what was expected: instead, they prospered. Unlike a number of similar rituals in the southern regions of Travancore and Cochin, which disappeared or were conveniently euphemised, Teyyam cults, well entrenched in complex networks of rural power, were able to resist reformist campaigns and adapt at the same time to changing socio-economic conditions. What is more, from the 1940s onwards, Teyyam began progressively to undergo a complete redefinition in the public eye to the point that their spectacular figures have nowadays become emblematic of Kerala culture in tourist publications –Teyyam photographs make good cover pictures.

Let us look at the reasons behind this dramatic change, the seeds of which are to be found in new sensibilities developed at the same period when denunciations were at their peak. Between the 1930s and 1950s, three different kinds of people – Western artists, Indian nationalists and Kerala Communists – all with their respective global attitudes, contributed in different ways and for different reasons to these changes in sensibility, leading ultimately to a radical reconsideration of Teyyam and similar rituals.

Marxists in Action

The specific development of the Communist party in Kerala enabled it to command mass support and eventually, led by its general secretary, the late E. M. S. Namboodiripad, it came to power in 1957 in the first general elections in the newly formed state of Kerala, following the reorganization of Indian States on a linguistic basis. Since then, Marxists in coalition with other parties have regularly headed the state government, alternating with Congress-led coalitions. In the 1930s the party was still at a formative stage around a small group of militants, but a new leftist sensibility was rapidly growing in the intellectual milieu of Kerala, especially among writers who favoured social engagement and who were to have a far-reaching influence in Kerala beyond Marxist sympathisers. Young writers like Takazhi, Kesava Dev and others were well acquainted with European and Russian literature and personally committed to a kind of social realism. They were concerned to portray the downtrodden, the destitute, thus creating new heroes who could never have found a place in earlier Malayalam literature. People born into low-status castes were thereafter no longer 'primitive' but 'oppressed' or 'repressed'. Short stories and novels from this new literature were widely read in a region where literacy was already comparatively high.

As a consequence, in the 1940s, Teyyam and certain other rituals involving spectacular elements came to be seen by some as a 'culture of the people', though in an ambivalent manner. On the one hand, entrenched as it was in the rural structures of power, Teyyam was condemned for legitimizing the existing land tenancy relationships, and therefore for perpetuating a local 'feudal' order. On the other hand, it was possible to see the stories of past heroes which were at the centre of many Teyyams as epics of resistance against such an exploitative order, and Teyyam costumes, music, songs and dance as the expression of the creativity of the masses. World War II gave local Marxists the occasion to test some practical consequences of these views.

As long as the pact between Germany and the USSR was in force, the Indian Communist Party opposed the war as an imperialist war. When the Germans attacked the USSR, the Party, in 1942, labelled the conflict a people's war and decided to support it. As a consequence, its imprisoned leaders came out of jail and the party was temporarily able to operate freely. Its militants turned towards popular rituals and theatres as media of communication and propaganda in order to reach the widest possible audience. As Dilip Menon writes (Menon 1994: 176–7):

> Folk arts were harnessed in the cause of anti-Japanese and anti-hoarding propaganda and the *ottan thullal, poorakkali, kolkali, teyyattam* [various Kerala rituals], all of these found patronage. In the aftermath of the depression, many of the less prosperous tharavadus [aristocratic houses of comparatively high-status castes, like the Nayars] had stopped sponsoring the *teyyattam* and other shrine performances. The leadership of the KCP [Kerala Communist Party], coming as they did from branches of the larger tharavadus, were in their element as patrons of the rural arts. Later in this decade, victims of police action would be lauded as heroes and martyrs, and many individuals incorporated within the *teyyattam* tradition of victims of injustice. Among the persons arrested in the fighting at Karivellur in 1946 was a *teyyattam* performer who 'used to dance Communism'.

Nowadays, instances of politicised Teyyam are still found, although they are certainly not the rule. This is particularly well documented in Wayne Ashley's work (1993), specifically aimed at understanding the 'recodings' to which Teyyam has been and still is subjected. Writing about a presentation of a Teyyam of the god Bhairavan (a violent form of Shiva) by a Marxist worker, in 1981, the author suggests that (Ashley 1993: 198):

> Code subversion characterizes Kuttumath's performance. There is an explicit attempt to strip the ritual of its efficacy by demonstrating that it can be performed outside the temple in a non-consecrated space without priests or offerings. Kuttumath performs teyyam in a symbolic ensemble

which serves to undermine its conventional meaning and function. None of the appropriate purification rituals are performed; nothing is done to 'honour' the deity ; nor does the dancer become possessed.

The aim, according to another party worker, is to liberate people from their 'belief in fate', by encouraging doubt when people see that the dancer can complete the performance unharmed. But the dilemma for Marxists is that liberation should not create unemployment. As Ashley elaborates on his informants' discourse (ibid.: 202–3):

> They feel that destroying the belief system and social relations which support the conditions for teyyam will put numerous performing families out of work. In their scenario for the future of teyyam its existence will be ensured within an emerging wage labour system. Money will replace birthright, privilege and obligation. Teyyam will no longer function solely as offering but will take another cultural path [...]. The stage will dominate over the shrine.

These perspectives, testifying to the complex imbrications between village gods and the proletarian cause (a supremely global project), probably could be seen as later developments in Marxist local thinking about Teyyam. In the 1940s, Party workers in Malabar had a more immediately instrumental approach. Nevertheless, the fact that they saw such a cult as an expression of 'people's culture', and as a form of communication endowed with artistic qualities, constituted at the time a decisive break with previous condescending or denunciatory attitudes. As a matter of fact, many subsequent Kerala folk-lorists, who have undertaken the patient collection and publication of Teyyam songs or the promotion of Teyyam at large, have been Marxist sympathisers.

Folklorists in Action

In Western countries, too, decisive changes in aesthetics had taken place since the end of World War I. Dadaism, cubism and surrealism, explicitly influenced by 'local', 'primitive' arts, had swept away former definitions of beauty among artists and their public. 'Primitive arts', in particular, though still deemed to be primitive, had become beautiful. They were now Art, part of a renewed and extended definition of culture and testifying to man's power of creativity. As such, local in origin as they were, they became endowed with a strongly affirmed universalist quality, inasmuch as a Western urban elite was able to appropriate them according to its own views. This aesthetic revolution took some time to come about in the theatre, although Diaghilev's Ballets

Russes had already shaken some certainties. It was not until the early 1930s that Antonin Artaud, after witnessing performances of Balinese theatre during the Exposition universelle of Paris in 1931, issued two manifestos (1932, 1933) which, under the title *Théâtre de la cruauté*, called for a new approach to drama. Although at the time it had comparatively little impact, it nevertheless underwent a general evolution and influenced the way 'primitive' arts, including dances and spectacular rituals, came to be seen anew. This was to have an important legacy, to which we will return at the end of this chapter.

This period correlatively saw a revival in rural cultural studies in Western countries, leading to the organization of international folk dance festivals throughout Europe (Vienna 1934, London 1935, Stockholm 1939). A young Indian ethnologist studying in Oxford, M. D. Raghavan, witnessed such a festival in 1931, held 'in the picturesque grounds of Blenheim Palace in the county of Oxford', a 'magnificent display' which acted upon him as 'an eye-opener', impressing him (Raghavan 1947: i–ii)

> with the great need for an alround [sic] revival of folk arts and of folk plays and dances here in India, where the advancement of rural studies is so vital to the welfare of her peoples.

Such a vocabulary, where valorisation and study of the local 'folk' was deemed to be in itself a tool for the betterment of India as a whole, was indeed new and anticipated developments which would take place only 10 or 20 years later. It was also to have direct consequences specifically for Teyyam. As far as I am aware, Raghavan was the very first to publish in English a eulogistic report about it in his booklet on *Folk Plays and Dances in Kerala* (1947), paving the way for the arrival of many folklorists. He was possibly also the first to denounce the expression 'devil-dancing' used formerly to denote Teyyam and similar rituals. According to him, this was 'scarcely appropriate to the sacred character of the performance' (ibid.: 3). His account (p. 23) emphasized the aesthetic characteristics of the cult (thoroughly negated by William, as we have seen):

> The dancers who belong to the hereditary professional classes of spirit dancers get such a mastery in the art, scarcely surpassed in other spheres of folk life. It is a living art enlivened by appropriate music, the resplendent costume, the make-up and open air carnivals.

A page further, his state of mind is still more explicit (p. 24):

> The diversity of deities and the variety of functions produce a rich and varied art. The decorative motifs are a study in themselves, disclosing as

they do an observance of stylistic canons and of forms of presentations indicating a long tradition of expression. The resplendent costumes and gorgeous colours harmoniously and artistically blended are a feature of the impersonation in North Malabar temples creating a rich pageant which stands supreme among the ritual art of South India, a pageant which is equalled, if not surpassed, only by the splendour of the Kathakali, which it so closely resembles. Every line and every symbol bespeaks tradition and a profound sense of design and method. The student of folk art and culture has much indeed to interest him in those displays and to ignore them or to dismiss them as of no moment is altogether to miss what really is a most alluring factor in the cultural, religious and social life of Kerala, a factor too which acts in some degree as a unifying force amid the diversities of Kerala society for the association between these annual festivals and the community is both sacred and intimate.

Instead of a being a mere particularizing force, folk culture becomes here a bond across parochialisms. The development throughout India of a similar sensibility led after independence to the multiplication of folklore studies and the valorisation of rural arts as unifying factors. This was taken up by nationalist actors who extended its significance beyond the local community.

Building the Nation

One of the most significant events in the development of politico-cultural pageants in India in the 1950s was probably the introduction of folk dances to the official celebrations of Republic Day in New Delhi. From 1953 onwards, nearly every year, folk dances from different parts of India were included in the parade together with shows of military power, technological advancement and economic achievements. Moreover, in 1954, a Folk Dance Festival was instituted. As Prime Minister Nehru put it (cited in Vidyarthi 1969: 81):

> The idea of several hundred folk dancers from different parts of India coming to Delhi brings home to them and to all of us the richness of our cultural heritage and the unifying bond which holds it together.

As Satish Deshpande noted, this was a period when development as an ideology was trying to ensure the mutual coherence of 'political legitimacy, cultural identity and class relations' (Deshpande 2001: 99). According to him, the Nehruvian years were an exceptional period characterized by '(relative) inward orientation' (ibid.: 98) in India, as opposed to a more general perception of globalizing processes in earlier or later years. During this era, the rhetoric 'had seemed to issue an inclusive invitation to all members of the nation to come and play the role of the secular-modern citizen devoted to the task of nation-building', although this citizen 'turns out upon examination to be at once familiar and elusive – a modern middle-class subject who continues to claim the pre-modern privileges of community, caste, gender and region' (ibid.: 104). This voluntarism in building the nation was not without some condescension for 'old habits and customs'. Nehru, emphasizing the common obligation to build the nation, thus addressed a group of Gond dancers in 1955 (cited in Ashley 1993: 269–70):

I have seen your folk dances [...] and I have found them quite enchanting. [...] You should not think that you have to [give up] your songs and dances. They are not bad. [...] You have to bear one thing in your mind that whether you reside here in Bastar or at Delhi or in any other part of the country, we are all sailing in the same ship in the sea. [...] Therefore we all have to do our jobs in close cooperation and to forge ourselves and our country ahead to achieve progress and prosperity.

The account and analysis by Ashley (1993: 250ff) of a Republic Day parade held much later, in 1984, underlines how such celebrations combined symbols and emblems which instilled a sense of pride in Indian nationhood, diverse but united and therefore strong. Folk dancers were there to 'remind India of its roots in the soil', as a 1985 parade newscaster put it (ibid.: 259). This was possible only through a radical selection, at an early stage, of the traits in 'folk' practices that could be shown to an urban audience during the festival, or that could be adapted to the constraints of a street parade. Although in 1953 'a thousand folk dancers had stormed Delhi with their riotous colour and infectious rhythm' (Vidyarthi 1969: 74), it was not long before new sets of costumes were designed and new arrangements made with, at times, urban 'folk dancers' replacing village ones (Vidyarthi 1969: 82, who denounces such trends). This was part of a complete reconstruction of 'folk culture' in terms of Indianness and urban-middle class taste. As Ashley explains (Ashley 1993: 255–6):

Moreover, as government officials, dance critics, and theatre practitioners elevated the cultural forms of specific groups, especially tribals (adivasis), to national status, and linked them to a pre-existing primordial national identity, the state increasingly dominated their everyday lives, encroached upon their lands, and rationalized their cultural practices. In the parade and Folk Dance Festival what proclaims to be a performative space wherein the 'tribal' and the 'folk' are held up as signifiers of an 'authentic Indian culture' is actually a post-colonial staging of the tribal – reformed and employed to stand for exemplars of national integration and harmony.

Ten years after Delhi, the Kerala government organized similar shows. The people of this state, formed in 1956, were yet to feel a common 'Kerala-ness'. In 1961 the government began to celebrate what was previously a rural (and quite feudal) festival, Onam, as Kerala's National Festival, which, for nearly two decades, has also been a 'Tourist Week Celebration'. Typically, the National Festival and Tourist Week includes street parades in the main cities, combining folk dances with decorated floats on various themes, and many Folk Arts Festivals in different venues in the main cities. Urban middle- and upper-class people, for the most part quite ignorant of the various rituals and performances practised in the different parts of Kerala, congregate at that time to witness rural 'folk' plays, dances and rituals staged in auditoriums.

The first involvement of Teyyam in such public celebrations seems to have been in 1960, when a group of dancers participated in the Republic Day extravaganza in Delhi.[11] Teyyam dancers participated again in many later years in this pageant, and were also at the opening of the IXth Asian Games in Delhi in 1982. They may have participated in the Kerala State sponsored Onam festival sometime before this latter date. In any case, by 1981 they were already so much part of the picture that half the photos in the programme distributed for the Tourist Week Celebration were of Teyyams. Similar photos were already illustrating the cover of a *Folk Arts Directory* published by Kerala Sangeet Natak Akademi in 1978, as well as the inside cover and first page of an official Public Relations Department publication about *Dances of Kerala* issued in 1980. This was definitely cultural respectability and recognition, and it has not ceased since.

We may note in passing an iteration of the iconic use of Teyyam at different territorial and cultural levels. Within North Malabar, festivals may gather Teyyams from different lineages, villages or castes, for which they act as their respective representatives. At the level of Kerala state, Teyyam can be an iconic marker of a restricted regional identity (i.e. North Malabar). For instance, Teyyams were used during a political demonstration in 1982, when delegations from different districts congregated in the streets of the capital, each one with a spectacular attraction: Teyyam was the one signalling the northern delegations. At the national level, in a Delhi parade or festival, the presence of Teyyam dancers represented the Kerala contribution to Indian culture as a whole. It is also mostly as emblems of Kerala culture that

Teyyams are presented in the more than 1,000 Internet sites which Google identified in September 2002, using the key words 'teyyam' or 'theyyam' (the electronic 'deterritorialization' dear to Appadurai has not invented this iconic use, but definitely provides it with wider possibilities). Lastly, at the international level, Teyyam was, for instance, one entry in the Year of India festival held in Paris in 1985, where it no longer represented Kerala as such, but India's folk culture.

Different social actors enable these changes at different levels of 'localities' to take place: journalists, dramatists, filmmakers, arts and crafts regional or national institutions, performers' associations, free-lance folklorists and academic scholars (Tarabout 2003). All these mediations, intricately interwoven, are necessary to build up a patrimonial reality and to pass from one level of 'locality' to another. In these shifts from village cult to regional or national heritage, and to theatrical performance abroad, drastic changes are operated by these mediators, not only in scale but in the very nature and meaning of what is performed: the power of a particular deity is no more the issue, while traditions of artistry are extolled at the cost of a complete reconfiguration of the practice itself. Such a transformation has often been termed 'commodification'.[12] But I think that this expression oversimplifies processes that are by nature multidimensional, unless 'commodity' is taken in an extended meaning implying, as Baricco (2002) underlined, that when we buy a brand 'we are buying a world', so that the work of the imagination is always there. This becomes apparent in the aims and role of the actors responsible for bringing Teyyam to public appreciation and enabling its circulation in the international market. What did they have in mind?

Scholars in Action

M. D. Raghavan's pioneering folklore study, inspired by a preoccupation with the welfare of Kerala and India's people, was followed in 1955 by a short description about Teyyam in S. K. Nayar's classic study (in Malayalam) of folk dances and plays, and by a study published in 1956 by K. G. Adiyodi (also in Malayalam). But it was not until the end of the 1960s that studies on Teyyam, both in Malayalam and in English, enjoyed a spectacular boom.

C. M. S. Chanthera was probably the first to publish a full-length study of Teyyam in 1968, in Malayalam, which included detailed first-hand observations and a collection of Teyyam songs. It was followed by a short paper by anthropologist Joan Mencher (in English) and by papers and books by historian K. K. N. Kurup (English, Hindi and Malayalam) in the early 1970s. All three authors might be said to have had Marxist sympathies. More works were to come later, from different perspectives, including many books in

Malayalam by M. V. Vishnu Namputiri, the main authority on Teyyam today in Kerala, and the anthropological research and publications of Ashley and J. R. Freeman. This scholarly activity produced valuable collections of Teyyam songs and stimulated contrasting responses, many informed by a general perception that 'tradition' was on the verge of extinction.[13] In practice, some were instrumental in bringing Teyyam to a wider public both inside and outside Kerala, and in gaining access to a wider market than the one provided in villages. In this process, as we have already seen, Teyyam was an icon for various imagined communities.

K. K. N. Kurup, of Kozhikode (Calicut) University, is one example of a scholar actively promoting knowledge of Teyyam. He wrote two books in English (1973, 1977) that were circulated in folkloric and anthropological circles and made Teyyam known to non-Malayalam-speaking audiences in India and abroad. Soon Kurup became the man to meet for foreigners interested in the study of Teyyam (together with A. K. Nambiar, from the Drama School of the same University). Kurup also publicised Teyyam through a government-sponsored booklet in English (1986), in which he makes clear his reasons for promoting it, referring to both Marxist analysis and regionalist discourse (pp. 15, 29, 32):

> The Tamil Sangam culture with variations still continue in this region. The dance of Velan had taken new forms and developed into the present-day cult of Teyyam over a period of 1,500 years. This uninterrupted continuity of the Sangam tradition makes Teyyam a prominent religious system of north Kerala. ...
>
> The Teyyam ritual dance is exclusively performed by the male members of the traditional caste groups like Vannan, Malayan, Velan, Mavilan, Pulayan and Koppalan. These sections belong to the Scheduled Castes and Tribes. They are the sole custodians of Teyyam art and dance. In that way it is the art of the depressed castes. Naturally they belong to poor economic background. As the artists belong to this particular social class, he [sic] commanded no status and position. ...
>
> The social system which patronised this art form, kept the artist bonded and submissive. The rigid social system of a caste-oriented society did not encourage the all-round growth of personality of the artist.

Teyyam, potentially a classical art of ancient Tamil culture, with a universal appeal, was thus nipped in the bud because of the local social system (pp. 39, 42):

> Although it incorporates some folk aspects, it is a developed art form and a systematic stylization had taken place in the course of its development.

[...] However, the Teyyam dance could not achieve the status of a classical theatre as its growth was arrested due to various factors of social, political and economic system of the region. Further, as the artists belonged to the depressed communities the status of the art form was belittled by a caste-ridden society. The classical arts like Kathakali had borrowed several aspects from Teyyam. There is a close resemblance between the Teyyam art and the Kathakali in make-up, costume, dance and musical instrument. [...] But the rural background and the position of the artists made the Teyyam an entirely different art of the poor, depressed and downtrodden.

Kurup's purpose in promoting Teyyam as art is thus manifold: to demonstrate that Teyyam is the true heir to ancient Dravidian culture, to suggest that it has the same aesthetic potential as classical art, and to denounce the social oppression that prevented it from fully blossoming. In this perspective, his cultural mediation is to be understood in connection with a complex work of the imagination, involving, for instance, ideas about progress that call not only for a better appreciation of the artistic heritage of Kerala, but also for the betterment of the socio-economic condition of the performers themselves.

Looking for Money and Consideration

Kurup's booklet ends by echoing the preoccupations of a famous Teyyam performer, winner of an award from the Kerala Sangeetha Nataka Akademi in 1975, who is said to have been the first 'to take the art form to different parts of Kerala and outside without ritual formalities as a theatrical performance' (p. 53–4):

> There is no future for Teyyam art and artists. It is dying and in a moribund state. The existing society would spend Rs 10,000 for a festival, but Rs 10 only for an artist. The social changes and the modernity had adversely affected the art and cult. However, as an art form it is to be preserved and encouraged.

As a permanent official and teacher at the Teyyam Institute of Kodakkat (which Ashley helped to establish), this performer has encouraged Teyyam studies by foreign students. 'He finds that their involvement in this field had given encouragement to some native scholars to study and analyse this dying art' (p. 56). Locally, there have been negative perceptions about all these developments, however, which have provoked social tensions. One dancer from one of the five institutes recorded by Ashley in 1984 was banned from performing in temples after his performance at the Delhi Asian Games in 1982 led to an accusation of 'selling out' Teyyam. As he said (Ashley 1993: 246–7):

I wanted [Teyyam] to be expanded outside of the temple. By opening an institute other castes can come and learn and it will be performed on a public stage. I want it to be appreciated on a mass scale. We want people to understand how difficult teyyam is to perform – and thus realize that we are not being paid enough.

There are thus several different factors contributing to what Ashley himself calls the 'commoditization' of Teyyam under the renewed forms of dance or theatrical performance. The possibility of staging Teyyam as an art form makes it a means for performers to raise their social and economic status, while still presenting in a dramatic way a rich array of ideological referents and purposes (for example, the valorisation of a 'Dravidian culture'). With this aim in mind, new ways of staging what is still called 'Teyyam' have been elaborated so that it may qualify for inclusion in the general marketing of cultural goods. The staging is now devoid of so-called 'ritual formalities', alienating to contemporary urban taste, as they were to modernists early in the last century. This 'sanitized' version typically shows to advantage the drumming, the dance steps and gestures, and above all the costume and make-up, the whole being designed to last less than the usual two hours of Western shows. In this version 'Teyyam' has recently reached international audiences.

Meeting the International Public

We may discern movement in two directions. In one direction foreigners come to the villages, in the other the villagers go abroad. The Ford Foundation has been engaged in a programme of support for 'traditional cultures' in order to respond to a perceived 'crisis of values' or 'the eroding social and cultural coherence of the modern world' (the Foundation's words), especially in Third World nations (Ashley 1993: 306ff). This can be seen as another discourse on the negative effects of globalization.

In this way the Foundation helped to produce a folk festival organized by Kozhikode University in 1984 in Kerala, in which Teyyam was prominently featured both in the form of decorative items such as costumes at the venue entrance, and as staged performances. The festival took place in a village school, and the audience comprised local villagers, Indian and foreign scholars, photographers and artists. What is significant for the present discussion is that one of the university organizers explained that the purpose of such festivals was 'to re-establish the villagers' umbilical attachment to these elemental forms which have in many ways been impaired by changes of time' (Sankara Pillai, cited in Ashley 1993: 320–1). In other words, the local was to be rescued by going global. Urban-educated scholars and artists, helped by the external funding of a concerned global agency, were there to help unsuspecting villagers to recover their true local culture against the attacks of globalization.

There was an additional loop in this global reaction to the global, in that one of the guests was Peter Brook, engaged in the preparation of his version of the *Mahabharata* epic. He had already come to Kerala the previous year to witness a Teyyam performance arranged specially for him in a village through the mediation of folklorist and drama school teacher A. K. Nambiar. For Brook, Teyyam could have been a source of inspiration for theatrical ideas of Indian origin, to which he might have lent a universal dimension. As far as I am aware, however, he did not make use of it.

This leads us to the second perspective in which the Teyyam spectacle has caught the international eye. In a significant development, we find a photograph of Teyyam on the cover of a French book entitled *Atlas de l'imaginaire* (Gründ and Khaznadar 1996). The authors are directors of a well-known cultural institution in Paris, the Maison des Cultures du Monde, which regularly produces musical, dance and theatrical performances by companies from all over the world. It invited a Teyyam troupe to perform in the street during the French Year of India in 1985, and again in 1989 to stage a more complete show in collaboration with a theatre company, a feature repeated in 2003 during the Seventh Festival de l'imaginaire. J. Duvignaud, in the Preface to the *Atlas* (1996), says:

> Away with your fads for the exotic, for tourism, for folklore …! Since 1982 the Maison des Cultures du Monde has been responding to the open-ended invitation bequeathed by Antonin Artaud: to reveal the plentiful and fascinating wealth of festivals, games, rituals and perfor- mances by which men living on earth today represent themselves and represent their dreams …

If this interpretation of Artaud's message seems somewhat eccentric, the reference to him is nonetheless not accidental. Producers and actors alike have tried in the recent past to take inspiration from his manifesto and to emphasize the physical and dramatic dimensions of theatrical shows. This has contributed to a recent interest in the study of rituals all over the world, treating them as forms of drama.[14] A recent development in this direction was the creation in 1995 by Gründ, Khaznadar and a few French scholars, under the aegis of UNESCO, of what claims to be a new academic discipline, 'ethno-scenology'.

Teyyam is well adapted for such a programme, and has contributed in its own way towards shaping it, but the perspective clearly differs from the one advocated by the Ford Foundation. Here, Teyyam becomes part of an international heritage of the imagination (as a matter of fact, a rather imaginative paper on Teyyam by F. Gründ appeared in 1989 in a magazine called *Internationale de l'imaginaire*). At the same time, this appraisal is made through a kind of romanticisation of ritual: for instance, the book quite complacently describes human sacrifice, an astonishing reversal of appreciation in contrast with earlier accusations of savagery. Actually, rituals are never shown on stage, but are merely evoked by commentaries in order to generate in the audience a kind of reverent awe that itself adds value.

Conclusion

Discussions of Teyyam involve widely differing points of view expressed at different levels of society. Although Teyyam is still mainly a village cult, most of these discussions relate to notions of globalizing: 'primitivity', irrationality, the imagination, popular culture, cultural heritage, worldwide social and cultural cohesion, etc. Social influences are diverse. Colonial administrators, Christian evangelists, reformist Hindu saints, local caste elites, Marxists, nationalists, folklorists, anthropologists, dramatists – all have something to say about Teyyam. What should be stressed is that these various discourses have all implied interpretations of 'the locality', and conceptions about the relationship of the locality with what are perceived as 'universals'.

The discourses also imply contextual references to the identities that Teyyam is supposed to define: the nation, the region, North Malabar, this or that caste, a particular religious system, the villagers' true culture, Dravidian artistry, mankind's innate power of expression, or just individual professional practice. Even performers themselves are often aware nowadays of various global aspects while preserving Teyyam as a village cult. Behind obvious appearances, things might therefore be more complex. My analysis has had to distinguish between concepts that seem often to articulate with each other contextually. An example can be seen in one of many Kerala newspaper reports about Teyyam. In words that should strike a familiar chord by now, journalist K. K. Gopalalakrishnan writes (*The Hindu*, 6 March 1994: x):

Although it is only performed in the relatively neglected northern part of Kerala, theyyam is the foremost of the ritual folklore art forms of the State. Its prominence is always beyond the superficiality of a mere ritual because it combines the significance of social unity, harmony and mutual respect with the highlights of the cultural heritage and bewitching aesthetic sense of the people.

We find here a combination of many concepts that the analysis above has distinguished. The author continues: 'The general belief, especially of the local inhabitants, is that theyyams are representatives of Gods and demi-Gods.' A caption below a photo is shorter: 'The locals believe ... etc.' Most interestingly, this reference to 'the locals' is based on something unsaid. The author evokes a Teyyam performed in 'an old once very affluent landlord family', without revealing that it is his own – a revealing example of a 'self-exoticizing' process (Battaglia 1999, p. 125) resulting from an internalisation of the kind of material discussed in this paper. As anthropologist J. R. Freeman suggests (Freeman 1991: 169):

> Thus, while my general impression is that the educated (particularly English-educated and urban) Hindus of northern Kerala are less likely to have belief or respect for teyyam-worship as a religious expression, it is also not unusual to find many, even among this group, who, at festival time, return to their ancestral homes or caste-shrines to participate in the rites.

Teyyam has now two intersecting realities: the cult (only in Malabar villages) and the staged demonstration (everywhere, including Malabar villages). In both forms it has been, and still is, a locus where contrasting meanings about the local and the global are projected, especially at the village level where all the various facets may be present. The connection between these meanings can imply a coexistence or, at times, an implicit misunderstanding. More often, it is a contextual shift. In some cases, too, it seems to rely on personal ambiguity and inner complexities, for in the work of the imagination at the individual level, the global world is within.

Notes

1 See for instance Dumont 1985; Hannerz 1989; Assayag 1998; 1999; Racine 2001; Terdiman 2001.

2 This chapter is the outcome of various oral presentations (Maison des Sciences de l'Homme, Paris, 1997; South Asian Anthropologists Group, London, 1999; London School of Economics, 2001). I wish to thank all the participants at these meetings for their comments. I also particularly thank C. Clémentin-Ojha and Mayuri Koga for their detailed remarks on an earlier draft. A related short paper for the general public has previously been published (Tarabout 1997).

3 For a detailed analysis of the mediations involved in the international 'marketing' of another South Indian ritual practice, and of matters associated with this development, see Tarabout 2003.

4 Because the region where it is still prevalent as a village cult is not an area of Kerala in which I have personally conducted research, I have to rely heavily on others' work – particularly that of anthropologists W. Ashley and J. R. Freeman – and on other

available material. Fortunately, Teyyam figures feature as contemporary symbols of Kerala culture, so there is no dearth of documents for at least the last 20 years.

5   Documentation on these cults is constantly growing in Malayalam, the language of Kerala, and in English. In English, the reader may refer mainly to the works of Freeman (1991 [by far the most comprehensive account]; 1993; 1998); Ashley (1979; 1993); Ashley and Holloman (1990); Kurup (1973; 1977; 1986); Balan Nambiar (1993); Paliath (1995); and Koga (2003).

6   Compare Blackburn 1985; see also Tarabout 2001.

7   Compare Nichter 1977 for the cults of the neighbouring district of South Kanara, which present strikingly similar traits.

8   As far as I am aware, reports from both administrators and travellers before the end of the nineteenth century are remarkably discreet on the subject, with the exception of a sixteenth-century description by Duarte Barbosa which might allude to a similar cult.

9   Which required him to report in detail about physical characteristics – such as the maxillo-zygomatic index or the distribution of hairs on the chest – following the then current practices of physical anthropology.

10 I use the expression 'new elite' here in a somewhat loose sense. What was new was their frequent English education, and the fact that their livelihood no longer depended on the land. In this they mostly differed from the rural elite, although they belonged to the same castes and sometimes even the same families.

11 I thank Mayuri Koga for kindly providing me with this information.

12 See for instance Appadurai 1986; Phillips and Steiner 1999.

13 See for instance Balan Nambiar (1995), a Kerala artist who has documented Teyyam by taking photographs on a large scale, before it is 'lost for ever'.

14 See for instance Schechner 1983.

Bibliography

Anonymous (1978) *Folk Arts Directory*. Trichur: Kerala Sangeetha Nataka Akademi.

Anonymous (1980) *Dances of Kerala*. Trivandrum: Government of Kerala, Department of Public Relations.

Appadurai, Arjun, ed. (1986) *The Social Life of Things. Commodities in cultural perspective*. Cambridge: Cambridge University Press.

Appadurai, Arjun (1996) *Modernity at Large. Cultural dimensions of globalization*. Minneapolis: University of Minnesota Press.

Ashley, Wayne (1979) 'The Teyyam Kettu of Northern Kerala', *The Drama Review*, 23, 2: 99–112.

—— (1993) 'Recodings: ritual, theatre, and political display in Kerala State, South India', unpublished PhD dissertation, New York University.

Ashley, Wayne and Regina Holloman (1990) 'Teyyam', in F. R. Richmond, D. L. Swann and P. B. Zarrilli, eds, *Indian Theatre: Traditions of performance*. University of Hawaii Press; 131–65.

Assayag, Jackie (1998) 'La culture comme fait social global? Anthropologie et (post)modernité', *L'Homme*, 148 : 201–4.

—— (1999) 'La "glocalisation" du beau. Miss Monde en Inde, 1996', *Terrain*, 32: 67–82.

Balan Nambiar (1993) 'Tai Paradevata: ritual impersonation in the Teyyam tradition of Kerala', in H. Brückner, L. Lutze and A. Malik, eds, *Flags of Fame: Studies in South Asian folk culture*. Delhi: Manohar; 139–63.

—— (1995) 'Photographing Teyyam', *India International Centre Quarterly*, summer-monsoon 1995 (special number: *Kerala, Progress and Paradox*): 131–42.

Baricco, Alessandro (2002) *Next. Petit livre sur la globalization et le monde à venir*. Paris: Albin Michel/Milan: Feltrinelli.

Barnard, Alan (2000) *History and Theory in Anthropology*. Cambridge: Cambridge University Press.

Battaglia, Debbora (1999) 'Toward an ethic of the open subject: writing culture in good conscience', in Henrietta L. Moore, ed., *Anthropological Theory Today*. Cambridge, Polity Press; 114–50.

Blackburn, Stuart H. (1985) 'Death and deification: folk cults in Hinduism', *History of Religions*, 24, 3: 255–74.

Deshpande, Satish (2001) 'From development to globalization: shifts in ideological paradigms of nation and economy in the Third World', in R. Melkote, ed., *Meanings of Globalization. Indian and French perspectives*. New Delhi: Sterling Publishers; 98–114.

Dumont, Louis (1985) 'Identités collectives et idéologie universaliste: leur interaction de fait', *Critique*, 456 : 506–18.

Fawcett, Fred (1901) 'Nâyars of Malabar', *Madras Government Museum Bulletin*, III, 3: 185–322.

Freeman, John R. (1991) 'Purity and violence: sacred power in the Teyyam worship of Malabar', unpublished PhD dissertation, University of Pennsylvania.

—— (1993) 'Performing possession: ritual and consciousness in the Teyyam complex of Northern Kerala', in H. Brückner, L. Lutze and A. Malik, eds, *Flags of Fame: Studies in South Asian folk culture*. Delhi: Manohar; 109–38.

—— (1998) 'Formalised possession among the Tantris and Teyyams in North Malabar', *South Asia Research*, 18, 1: 73–98.

Frykenberg, Robert E. (1988) 'Fundamentalism and revivalism in South Asia', in J. W. Björkman, ed., *Fundamentalism, Revivalists and Violence in South Asia*. Delhi: Manohar; 20–39.

—— (1989) 'The emergence of modern "Hinduism" as a concept and as an institution: a reappraisal with special reference to South India', in G. D. Sontheimer and H. Kulke, eds, *Hinduism Reconsidered*. Delhi: Manohar.

Ganguly-Scrase, Ruchira and Timothy J. Scrase (2001) 'Who wins? Who loses? and Who even knows? Responses to economic liberalisation and cultural globalization in India', *South Asia*, XXIV, 1: 141–58.

Gründ, Françoise (1989) 'Le Teyyam du Kérala', *Internationale de l'imaginaire*, 12.

Gründ, Françoise and Chérif Khaznadar (1996) *Atlas de l'imaginaire*, Paris/Lausanne: Maison des Cultures du Monde/Favre.

Hannerz, Ulf (1989) 'Culture between center and periphery: toward a macroanthropology', *Ethnos*, 3–4: 200–16.

Harriss, John (2001) 'Globalization and the world's poor: institutions, inequality and justice', *Economic and Political Weekly*, XXXVI, 23 (9 June): 2034–7.

Hensman, Rohini (2001) 'Religious sentiment and national sovereignty. Resisting Talibanisation', *Economic and Political Weekly*, XXXVI, 23 (9 June): 2031–3.

Koga, Mayuri (2003) 'The politics of ritual and art in Kerala: controversies concerning the staging of *teyyam*', *Journal of the Japanese Association for South Asian Studies*, 15: 547–79.

Kunhappa, Murkot (1980) *Sree Narayana Guru*. Delhi: National Book Trust.

Kurup, K. K. N. (1973) *The Cult of Teyyam and Hero Worship*. Calcutta: Indian Publications (Indian Folklore Series No. 21).

—— (1977) *Aryan and Dravidian Elements in Malabar Folklore: A case study of Ramavilliam Kalakam*. Trivandrum: Kerala Historical Society.

—— (1986) *Teyyam*. Trivandrum: Government of Kerala, Department of Public Relations.

Menon, Dilip (1994) *Caste, Nationalism and Communism in South India. Malabar, 1900–1948*. Cambridge: Cambridge University Press.

Osella, Filippo (1993) 'Caste, class, power and social mobility in Kerala, India', unpublished PhD dissertation, London School of Economics.

Nichter, M. (1977) 'The Joga and Maya of the Tuluva Bhuta', *The Eastern Anthropologist*, 30, 2: 139–55.

Paliath, J. J. (1995) *Theyyam. An analytical study of the folk culture, wisdom and personality*. New Delhi: Indian Social Institute.

Phillips, Ruth B. and Christopher B. Steiner, eds (1999) *Unpacking Culture. Art and commodity in colonial and postcolonial worlds*. Berkeley and Los Angeles: University of California Press.

Racine, Jean-Luc (2001) 'On globalization: beyond the paradigm. States and civil societies in the global and local context', in R. Melkote, ed., *Meanings of Globalization. Indian and French perspectives*. New Delhi: Sterling; 1–40.

Raghavan, M. D. (1947) *Folk Plays and Dances of Kerala*. Trichur: The Rama Varma Archaeological Society.

Sarveswaran, P. (1980) 'Sri Vaikunda Swamikal. A forgotten social reformer of Kerala', *Journal of Kerala Studies*, VII, 1–4: 1–10.

Schechner, Richard (1983) *Performative Circumstances. From the avant-garde to Ramlila*. Calcutta: Seagull Books.

Tarabout, Gilles (1997) 'La mise en culture des rites', *Cultures en mouvement*, 5: 40–3.

—— (2001) 'Ancêtres et revenants. La construction sociale de la malemort en Inde', in B. Baptandier, ed., *De la malemort en quelques pays d'Asie*. Paris: Karthala; 165–99.

—— (2003) 'Passage à l'art. L'adaptation d'un culte sud-indien au patronage artistique', in Y. Escande and J.-M. Schaeffer, eds, *L'esthétique: Europe, Chine et ailleurs*. Paris: Editions You-Feng; 37–60.

Terdiman, Richard (2001) 'Globalization and cultural studies: conceptualization, convergence, and complication', *Comparative Studies of South Asia, Africa and the Middle East*, XXI, 1–2: 82–7.

William, V. (1944) 'Devil dances of North Malabar (Thirayattam or Theyyam Tullal)', unpublished dissertation submitted for the degree of Bachelor of Divinity, Bangalore United Theological College.

10

GLOBALIZING HINDUISM: A 'TRADITIONAL' GURU AND MODERN BUSINESSMEN IN CHENNAI

C. J. Fuller and John Harriss

Affirming the Sanatana Dharma and Recording the History of a Billion-Strong Global Religion in Renaissance.[1]

The need for cultural revival in India is the need of the hour. How are we to hand over our cultural values to our next generation when westernization is the current trend via the media, social and peer pressures [sic]. The Indian cultural forms will disappear from this nation if its constituent elements are not understood and imbibed by our next generation.[2]

The first of the two epigraphs above is the masthead on the website of *Hinduism Today*, a magazine published in Hawaii since 1979, which enjoys a wide readership among overseas Hindus, especially in the United States. Using the standard modern phrase *sanatana dharma* or 'eternal religion' to refer to Hinduism, the epigraph is a striking example of how Hinduism may be proclaimed as a genuine global or world religion, flourishing as never before. The second epigraph comes from the website of a religious trust in Chennai (Madras) and it announces the *Vedic Heritage Teaching Programme (VHTP)*, which was designed in America but is also being promoted in India. The epigraph, which equates 'Indian' culture with the ostensibly Vedic Hindu religious tradition, expresses a profound anxiety that westernization may soon lead to its extinction.

Optimistic confidence about global Hinduism and pessimistic concern about Hindu Indian culture are obviously antithetical. Nevertheless, they belong to the same discourse of globalized Hinduism and highlight a crucial ambiguity that runs through it. This ambiguity is at the heart of our discussion, which focuses particularly on Swami Dayananda Saraswati, a Hindu holy man and patron of the *VHTP* who is popular among modern big businessmen in Chennai.[3]

The Chennai businessmen belong to the upper managerial-professional segment of the middle class. As Satish Deshpande comments, 'much of the celebratory rhetoric about globalization emanates from, and is aimed at, this group' (2003: 150). Indeed, we argue, there now exists a new, globalized upper-middle class made up of 'non-resident Indians' or NRIs, together with prosperous Indians in India, mostly resident in major cities, whose work, education and lifestyle link them closely to their relatives, colleagues, friends and other associates in the NRI population. Many of these Indians also travel abroad frequently or have returned home after several years working overseas. The NRI category emerged in the early 1970s (Rajagopal 2001: 241–2); in America, and to a lesser extent in Britain and some other countries, NRIs have become one of the most prosperous, professionally successful and best-educated of all ethnic minorities.

In statistical terms, the NRI population has made only a small difference to Hinduism's worldwide distribution, because the overwhelming majority of Hindus still live in India. Financially and ideologically, however, the NRIs' impact has been far more decisive. The powerful Hindu nationalist organization known as the Vishwa Hindu Parishad (VHP) or World Hindu Council was founded in India in 1964, and the VHP of America was active by 1969 (Rajagopal 2001: 239). The rise of Hindu nationalism is a vital element in the contemporary development of overseas Hinduism and vice versa (Bénéï 1998), but it is not the whole story and in its earlier years, especially in America, the VHP was not a stridently political organization. Moreover, one key point is that the VHP's name – even to many Hindus who do not support the organization – is a sign of a new truth: the emergence of a global diaspora whose Hinduism is a world religion on equal terms with Christianity or Islam. This idea, as we have seen, is expressed on the masthead of *Hinduism Today*'s website.

Easily accessible from *Hinduism Today*'s website is a directory of 'saints, sages, swamis and satgurus', 'divine mothers' and Hindu religious organizations (ashrams, monasteries, teaching centres, etc.).[4] In this directory are many religious personages who live and work outside India or are based both in India and overseas, notably in the United States. Since Swami Vivekananda's famous visit to Chicago in 1893, travelling holy men have been a familiar phenomenon, but in the last two or three decades they have flourished as never before and they are key agents in the process of globalizing Hinduism. One of them is Swami Dayananda Saraswati.

Swami Dayananda Saraswati and His Activities

Swami Dayananda Saraswati (who is not to be confused with his namesake, the founder of the Arya Samaj) was born in 1930 in a village in Thanjavur District, Tamil Nadu.[5] He was his Smarta Brahman parents' second son and was named Natarajan; his father died when he was young, so that he was mainly brought up by his mother. As a schoolboy, Natarajan reacted vigorously to the anti-Hindu and anti-Brahman Dravida Kazhagam movement, and in his own eyes, his experience as a young Brahman defending himself and his religion against overwhelming hostility had a formative influence on his life. After finishing school, the young Natarajan went to Madras to find work, like so many other rural Brahmans in the 1940s. He trained as a stenographer and taught himself English, worked for a Hindu magazine which sought to combat the Dravidian movement's publications, served for a short time in the Indian Air Force, and finally became a typist in a large company.

In 1952 Natarajan went to hear Swami Chinmayananda lecturing at a *jnana-yajna* ('knowledge-sacrifice') session in Madras. Chinmayananda was the leading disciple of Swami Shivananda, founder of the Divine Life Society, and his lecture tours attracted large crowds across India in the 1950s. Chinmayananda's aim was apparently to 'convert Hindus to Hinduism', especially the 'faithless' educated class (McKean 1996: 178). Natarajan's life was transformed by Chinmayananda's teaching; he volunteered to work for him and started learning the Veda, and in 1953 he became the secretary of the newly-founded Chinmaya Mission. He later gave up his typing job and also resisted his mother's attempts to find him a wife. In 1962 Chinmayananda suddenly initiated Natarajan as a sannyasi, an ascetic renouncer, a transformation that seemed natural to him but caused his mother and brothers great distress. Swami Dayananda was presumably given his new name at this time.

In 1963 Chinmayananda asked Dayananda to teach in Sandeepany Sadhanalaya, the Mission's centre in Bombay (now Mumbai). After about a year, however, Dayananda left Bombay and eventually arrived in Rishikesh, the famous north Indian pilgrimage centre at the head of the River Ganges. He stayed there for three years, concentrating on his religious studies and living in a hut that is now the site of his Rishikesh ashram. In 1964 Chinmayananda presided over the foundation of the Vishwa Hindu Parishad in Sandeepany Sadhanalaya, and in 1966 the VHP held its first World Hindu Conference at the great Kumbha Mela festival in Allahabad, when Dayananda was reunited with Chinmayananda. Dayananda rejoined the Chinmaya Mission in 1967; he continued with Mission work and the *jnana-yajna* tours for five years, until he returned to teach in the Bombay centre in 1972.[6]

A few years later, Dayananda replaced Chinmayananda on a lecture tour
to the United States, and after his third visit there, he was invited by his
mainly American followers to teach a course on Hinduism in California. By
1982, Dayananda was working independently of the Chinmaya Mission and
making repeated visits to America. In 1987 he began to teach in a new centre in Saylorsburg, Pennsylvania, founded by a combination of US and NRI
devotees. In India, two centres for residential teaching were established – in
Rishikesh (built in its modern form in the 1980s) and Coimbatore (1990) –
and throughout the country Dayananda and other swamis, who are his disciples, now give regular lectures and courses to both adults and children. In
practice if not in name, Dayananda now heads an established Hindu mission,
similar to the Chinmaya Mission or the Divine Life Society, which has its own
teaching-centres-cum-ashrams in India and the United States, as well as other
educational programmes; a growing cohort (more than 250 worldwide) of
sannyasis and other former students who spread their guru's teachings, which
are also reproduced in a steady output of publications; a large following of
mainly middle-class supporters and disciples in both India and America,
whose donations provide substantial financial support; and, last but not least,
several promotional websites. In Chennai, the Sastraprakasika Trust supports
and publicises Dayananda's activities, and sells publications and tapes through
its well-organized website. Separate websites are run by the centres in
Rishikesh and Saylorsburg, and the Center for Traditional Vedanta set up in
the USA under Dayananda's patronage.[7]

In every context, Dayananda is styled as a 'traditional teacher of Brahma
Vidya or Advaita Vedanta', and his teaching centres are specifically said to be
designed for the 'traditional teaching of Vedanta and Sanskrit'. The archaic
name of the Saylorsburg and Coimbatore centres – Arsha Vidya Gurukulam –
also pointedly emphasizes traditional teaching by a guru of the knowledge
(*vidya*) deriving from the ancient sages (*rishi*). Seen in comparative perspective,
however, Dayananda is a quintessentially modern guru, who teaches in
English – although some of his fellow swamis do teach in Indian languages –
and has a middle-class following in India and America, just like his own guru
Chinmayananda (van der Veer 1994: 136–7).

In its essentials, Dayananda's teaching is also typical of contemporary
Vedantic Hinduism or neo-Vedanta: it is monistic, being premised on the indi-
vidual soul's identity with the Supreme Being, and it insists on the primacy of
the Veda as the source of the 'eternal' *sanatana dharma* from which all religions
later developed – not only Hinduism but other faiths such as Christianity and
Islam as well. The Veda is also the foundation of Indian culture and society.
Dayananda's apparent intention, however, is to distinguish himself from other
Hindu holy men as above all else a traditional teacher, who is specifically

committed to the value of Sanskrit. The Saylorsburg website, for instance, describes him as an 'outstanding teacher of the Brahma Vidya ... not a preacher giving sermons, nor is he a missionary trying to spread a particular belief. Also he is not a mystic promising subjective experiences.' Compared with the Shankaracharyas of Kanchipuram, the most prominent and influential religious leaders in Tamil Nadu (Fuller 1999: 47–51) – or their rivals, the Shankaracharyas of Sringeri – Dayananda can communicate with English-speaking middle-class Indians much more directly, but like them, he is a Brahman renouncer who stands for tradition and orthodoxy. He thereby distances himself, too, from popular, non-Brahman religious cults in Tamil Nadu, like that of the goddess Parashakti and her 'god-man' Bangaru Adigalar of Melmaruvathur. Dayananda is also very different from eclectic god-men like the immensely popular, miracle-working Sathya Sai Baba or fashionable gurus like SriSri Ravishankar, who promotes his 'Art of living' from an American base but attracts a middle-class following in Chennai.[8]

In recent years, Dayananda has hardened his support for the VHP and the Hindu nationalist movement. Thus in 2002, when the controversy over Rama's temple in Ayodhya erupted again, Dayananda – then president of the Hindu Dharma Rakshana Samithi (Hindu Religion Protection Society) – was reported to have 'thundered at a public meeting' in Chennai that building the temple is a non-negotiable matter and Muslim leaders must 'yield to the majority' so that *dharma* can be reasserted in India.[9] Dayananda has also been persistently aggressive towards Christianity in his lectures, and he supported the Tamil Nadu government's controversial ordinance banning 'forcible' conversions, which was issued in 2002.[10] Dayananda has taken a leading role in the activities of the VHP of America, which sponsored the first Dharma Sansad, a meeting of Hindu religious leaders in the USA, at Saylorsburg in August 1998, and a year later he was one of four prominent swamis advertised as leaders of a 'whirlwind' pilgrimage from Los Angeles to New York to promote Hindu *dharma* across the United States (although later reports imply that he did not actually take part).[11]

The activities pursued by Dayananda or given his patronage are extensive, and his disciples and followers in India and the United States – men and women, adults and children, domiciled Indians, NRIs and white Americans – have diverse backgrounds, outlooks and interests, even if they are all broadly middle-class. About most of them, however, we lack detailed data, and this chapter instead focuses on the men running large or successful modern businesses in Chennai who count themselves as Dayananda's followers. A principal question to be explored is how and why there is apparently an elective affinity between Dayananda's teaching and the businessmen's socio-economic values and interests. To answer this question we look at some aspects of the businessmen's religious beliefs and practices, and Dayananda's activities in Chennai, before examining the kind of Hinduism that he is promulgating.

Chennai Businessmen and their Religion

Our evidence comes from interviews conducted in 2000 by John Harriss with 40 big businessmen in Chennai. This group included the chairmen or managing directors of Chennai-based firms listed in *The Economic Times*' rankings of the Top 500 Indian companies, as well as entrepreneurs in the city's rapidly developing software industry. Harriss's aim was to replicate Milton Singer's research, carried out in 1964 in Madras and described in his book, *When a Great Tradition Modernizes* (1972).[12]

Singer interviewed several men described as 'the industrial leaders of Madras' about their religious beliefs and practices, and he says that in general they conformed with the self-description given by one of them: 'a fellow who is not an orthodox Hindu but who believes in the essential tenets of Hinduism'. Singer characterized their religion as an 'industrial theodicy', in which beliefs and ethics were emphasized (Singer 1972: 342):

> In this sense, the effect of industry is to change the traditional conception of the essentials of Hinduism from an emphasis on correct ritual observances and family disciplines to an emphasis on philosophical principles, devotional faith and right conduct.

According to Singer, the 'main difference among the [Hindu industrialists] is between those who have been influenced by Gandhi's reinterpretation of the *Bhagavad Gita* and other scriptures' – mostly through the idea that modern work can be a moral duty and 'sacrifice' – 'and those who are influenced by the more traditional gurus and teachers' (ibid.: 340), notably the Shankaracharyas of Kanchipuram and Sringeri. The businessmen, we are also told, viewed their success 'as a product of devotion to their calling and duty' and their 'careers as one path to salvation', so that their own and their companies' prosperity are 'expressions of divine will'; these opinions are endorsed by 'spiritual advisors' and 'pandits' (ibid.: 352–3). Among the businessmen, about half of whom were Brahmans (ibid.: 284), Singer felt that religion was regarded as a private matter, and he claimed that they 'compartmentalized', treating 'business and religion [as] different and separate spheres' (ibid.: 320). Singer derived some support for these arguments from an interview with Sri Chandrasekharendra Saraswati, the senior Shankaracharya of Kanchipuram, who became known as the Paramacharya (and died in 1994, aged 100). It was the Shankaracharya's view, for example, that 'formal and organized religion and "congregations" had waned, but that personal faith had increased.'[13]

Interviews at the turn of the twenty-first century with men in the same positions as those whom Singer met, including a good many from the same families, suggest a significantly different picture. Most strikingly, Singer never referred to experiences of the miraculous or the presence of 'god-men', although these are important to many contemporary businessmen. According to Singer, in the 1960s the industrial leaders' relationship with the Shankaracharyas was primarily about their philosophical teaching. In 2000, however, some businessmen told stories about miracles by the Paramacharya, as well as by 'god-men' such as Swami Rajagopala, who has an ashram in the Chennai suburb of Nanganallur and a considerable following among NRIs in the United States.

An example concerning the Paramacharya comes from a discussion with a prominent scientist, Govinda (pseudonym), who also runs a highly successful business. This man, like many others, has a picture of Chandrasekharendra on his desk. Govinda referred to a time when he was having a lot of trouble in his business from the then Chief Minister of Tamil Nadu over the Urban Land Ceilings Act. Govinda went to visit the Paramacharya, who said to him, 'What is this? You've come to me just for information? There is no problem.' Govinda returned to Chennai to be informed that the Chief Minister wanted to have breakfast with him, and he got the go-ahead for the project that he had long been seeking without success. On another occasion he and his wife visited the Paramacharya with their youngest daughter who was then unmarried. At that time Govinda's wife was anxious about her marriage. The Paramacharya gave her a coconut. Govinda and his wife did not know why, but within seven days the daughter's marriage was arranged. As far as Govinda is concerned, the Paramacharya was a living god (cf Harriss 2003: 353–4).

In the case of Swami Rajagopala, a pamplet produced by his American-based devotees recounts his story, which includes this account of the origin of the Shri Rajarajeshwari image now installed in his ashram's temple. Interestingly, the Paramacharya is involved in the miracle as well.

27 September 1957: 012 Thaiyappamudali Street, Madras. ... About 10 pm Sri Rajagopala Swami is offering oblations into the sacred fire. ... About midnight two devotees emerge from the worship room and report to the Swami. 'Come and see! There is something bright and shiny floating over the sacred fire!' The Swami goes in to take a look. Indeed, among the flames ... are floating a number of shiny gem-like stones. The Swami inserts a plate below them. As soon as they touch the plate they become heavy and the plate tilts to one side. ... The very next day, the gems which

floated on fire are taken to the Sage of Kanchi, Sri Chandrasekharendra Saraswati. He who came to the aid of the Swami in the spiritual path just as a guru would, looks at these gems and in his divine sight, the biggest gem becomes as the Divine Mother Herself ... just as the sage pronounced. Within one year, the big gem transforms itself into the like-ness of Sri Rajarajeshwari bearing conch, discus, sugarcane bow, and flower arrows.[14]

Miraculous occurrences in the god-man's life-story, as well as during worship in the ashram's temple, are strongly associated with the reverence that people feel for Rajagopala. Among Chennai businessmen there are devoted followers, too, of both Shirdi Sai Baba and Sathya Sai Baba, whose crucial associations with the miraculous are discussed by Lawrence Babb (1987: Part 3) and Deborah Swallow (1982), as well as in hagiographic accounts by devotees (e.g. Seshadri 1999). Moreover, contrary to Singer's suggestions about 'industrial theodicy', for many of the business leaders, in common with most middle-class people in Chennai, public ritual observance and support for temples have never ceased to be important. Thus members of the Shri Vaishnava Brahman TVS family (the greatest of the Chennai business groups) have long given generous financial aid for renovating major temples, both Vaishnava and Shaiva, in Chennai, Madurai (the group's original home-base) and else-where in Tamil Nadu. Singer's notes on his interviews show that he generally focused on his respondents' views on *dharma*, *karma* and *moksha*, rather than on their religious practice and experience, so that the absence of data on the lat-ter, as well as his idea of 'industrial theodicy', may have been products of his line of questioning.[15] Certainly, though, there are no significant references in Singer's book or notes to 'god-men', ritual observances, temple-building or indeed the study of Vedanta – although there are quite a few references to the *Bhagavad Gita*, and relatedly to the idea of 'Do your Duty. Success depends on effort and the will of God.'

In comparison with Singer's account, our recent evidence shows more diverse, as well as more public, religiosity among businessmen in today's Chennai, where there is, in Maya Warrier's phrase (2003: 248), a 'dense reli-gious supermarket' from which individuals pick and choose according to their personal preferences.[16] The trends apparent in the differences between Singer's observations and our own are also reflected in changes at the Kanchipuram monastery. The late Paramacharya, Chandrasekharendra, whom Singer met, was widely respected for his asceticism. In contrast, his successor, Jayendra Saraswati, who is currently the senior Shankaracharya, aspires to 'the imperial swami model', and the monastery has entered 'a more customer-centred phase, accompanied by its own mystification of the acharya, parcelling out his charisma when deemed appropriate'.[17] Today, therefore, the Shankaracharya of Kanchipuram – once the epitome of Brahmanical ascetic orthodoxy in Tamil Nadu – is actively promoting himself and the monastery, although by doing so he also attracts considerable criticism from more conservative Hindus.

We cannot discuss here the full diversity of the religious market in present-day Chennai. Swami Dayananda, however, is attractive to businessmen of a rather more philosophical bent, whose religious interests and activities are focused around him. These men explicitly describe Dayananda as a teacher, not a 'god-man' like Swami Rajagopal, and they are, in their own self-descriptions, 'followers of the Vedic Heritage', or perhaps more accurately of neo-Vedanta. They are also attracted to Dayananda because he seems able to apply his Vedantic learning to practical problems. Arvind Rajagopal describes his own reaction to Dayananda, whom he heard in Berkeley in the 1980s, in similar terms. He was[18]

> energetic and engaging: he inspired trust and confidence. One got the sense that here was someone pious and learned in the scriptures who was yet at ease in the modern world of affairs, and thus capable of providing practical advice relatively free of the frustrating do's and don'ts, pre-scriptions and proscriptions, that those in conventional households grow up with.

Dayananda's religious teaching, as we note below, also resonates with contemporary (especially US) self-help and management ideas. Dayananda is sometimes invited to speak on business management, as he did at a function to launch a new software company in Chennai. At least two of the leading business houses fund the Sastraprakasika Trust, which propagates his teaching, and they and other businesses sponsor events such as the annual series of lectures on Successful Living that Dayananda gives in Kamaraj Hall, Chennai's largest auditorium. Two of Dayananda's disciples living in Chennai give regular courses on Vedantic philosophy, which also pick up on the theme of 'successful living'.

One of these courses was taught in 2000 on Sunday afternoons in a school hall in Adyar, south Chennai, a prosperous, upper-middle-class neighbour-hood. The classes, conducted by Swami Paramarthananda on the *Bhagavad Gita* in English, though with occasional forays into Tamil, were always well attended by a diverse and decidedly middle-class audience of two or three hundred people. Older people were strongly represented, but there were also a lot of young women and significant numbers of fairly young professionals of both sexes. The classes' stated aim was to show how the Vedanta helps us to develop a new vision of life – 'the Vedanta is a painful, time-consuming reassessment of life' – and also helps us to be happy in spite of the situations in which we find ourselves. Paramarthananda worked steadily through the *Gita*, emphasizing its relevance to modern life and occasionally using very mundane examples to illustrate the notion of detachment. We should think, he said, not 'I need a cup of coffee,' but 'A cup of coffee would be agreeable, although it's not important whether I have it or not.' He referred frequently to the virtues of self-control and moderation in everything, and to how the *Gita* teaches us self-confidence: 'Never look down upon yourself. If you feel diffidence, think of yourself as part of God.' Another important idea that he stressed was that we should not be fatalistic: 'The Veda is anti-fatalist [and] it says "Always take charge of your life".'

Two business leaders who are particularly devoted to Swami Dayananda are both men of about forty, who took MBAs at prestigious US universities after first studying engineering and accountancy (respectively) in local colleges in Chennai. Both are now enterprising and innovative chief executives of companies within their family business groups, responsible for introducing new methods of industrial organization and for branching out into the 'new economy' in the software industry. The two men travel widely and are, as we have witnessed, entirely comfortable in a western environment. In short, both might be described as thoroughly 'modern' men who are quite at home in the globalizing world. But they are also very serious about their religion, and they and their wives are active in religious observance and scriptural study, which they prefer to do in English because, as one of them admitted, they find it difficult to follow complex ideas in Tamil. Both men have longstanding family connections with the Shankaracharya of Sringeri, but say that they derive their knowledge of the Vedas from Dayananda, who is regarded as particularly responsible for the religious revival, attributed to the 'Vedanta Movement', which they now see in Chennai. The businessmen are attracted by what they perceive to be the 'scientific' nature of Vedic teaching. One of them explained that, like mathematics, the Veda is based on a very few axioms, of which the most important is that 'God is infinite', and much is said to follow logically from this basic proposition. Both men have generally moderate though socially conservative views, and clearly they were also reassured by Dayananda's teaching about the legitimacy of their wealth. One was obviously uncomfortable with questions about caste and inequality in Indian society and sought to justify caste practices as being no different in substance from what occurs in other societies.

Dayananda himself is – or can be – a charismatic speaker, with a gift for comedy and metaphor. These qualities were apparent at a public meeting addressed by Dayananda in 2000, which was attended by several of the business leaders we are discussing. Dayananda spoke in English to a huge audience of men and women, young and old, on the theme of 'Hinduism – what it means and what it does not'. The meeting was organized by an association founded in 1999, the Citizen's Committee for Dharma Rakshana Sammelan, which has the aim of opposing religious conversion – perceived as an act of violence against Hinduism.[19]

In his lecture Swami Dayananda spoke brilliantly and wittily in celebration of the knowledge contained within the Hindu tradition, often by making mocking comparisons with 'religions of the Book'. He concluded this part of his address (to prolonged applause) with the words, 'I am happy that I am a Hindu, and that I am not afflicted by guilt.' Then he turned to the issue of conversion. He spoke about the launching of charities in remote, tribal areas to teach people there – who are *not* 'non-Hindus' – that what they are doing is right, and to support them in resisting the attentions of missionaries from other religions. 'Indians need no lessons in giving,' he said, and Christians have no monopoly on compassion. Furthermore, 'Conversion is a violence. You [Christians] betrayed the trust we placed in you when you came and built your churches, when you started to convert. Conversion does violence to the person. I say, put a freeze on conversion.'[20] And he concluded with the words, 'Strength is being what you are. You are a nobody if you don't know that. It is in this sense that Hindus must be strong.'

Significantly, in his address Dayananda was continually switching between 'Hindus' and 'Indians', and in part of it he expressed unequivocal support for militant Hindu nationalism (cf Harriss 2003: 357–9). As noted above, he has also supported banning 'forcible' conversions. We do not know how Dayananda's followers are responding to his advocacy. Yet it is noteworthy that the Sastraprakasika Trust in early 2002 chose to put on its website a press report which, without actually condoning the violence then being waged against Muslims in Gujarat, shifted the focus to the notion of a Muslim conspiracy behind the Godhra atrocity that started the killings. Moreover, although he, like others, clearly abhorred violence, one of the Chennai businessmen once told Harriss, 'You know, in my heart I am with the RSS.' In analysing Dayananda's appeal, however, the most important point here is his insistence that it is by being 'more truly' or 'more fully' themselves as Hindus – 'Strength is being what you are' – that Indians can best tackle the problems of the modern world. The clear implication is that Indians do not become 'modern' by becoming more 'western', but rather by becoming more thoroughly imbued with their own, primarily religious, Hindu cultural tradition. In other words, tradition *is* modernity, if you make it so. This is the potent idea that attracts some of the businessmen, and for many upper-middle-class people it is an interest in their own tradition and a commitment to their own religion that primarily account for sympathy with the RSS and Hindu nationalist ideology, not the other way round.

In his address, Dayananda briefly compared Hinduism with physics, but he generally says rather little about science and has insisted that the Vedanta must be distinguished from science because it is a means of knowledge independent of perception and inference.[21] Some businessmen in Chennai, however, including those with technical qualifications, understand Dayananda to be stating that the Vedantic tradition is scientific because it is primarily about the logical working out of some elementary principles, so that, like science, it is dynamic and always evolving. The religions of the Book, on the other hand, seem static because they are so dependent upon a written canon and ancient custom. Hence the Hindu tradition is perceived as more fully 'modern', for it is more scientific than the dogmatic traditions of Christianity or Islam. In fact, this idea has long been part of Hindu reformist thinking and its most vigorous advocate was the earlier Dayananda Saraswati, founder of the Arya Samaj. He insisted that the Veda was superior, as a sci-entific body of knowledge, to the Bible and Qu'ran, and in one debate in 1877 with Christian and Muslim clerics he polemically forced his point home (Prakash 2000: 92–4). Very possibly, today's businessmen in Chennai are hear-ing in their Dayananda's words ideas about science that have actually been current for more than a century. But what they are also hearing is his appar-ently pragmatic wisdom about the pressures of everyday life. Dayananda's messages about 'successful living', which were prominent in Paramarthanda's *Gita* classes as well, are clearly attractive to men who also read the rather sim-ilar mantras of leading business gurus, such as Tom Peters.[22] This similarity is not coincidental, as we shall see by considering some aspects of Dayananda's teaching in greater depth.

Dayananda's 'Traditional' Teaching

In many respects, as already noted, Dayananda teaches modern Vedantic Hinduism, which is monistic and emphasizes the authority of the Vedas and especially the Upanishads as the 'end of the Veda' (Vedanta) – although par-ticular attention is also paid to the *Bhagavad Gita* (described by one Chennai businessman as the 'ABC of the Vedas'). Much of Dayananda's teaching has been published as edited transcripts of his lectures produced by his students. The publications can be divided into three main categories. First, there are the three tomes of the *Bhagavad Gita* 'home study course' (1,600 pages in total). Second, there are the longer books (100 pages or more) that are mostly trans-lations and commentaries on specific texts, such as the *Gita* or *Sri Rudram*, although there is also an *Introduction to Vedanta* based on classes given in the

USA. And third, there are short pamphlets containing transcripts of a few lectures on particular topics, or miscellaneous collections of homilies, prayers or question-and-answer sessions. In addition, numerous tape-recorded cassettes of Dayananda's lectures are available, as well as a few audio-clips on the Sastraprakasika website.[23]

Another important publication is the *Vedic Heritage Teaching Programme* (*VHTP*) compiled by Sunita and Sundar Ramaswamy, two of Dayananda's Indian disciples resident in the United States.[24] This ambitious programme, endorsed by Dayananda in his foreword, consists of teaching manuals and children's workbooks, as well as cassette tapes of scriptural texts, and is designed to teach Hinduism to children aged six to fifteen over a ten-year period. In general, the *VHTP* is much better written than the other publications referred to above.

One significant feature of many of the books and pamphlets, as well as the *VHTP*, is that they reproduce Sanskrit textual passages in both Devanagari script and standard scientific transliteration; Indian names and terms in the body of the English text are also systematically transliterated. Plainly, this scholarly concern for Sanskrit is partly intended to highlight the authentically traditional character of Dayananda's teaching. Yet despite the ostensible scholarship, the commentaries on scriptural texts are neither very profound nor often very clear.[25] On the other hand, this probably does not matter to Dayananda's followers, because it is much more important that the crucial premise of monism – that all beings are ultimately inseparable from the one Supreme Being – is repeatedly restated through simple analogies, even if they are actually unclear or misleading.

Moreover, Dayananda's authenticity as a traditional teacher is demonstrated by his fluent discourses on scriptural texts, verses of which he can readily quote and recite verbatim from memory. This in turn means that his 'pearls of wisdom' (to cite one of his pamphlet's titles) on a wide range of religious, moral, social, economic and political questions are given credibility in his followers' eyes. Nonetheless, Dayananda's answers to these questions owe at least as much to popular western, especially American, ideas as to the Vedanta, so that there are many implicit references to notions of individual self-help and the power of 'positive thinking'. In this respect, Dayananda's approach is not unusual; Vasudha Narayanan (1992: 171–2) mentions, for example, 'a supreme stress management program spiritual workshop' led by a swami in the Penn Hills temple in Pennsylvania, and one of the temple's youth camps whose theme was 'positive thinking and living'. Quite often, too, ideas that are primarily Christian in origin make an appearance. A patent example is the pamphlet on 'morning meditation prayers' for Dayananda's students in the USA, which is actually based not on any Hindu source but on a slightly modified version of the famous 'serenity prayer' that was adopted by Alcoholics Anonymous.[26]

More significant is the explication of key concepts. For instance, in an audio-clip Dayananda says that *moksha* means seeking freedom in life, without which everything seems meaningless. In a dialogue with a student, he explains that: [27]

> My concept of *moksha* is freedom from the sense of limitation and the sense of dependence for your security and happiness. It is not my concept – it is the Vedantic concept. ... [It means] freedom from the sense of inadequacy.

This might be equated with the definition given by S. Radhakrishnan, the most influential twentieth-century philosopher of Vedantic monism: '*Moksha* is spiritual realization. ... *Moksha* is self-emancipation, the fulfilment of the spirit in us in the heart of the eternal' (1971: 58).

But Dayananda's interpretation more obviously reflects a less spiritual, more this-worldly idiom that echoes contemporary western ideas about individual self-fulfilment, and in the dialogue just quoted, he insists that: 'The problem of sense of inadequacy is not a social problem but is an individual problem.'[28] Much the same point was made, through a reference to *karma*, in Dayananda's Chennai address (Harriss 2003: 358–9). Furthermore, *moksha* for Dayananda is not a very remote and difficult goal, whereas in the orthodox Brahmanical tradition, in P. V. Kane's words, to know and become identified with the Godhead is the ultimate objective (Kane 1977: 1631):

> This can be achieved by one's own efforts, but [it] ... is most difficult and requires the aspirant to give up egotism, selfishness and worldly attachments.

Compared with these demands, Dayananda's followers should surely have no more trouble pursuing his version of liberation than most people who try to overcome feelings of inadequacy by consulting a personal therapist, for, not coincidentally, *moksha* has been redefined as a psychological state that is fairly easy to attain, instead of a formidable objective that is achieved only through awesome austerities or superabundant devotion.

Dayananda's outlook on this 'individual problem' appears to be at the heart of his appeal to Indian middle-class people and businessmen in particular. The epigraph on the title page of *Pearls of Wisdom* reads: 'There is no failure in life. There are only varieties of experience. We learn from experiences, not from failure.' In a repetitious (and uncharismatic) lecture on 'Indian philosophy and contemporary management' delivered in 1999 and sponsored by a leading company in Chennai, Dayananda sought to develop this argument about failure and derive it from the *Bhagavad Gita*. In the *Gita*, Krishna says that he manifests himself in human beings in the form of desires (which he does, though he qualifies this by referring to desires that are not inconsistent with righteousness [7.9]), and Dayananda claimed that this means that desire is a human privilege and a manifestation of divinity that actuates people to do things. In life, though, unfulfilled desires normally outnumber fulfilled ones, so that people feel a sense of failure and inadequacy. Krishna, however, teaches us to control desires. (Actually, he tells us to renounce desires in order to obtain peace [2.55, 71], as is indeed confirmed in Dayananda's commentary.)[29] Krishna therefore gives us a 'programme for living', 'a plan for life', which ensures that if desires are kept under control, the process of trying to fulfil them – whether successfully or not – is enjoyable and we can learn from it. Hence there are 'varieties of experience', not 'failures'. By the same token, working to try to achieve success is an enjoyable, educational experience, and controlling the human privilege of desires is managing the self; if everyone in a company does this, then the management needs only to communicate its needs to employees, because the latter actually manage themselves and enjoy their own work. Finally, Krishna teaches that when people enjoy the process of working, they are following their *dharma* and do not 'cut corners' – Dayananda's folksy translation of *adharma*.

Before his lecture – which converts religious teaching into a kind of tool-kit for coping successfully with everyday life and work – Dayananda was introduced by a director of the company as a great Vedantic thinker and a great teacher of ordinary people on both theological and practical matters. Yet to interpret Krishna's address to Arjuna before the *Mahabharata* battle as a functionalist plan for good management is surely banal, and it is hard to believe that it really helped any businessmen in the audience to improve their companies' management, even if they were pleased to hear that their activities might have divine approval. On the other hand, to focus too specifically on the content of Dayananda's teaching on management is to miss the point, for his appeal primarily lies in his exemplary personage as a Brahman teacher who, in spite of his ascetic renunciation, nevertheless engages with the affairs of the modern world and presents them as if they were or could be made compatible with the Vedanta. Delivered by such a personage, a lecture about Krishna as a management guru is heard as proof that modern business and the Veda are mutually compatible, whereas a similar set of homilies about desire, failure and so on would probably be ignored if they were uttered by someone of less stature.[30]

Business Success and Dayananda's Appeal in Chennai

Although Dayananda may address today's Chennai businessmen on failure and how to redefine it as experience, his attractiveness to them is probably significantly related to their self-confidence about themselves and their work, which they share with so many of the American NRIs who are also attracted to him. Admittedly, Singer's evidence suggests that the Chennai businessmen whom he studied in the mid-1960s displayed a similar self-confidence, although it is hard to believe that they were all as sure about divine will as he suggests, but, as we pointed out, Singer makes no reference to any modern gurus. Assuming this is not an oversight and that Singer's evidence is reliable (cf Harriss 2003: 334–5), however, why should businessmen today be attracted to a guru like Dayananda, whereas their predecessors were content with the Shankaracharyas or their own understanding of Gandhian ideas?

One important part of the answer is that the economic, political and religious situation has changed enormously. In the 1960s Indian businessmen, even in major industrial companies and notwithstanding their foreign collaboration agreements, mainly operated within the highly-regulated heavily-protected market of the Nehruvian planned economy. By the 1990s, following economic liberalization, the opening up of India's markets, and much more extensive international investment, trade and collaboration, businessmen were operating in a far more competitive global economy. Many of them, like the Indian business press, are concerned to 'show what Indian business can do' in the globalizing economy, and most importantly, many believe that they can be successful. For the Chennai businessmen, if not for all Indians, the old question of whether Indians could actually do as well as foreigners in the modern world has been answered by the economic success achieved by some of them both in India and abroad, especially in the United States.

Accompanying the changes in the Indian economy since the 1960s have been equally significant political changes, as Nehruvian socialist secularism and Congress hegemony have given way to religious nationalism and the BJP, together with a host of regional parties.[31] Within Tamil Nadu since the early 1990s – first during Jayalalitha's AIADMK regime (1991–6), but afterwards under Karunanidhi's DMK (1996–2001) and the AIADMK again since 2001 – there has been a wave of Hindu revivalism that is, to a significant extent, both cause and effect of the impact of Hindu nationalism on the state (Fuller 2003: 119–37). The Tamil Nadu government has become an active promoter of Brahmanical, Sanskritic Hinduism, especially in the temples, and its policy, combined with many people's growing prosperity, has led to an ever-rising number of spectacular temple renovation rituals (*kumbhabhisheka*), as well as considerable expenditure on extending old temples and building new ones. No figures exist to prove it, but at least in the major urban centres where middle-class affluence is concentrated the evidence suggests that increasing numbers of costly, elaborate rituals are also being held in both temples and homes. Similarly, the number of gurus and other Hindu religious personages who are active probably continues to grow, and all kinds of religious activities – from learned debates to new local festivals – are flourishing as never before. Dayananda, notwithstanding his devotees' special claims on his behalf, is actually only one of many holy men active in contemporary Hindu revivalism in Tamil Nadu.

In general terms, therefore, in Tamil Nadu as in much of India, the public sphere has been transformed during the last ten to fifteen years, so that it has become increasingly religious in tenor, and Hindus have become increasingly assertive about celebrating their religion publicly. They have also become more assertive about their own identity as Hindus in opposition to Muslims and Christians. These changes have taken place among Chennai businessmen, just like other Hindus, irrespective of how much support they extend to the Hindu nationalist movement. For the men studied by Singer, religion was a more private matter and more often left to wives and children (1972: 333) than it is for their successors today, who expressly disapprove of 'compartmentalizing' public business apart from private, home-based religion.

To return to Dayananda: like countless other holy men active in contemporary India, he seeks to explain how and why traditional Hinduism (as he portrays it) remains valid and important in the modern world because, properly understood, the Vedanta actually is modern. For many leading Hindus, at least since the late nineteenth century, denunciation of western materialism and eulogy of Indian spirituality has been a central theme, but in Dayananda's teaching – apart from his criticisms of Christianity and Islam – any denunciation is mild. This is consistent with the fact that businessmen in Chennai – and presumably most of his other followers – display none of the anxious antipathy towards the west and its capitalist lifestyle found in many less-favoured sections of the Indian middle class. The reasons are of course obvious: unlike the majority of Indians who have no real experience of the west, many of the businessmen have studied, worked and lived in western countries, usually the United States; they often go there for business or pleasure as well, and they send their children there for education. These men, as we have said, now belong to a transnational Indian managerial-professional upper-middle class, for whom the west – especially America – is simultaneously an icon of modernity and a familiar place where they are comfortable and successful. Dayananda's message is therefore not anti-western, even though it insists on the value of Hinduism for Indians living in the west. As Rajagopal comments (2001: 247):

Hindu spiritualism is seen as providing a necessary counterweight to the ills of a materialist society and, at the same time, as redeemable by the standards of that society itself.

A similar idea was voiced by one Chennai businessman:

> You don't find Indian businessmen running off to psychoanalysts like Americans, because they are able to find comfort in religion. Religion is a buffer against problems.

Furthermore, the Chennai businessmen do not display anxiety about a rapidly changing, highly competitive social world – and the need to validate their own prosperous position within it – that various scholars have seen as one important reason why Sathya Sai Baba and some other miracle-working religious virtuosi were so attractive to their predominantly urban middle-class followers, at least in the 1970s (Babb 1987: Part 3; Kakar 1983: Chapter 7; Swallow 1982; cf Fuller 1992: 177–81). Maya Warrier (2003) criticises this scholarship because in her study of the extremely popular female guru Mata Amritanandamayi of Kerala, and her middle-class devotees, she saw no evidence of anxiety among them. Our findings are the same as Warrier's. For the businessmen and their family members who are devotees today of Sathya Sai Baba (or Shirdi Sai Baba), or those (mentioned above) who like to stress the miraculous powers of the Paramacharya or Swami Rajagopala, social anxiety is also not a salient factor.

In general, though, however untroubled they may be about their own prosperity, Chennai businessmen can be defensive about social inequality. Moreover, they do not want to hear a message antagonistic to their class interests, and on economic and political inequality, Dayananda – like the overwhelming majority of other holy men – maintains a 'persistent and strategic silence' (McKean 1996: 268) in his lectures. Not only does he avoid inflammatory diatribes about western materialism, Dayananda also preaches a socially conservative message that makes him, if only for negative reasons, congenial to businessmen. In addition, unlike the majority of contemporary Hindu holy men, Dayananda is a Brahman by birth, even though he does not make a lot of it. For almost all members of the Chennai upper-middle class, however, irrespective of their caste background, Brahmans retain a cultural-cum-religious pre-eminence that enhances Dayananda's authority as a guru and traditional teacher.

The 'Cultural Vacuum' and 'Generic' Hinduism

However successful they may be, one important issue about which the Chennai businessmen freely admit to being worried is that they know less than they should about Hinduism, and that their children are likely to grow up knowing next to nothing about it. That is why, as this chapter's second epigraph emphasized, 'cultural revival' is 'the need of the hour' to prevent the extinction of the Vedic Hindu religious tradition. In his foreword to the *Vedic Heritage Teaching Programme*, Dayananda explains that 'religious culture' used to be 'imbibed naturally from one's home and the cultural atmosphere of the immediate community. Not any more. ... So the children have to be taught methodically the religious cultural forms and their meaning, in a class-room situation.' These worries are not of course entirely new among more westernised, middle-class Indians, but they have intensified in recent years.

In its advertisement for the *VHTP*, the Saylorsburg centre's website has a similar message to the Trust's, but of course it is appealing directly to NRIs:

> [For the] second-generation Indian children ... the home is composed of a nuclear family wherein parental responsibilities are diverse. Western society, too, offers many alternative beliefs and ways of living. Given this situation, teaching the Vedic heritage to children emerges as an essential part of life in an immigrant Indian family or community.

The crucial point here is that the problem of religious cultural transmission is now seen as more or less identical in India and abroad. Thus the *VHTP* is explicitly designed as a response to the dangers of 'the encroaching Westernisation of India', as well as to the 'cultural vacuum' and 'increasing loss of cultural identity' faced by Indians outside India, to cite the white American's editorial note.

The *VHTP* is an ambitious project, which may in practice be over-ambitious. It comprises three large-format books for teachers – which cover mythology, theology, *dharma* and the *Bhagavad Gita* – seven children's workbooks, one book on worship containing prayers and textual passages, and three cassette tapes on which the latter are recorded. Taken as a whole, the *VHTP* propagates the 'generic' neo-Vedantic Hinduism that Narayanan (1992) identifies as dominant among 'young urban professional Hindus' in America. Emphasized particularly are 'a symbolic or psychological explanation of religious phenomena, a syncretic approach to the deities and rituals, and [discussion] on the perceived connections between religion, western psychology, and stress management' (1992: 172–3). Paradigmatic, too, is the proposition that all rituals have inner, symbolic meanings that actually show that science and Hinduism are compatible (ibid.: 174; cf Rajagopal 2001: 247). The reformulation of Hinduism in America can be seen as one part of its general transformation in the modern world, and there are also clear parallels with the modern history of other religions. Thus, as we have already seen, in the nineteenth century, the earlier Dayananda Saraswati was insisting that science and Hinduism are compatible because the Veda is itself 'scientific'; very similar claims about scientific compatibility have often been made by modern Buddhists or Muslims. Nonetheless, in its particular combination of features, Narayanan's concept of 'generic' Hinduism does identify a distinctively NRI-American form of the religion.

Another characteristic feature of generic Hinduism is the 'controlled diet' of myths about the deities, so that single, 'true' story-lines are highlighted, and alternative versions and meanings are eliminated, just as they are in the *Amar Chitra Katha* comic-book versions of Hindu mythology so popular with children in India (Narayanan 1992: 169; cf Hawley 1995). In the *VHTP* (like the comic-books), sex, violence and 'dysfunctional' behaviour in the deities' families are eliminated. Thus, for example, Daksha's sacrifice and Sati's death are recounted without any mention of Shiva's terrible, anguished rage, and when Krishna played his flute, we are told, 'all the *gopis* rushed to him leaving their household chores unfinished,' which effectively washes away any eroticism in their moonlit dance with the god.[32]

On the other hand, for many if not most Hindus today, Krishna is a morally upright god, not an adulterous lover, in line with a more general trend to portray all Hindu deities as moral exemplars. In this respect, therefore, the *VHTP*'s versions of myths are not exceptional. But it is also possible that converting Radha and the *gopis* into housewives portrays them as closer to an American Hindu wifely norm, and the expurgation of Hindu mythology may be reinforced by the impact of American family and gender ideology.[33] Thus Prema Kurien explains that the 'idealized' traditional family 'is a central icon in the construction of an American Hinduism', although women, in their role as transmitters of tradition, can 'reinterpret the patriarchal images more in their favour and construct a model of gender that emphasizes the importance of male responsibilities' (1999: 650). Significantly, the *VHTP*, even in its exegesis of the *Laws of Manu*, emphasizes men's duties towards women and the equality of the sexes in its section on 'women in Vedic culture'.[34]

The *VHTP*'s generic Hinduism, notwithstanding its simplifications, is mixed in with a preoccupation with Sanskrit accuracy, as already mentioned, as well as some fairly complicated discussion of Hindu philosophy. In Chennai, the *VHTP* is being used in some private schools popular with middle-class parents, notably the Arsha Vidya Mandir, founded in 2002 with the blessings of Dayananda and the Shankaracharya of Sringeri, and older Bala Vidya Mandir. Speaking in 2003, both schools' principals saw the programme as a valuable resource for overcoming the serious ignorance about Hindu religion and culture manifest in middle-class homes, but they also regarded it as hard to use, partly because its level of difficulty is so variable. One of the schools has therefore produced its own teachers' manual to supplement those supplied by the *VHTP*; both principals also send teachers to special training workshops, although one of them pessimistically commented that several years' training would actually be required before the *VHTP* could be used properly.

More detailed research would be needed to assess the pedagogical effectiveness of the *VHTP* in schools or at home. On the other hand, the programme certainly is a serious attempt to deal with the perceived problem of teaching traditional religious culture to middle-class and NRI children. Furthermore, even if the *VHTP* is not unique, its 'teach-yourself' cassette tapes are a rare example of using modern technology to reproduce the oral teaching of texts as found in religious schools (cf Fuller 2001). This case of 'secondary orality' – oral transmission fostered by electronics, not by the absence of writing or printing – indirectly draws attention to the lack (as far as we can tell) of any Hindu websites for teaching scriptural texts, so that the *VHTP* displays a greater commitment to traditional Hindu religious teaching, as emphasized by Dayananda, than anything apparent on the World-Wide Web.[35]

Taken as a whole, the *Vedic Heritage Teaching Programme* exemplifies a mixture of Sanskrit perfectionism and simplified, generic Hinduism that closely mirrors the structure of Dayananda's own teaching, itself characterized by an often dissonant combination of authentic Sanskrit quotation and simplified or Americanized Vedanta. Nonetheless, in this combination lies Dayananda's special appeal as an exemplary, traditional, Brahman ascetic teacher who can speak about modern affairs and present them in the light of the Veda, which is truly modern, even though it is also ancient revelation. Such a combination is not entirely new, but in some significant respects it is a response to contemporary globalization.

Conclusion: Globalization and Hinduism

In his discussion of NRIs, Rajagopal argues that because Hindus are an ethnic minority in the United States, the meanings of 'Hindu' and 'Hinduism', and the characteristics of Hindu nationalism vary from those in India (ibid.: 263–70; cf Kurien 2002: 114–16). In many respects he is undoubtedly correct, but in the particular case under discussion it is more salient that the Chennai businessmen and their family members are attracted to a style of Hinduism that is also popular with NRIs. Thus, we contend, a distinctive characteristic of Dayananda's teaching is that it chimes with the perceived needs of a globalized, upper-middle class of Hindus living both in India and overseas. This teaching celebrates the transformation of Hinduism into a universal, world religion that is going from strength to strength, but it is simultaneously predicated on the notion that westernised Indians now face the same problem as NRIs, especially in America, for they and their children are all endangered by a 'cultural vacuum' that may undermine the religion in spite of its global 'renaissance'. To bridge this gap between strength and potential weakness and to appeal to all his followers, Dayananda promulgates a generic Hinduism that in many respects is American-made, combined with a sizeable quotient of Sanskrit scripture, the authentic core component of the eternal, Brahmanical Hindu tradition and, for Hindu nationalists, all Indian civilisation as well.

Dayananda is engaged in a form of 'reintellectualisation' of Hinduism, to borrow Dale Eickelman and Jon Anderson's term for a new way of presenting Islamic doctrine to a new public that includes large numbers of transnational migrants by using new media, most recently the Internet (cf Anderson 1999). A key feature of this reintellectualisation is that the thinkers responsible for it – Dayananda in our Hindu case – 'successfully join global and local communities of discourse and reach wider audiences than their predecessors' (Eickelman and Anderson 1999: 12). Obviously, there are major differences between Hinduism and Islam; in particular, whereas Hindus are overwhelmingly concentrated in India, the homeland of their religion, the new 'Muslim publics' discussed by Eickelman and Anderson bring together Muslims from many different nations, none of them dominant over all others, and in certain respects globalization encourages a 'decentering' away from the Arabian peninsula (cf Eickelman and Piscatori 1996: 137).

Yet new Hindu publics are emerging too, and one of them is formed by the globalized upper-middle class to whom Dayananda appeals. Thus when he mixes the language of self-help and English homilies imported from America with the words of Krishna and Sanskrit quotations, he is developing a new way of presenting Hinduism that chimes with what his business audience in Chennai wants to hear. To these businessmen and those close to them, Dayananda's version of Hinduism confirms that their confidence in their own success and position in the world is well-placed, but also that their own and their children's ignorance of Hinduism is an outcome of westernization and globalization that can be overcome.

Notes

1 *Hinduism Today* website: www.hinduism-today.com.
2 Advertisement for *Vedic Heritage Teaching Programme* on Sastraprakasika Trust website: www.sastraprakasika.org.
3 For encouraging and critical comments on an earlier draft of this chapter, we thank Jackie Assayag, Véronique Bénéï, Henrike Donner, Haripriya Narasimhan, Arvind Rajagopal and Chakravarti Ram-Prasad. For financial support for the research in Chennai, we thank the Economic and Social Research Council.
4 The directory is at: www.hindu.org/teachers-orgs/. It is part of the larger Directory of Hindu Resources Online: www.hindu.org.

5 The biographical sketch is based on *Swami Dayananda Saraswati: The traditional teacher of Brahma Vidya* (Chennai: T.T. Maps and Publications, n.d.), which was compiled by a devotee, Padma Narasimhan, and published in around 1990.

6 On the VHP's foundation and early years, and on Chinmayananda's pioneering work for the VHP of America, see Katju (2003: Chapter 2, 157–8).

7 These websites are: www.sastraprakasika.org; www.arshavidya.org (Saylorsburg, through which the Rishikesh website can be quickly accessed); www.pramana.org (Center for Traditional Vedanta).

8 Audio-clips of Ravishankar's platitudes can be heard on his website: www.artofliving.org.

9 *New Indian Express*, 25 March 2002, as reproduced on the Sastraprakasika website.

10 Dayananda, while claiming that the ordinance upholds basic human rights, insisted that the 'denigration of one's religion and the humiliation that accompanies the conversion experience are violations of the dignity assured to every human being'. This statement, made in March 2003, was accessed through the *Hinduism Today* website by searching for 'Dayananda'.

11 Reports posted on www.hinduism-today.com/1999/2/index.html and (accessible through the search facility) the VHP of America website: www.vhp-america.org. No reports of Dharma Sansad meetings or pilgrimages after 1999 have been posted on these websites, consulted in summer 2003.

12 The research is described in detail in Harriss (2003).

13 This quotation comes from Singer's notes which are in his collected papers in the Regenstein Library, University of Chicago.

14 Quotation from the booklet *Sarvamangla Sri Rajarajeswari Ashram*, published by P. K. Seshan, Diamond Bar, California.

15 The relevant notes are in Box 129 of the Singer Papers in the Regenstein Library.

16 Jackie Assayag (personal communication) also comments on how our evidence suggests a kind of 'bricolage' of different elements of thought and practice in the religious market.

17 Quotations from Arvind Rajagopal (personal communication). The Kanchipuram monastery now has a website too: www.kamakoti.org.

18 Arvind Rajagopal (personal communication).

19 This committee is presumably linked to the Hindu Dharma Rakshana Samithi mentioned above.

20 Swami Dayananda's views on conversion are also set out in a pamphlet *Conversion is Violence*, published by Sruti Seva Trust, Arsha Vidya Gurukulam, Coimbatore.

21 See, for example, his pamphlet *Pearls of Wisdom* (pp. 4–5), published by Sri Gangadhareswar Trust, Swami Dayananda Ashram, Rishikesh.

22 Tom Peters is the author of *Thriving on Chaos: A handbook for a management revolution* (1991), *Reinventing Work: The Brand You50* (1999), and over 70 other titles listed in 'best-selling' order on Amazon's website.

23 In August 2002, the website listed for sale 23 books and pamphlets (plus two video CDs) by Dayananda, although this is not a complete inventory of his publications; in its list of cassettes, it also listed 66 titles by Dayananda in English, plus about 150 more by three fellow teachers in English or Tamil.

24 Published by Sri Gangadhareswar Trust, Swami Dayananda Ashram, Rishikesh.

25 Many examples could be cited, but the following passage of commentary intended to elucidate monism is typical: "'All that is here is *Brahman*". … So, too, every object like sun, moon, earth, space and time, is not separate from *Brahman*, even though each object has its own something to refer [sic] and it is that which is referred to by the words sun, moon, earth, space and time. … Between a word, *vacaka*, and its meaning, *vacya*,

there is an invariable relationship. Even if you don't have a name for a form of clay, can you imagine the form without imagining the substance? This is what is the non-separate relationship between name and form [sic]. If all forms are *Brahman, Isvara*, then all names are of *Isvara*. And therefore, in one name which includes all names, I can see the entire *jagat* [world] being non-separate from *Isvara*' (*Talks on Sri Rudram* [pp. 4–5], published by Sri Gangadhareswar Trust, Swami Dayananda Ashram, Rishikesh). The linguistic argument in this passage is specious, but even if it were not, the logic of the conclusion about Ishwara, the supreme God, would still be opaque.

26 *Morning Meditation Prayers*, published by Sri Gangadhareswar Trust, Swami Dayananda Ashram, Rishikesh. The modified serenity prayer is: 'O Lord, may I have the maturity to accept gracefully what I cannot change; may I have the will and effort to change what I can; and may I have the wisdom to know the difference between what I can and can not change.'

27 *Dialogues with Swami Dayananda* (p. 12), published by Sri Gangadhareswar Trust, Swami Dayananda Ashram, Rishikesh.

28 *Dialogues with Swami Dayananda* (p. 14).

29 *The Teaching of the Bhagavad Gita* (pp. 41–3), published by Vision Books, New Delhi; this book was edited by one of Dayananda's American students.

30 Deepak Chopra, a well-known Indian management guru, gave a talk in Syracuse, New York, in 2000. Haripriya Narasimhan (personal communication) informs us that an Indian friend who heard the talk told her that Chopra just said the same as their grandmothers, but coated in English jargon and Sanskrit tags. The same comment could be made about a lot of what Dayananda says, even though his style differs from Chopra's. See also Rajagopal's description of the 'avid crowd of engineers' who listened to a 'Upanishadic management consultant' at a Hindu nationalist organisation's summer camp in the United States (2001: 261).

31 In the 2004 general election, a Congress-led coalition defeated the BJP and its allies. This was a significant reverse for the BJP, but the real winners were regional parties, rather than the Congress.

32 For these two stories, see *VHTP* (1: 64–5, 82). In the *Amar Chitra Katha* comic-books, although sex is removed from the text, the pictures – as in the story of Mirabai and Krishna – can be romantic and erotic (Hawley 1995: 118–20), but this is not so for the rather crude pictures in the *VHTP*'s children's workbooks.

33 Radha does not appear to have become a 'New Age' goddess of power and sex in America like Kali, who is now being 'Indianized' by NRI Hindus 'endeavouring to rein in what they perceive as excesses of feminist and New Age interpretations of the Goddess' (McDermott 2003: 285, 287–8). More generally, even though Dayananda has many white American devotees, his style of teaching is obviously antipathetic to New Age fantasies and no 'Indianization' process has ever been necessary.

34 See *VHTP* (2: 167–70).

35 The situation is curious, because recitations of the *Rudram* and other key Sanskrit texts are widely available on cassette tapes and compact disks. Although there are some Sanskrit prayers on the Internet, much more common are devotional hymns (*bhajan*). These can be found on sites accessible through Directory of Hindu Resources Online: www.hindu.org. It is an interesting contrast that one of the biggest Islamic websites – IslamiCity.com-Islam and the Global eCommunity – provides both high-quality recitation of the Qu'ran and a simulation of its traditional oral teaching: www.islamicity.com (Qu'ran button).

Bibliography

Anderson, Jon W. (1999) 'The internet and Islam's new interpreters', in Dale F. Eickelman and Jon W. Anderson, eds, *New Media in the Muslim World: The emerging public sphere*. Bloomington: Indiana University Press; 41–56.

Babb, Lawrence A. (1987) *Redemptive Encounters: Three modern styles in the Hindu tradition*. Delhi: Oxford University Press.

Bénéï, Véronique (1998) 'Hinduism today: inventing a universal religion?' *South Asia Research*, 18: 117–24.

Deshpande, Satish (2003) *Contemporary India: A sociological view*. New Delhi: Viking Penguin.

Eickelman, Dale F. and Jon W. Anderson (1999) 'Redefining Muslim publics', in Dale F. Eickelman and Jon W. Anderson, eds, *New Media in the Muslim World: The emerging public sphere*. Bloomington: Indiana University Press; 1–18.

Eickelman, Dale F. and James Piscatori (1996) *Muslim Politics*. Princeton: Princeton University Press.

Fuller, C. J. (1992) *The Camphor Flame: Popular Hinduism and society in India*. Princeton: Princeton University Press.

—— (1999) 'The Brahmins and Brahminical values in modern Tamil Nadu', in Ramachandra Guha and Jonathan P. Parry, eds, *Institutions and Inequalities: Essays in honour of André Béteille*. Delhi: Oxford University Press; 30–55.

—— (2001) 'Orality, literacy and memorization: priestly education in contemporary South India', *Modern Asian Studies*, 35: 1–31.

—— (2003) *The Renewal of the Priesthood: Modernity and traditionalism in a South Indian temple*. Princeton: Princeton University Press.

Harriss, John (2003) 'The Great Tradition globalizes: reflections on two studies of the "industrial leaders" of Madras', *Modern Asian Studies*, 37: 327–62.

Hawley, John S. (1995) 'The saints subdued: domestic virtue and national integration in *Amar Chitra Katha*', in Lawrence A. Babb and Susan S. Wadley, eds, *Media and the Transformation of Religion in South Asia*. Philadelphia: University of Pennsylvania Press; 107–34.

Kakar, Sudhir (1983) *Shamans, Mystics and Doctors*. Boston: Beacon Press.

Kane, P. V. (1977) *History of Dharmasastra*, Vol. 5, Part 2. Poona: Bhandarkar Oriental Research Institute.

Katju, Manjari (2003) *Vishva Hindu Parishad and Indian Politics*. New Delhi: Orient Longman.

Kurien, Prema (1999) 'Gendered ethnicity: creating a Hindu identity in the United States', *American Behavioral Scientist*, 42: 648–70.

—— (2002) '"We are better Hindus here": religion and ethnicity among Indian Americans', in Pyong Gap Min and Jung Ha Kim, eds, *Religions in Asian America: Building faith communities*. Walnut Creek, CA: Altamira Press; 99–120.

McDermott, Rachel F. (2003) 'Kali's new frontiers: a Hindu Goddess on the Internet', in Rachel F. McDermott and Jeffrey J. Kripal, eds, *Encountering Kali: In the margins, at the center, in the West*. Berkeley: University of California Press; 273–95.

McKean, Lise (1996) *Divine Enterprise: Gurus and the Hindu Nationalist Movement*. Chicago: University of Chicago Press.

Narayanan, Vasudha (1992) 'Creating the South Indian "Hindu" Experience in the United States', in Raymond B. Williams, *A Sacred Thread: Modern transmission of Hindu traditions in India and abroad*. Chambersburg, PA: Anima Books; 147–76.

Prakash, Gyan (2000) *Another Reason: Science and the imagination of modern India*. Delhi: Oxford University Press.

Radhakrishnan, S. (1971 [1927]). *The Hindu View of Life*. London: Unwin Books.

Rajagopal, Arvind (2001) *Politics After Television: Religious nationalism and the reshaping of the Indian public*. Cambridge: Cambridge University Press.

Seshadri (1999) *God in Our Midst: Poomvathar Sri Sathya Sai Baba*. Chennai: Amra Publishers.

Singer, Milton (1972) *When a Great Tradition Modernizes*. London: Pall Mall Press.

Swallow, Deborah A. (1982) 'Ashes and powers: myth, rite and miracle in an Indian god-man's cult', *Modern Asian Studies*, 16: 123–58.

van der Veer, Peter (1994) *Religious Nationalism: Hindus and Muslims in India*. Berkeley: University of California Press.

Warrier, Maya (2003) 'Processes of secularization in contemporary India: guru faith in the Mata Amritanandamayi Mission', *Modern Asian Studies*, 37: 213–53.